Canadian Newcomer Series

You're Hired...
Now What?

An Immigrant's Guide to Success in the Canadian Workplace

Lynda Goldman

Funded by/Financé par

Citizenship and Immigration Canada

Citoyenneté et Immigration Canada

Canada

OXFORD
UNIVERSITY PRESS

OXFORD

UNIVERSITY PRESS

70 Wynford Drive, Don Mills, Ontario M3C 1J9
www.oupcanada.com

Oxford University Press is a department of the University of Oxford.
It furthers the University's objective of excellence in research, scholarship,
and education by publishing worldwide in

Oxford   New York

Auckland   Cape Town   Dar es Salaam   Hong Kong   Karachi
Kuala Lumpur   Madrid   Melbourne   Mexico City   Nairobi
New Delhi   Shanghai   Taipei   Toronto

With offices in

Argentina   Austria   Brazil   Chile   Czech Republic   France   Greece
Guatemala   Hungary   Italy   Japan   Poland   Portugal   Singapore
South Korea   Switzerland   Thailand   Turkey   Ukraine   Vietnam

Oxford is a trade mark of Oxford University Press
in the UK and in certain other countries

Published in Canada
by Oxford University Press

Library and Archives Canada Cataloguing in Publication

Goldman, Lynda, 1952–
You're hired—now what? : how to survive and thrive at a Canadian job /
Lynda Goldman.

(Canadian newcomer series)
Includes index.
ISBN 978-0-19-543218-3

1. Business etiquette—Canada. 2. Courtesy in the workplace.
3. Immigrants—Employment—Canada.
I. Title. II. Series: Canadian newcomer series

HD8108.5.A2G65 2009   650.1'3   C2008-908100-5

Cover credits (clockwise from top left):
iStockphoto.com / Jacob Wackerhausen; iStockphoto.com / Springboard, Inc.;
Cathy Yeulet / BigStockPhoto.com; hana / Datacraft; iStockphoto.com / Claire Desjardins

This book is printed on permanent acid-free paper.

Printed and bound in Canada.

1 2 3 4 – 13 12 11 10

Table of Contents

Foreword   vii

Introduction   viii

Section 1: Getting Started   1

Chapter 1—How to Work Well in Canada   2
- Canadian culture in the workplace   3
- Professional behaviour in Canada   4
- Sharing ideas and learning about Canada   5
- Canadian work values compared with values in other cultures   7
- How to work successfully in Canada   8

Chapter 2—Understanding Your Workplace Culture   23
- Learning about your workplace culture   24
- Getting oriented to your workplace   30
- Finding out your rights and benefits   32
- Finding out the norms in your workplace   35

Chapter 3—Setting the Stage for Success   40
- How to prepare for your first days on the job   41
- How to make a great first impression   43
- Meeting people and establishing good working relationships   45
- Setting up your workspace   48
- How to start off on the right foot   50
- Eight tips to get on track in the first two weeks   54

Chapter 4—Projecting a Professional Image   58
- How to dress for success in Canada   59
- What to wear in your industry and company   61
- Business clothing for the Canadian climate   71
- How to look up-to-date   78
- What you should know about grooming   79
- What to wear for business occasions   83

Section 2: Communicating on the Job   85

Chapter 5—Actions Speak Louder Than Words   86
- Non-verbal communication in the Canadian workplace   87
- Understanding people's gestures and postures   92
- How to use body language to connect with people   97
- How to use body language to look like a leader   101
- Body language that makes a great first impression   104

Chapter 6—Business Talk on the Job   106
- Canadian communication styles   107
- Canadian conversation patterns   110
- Business buzzwords   115
- How to talk with your manager   118
- How to talk with co-workers   123
- Using the right words   125
- How to improve your speaking ability   128

Chapter 7—Telephone Tips   131
- How to be effective on the telephone   132
- How to begin and end business calls   135
- How to talk with receptionists   137
- How to answer the phone for business calls   138
- Telephone courtesies   139
- How to leave effective voice messages   142
- Cellphone protocol   145

Chapter 8—Business Writing that Gets Results   150
- Five easy steps to business writing   151
- How to write an email   154
- How to write a business memo   166
- How to write a fax   169
- How to write a business letter   171
- How to write a thank-you note   176
- How to write clearly and professionally   178

Section 3: Working Relationships   183

Chapter 9—Getting Along with Co-workers   184
- How to get along with co-workers   185
- What not to do at the office   191
- Working well in a team   194
- Office courtesies—the everyday things that count   198
- The holiday season at work   204

Chapter 10—Good Boss / Bad Boss   208
- Understanding your boss   209
- How to develop a positive relationship with your manager   211
- Good boss, bad boss—different supervising styles   218
- How to manage problems with your manager   224
- How to handle a performance review   227

Chapter 11—Client Relations and Business Etiquette   234
- Working well with clients   235
- Making a good impression at a client's office   238
- Business etiquette for the 21st century   241
- Business dining etiquette in Canada   241
- Hosting a business meal   250

Chapter 12—Office Politics, Gossip, and Romance   253
- Dealing with office politics   254
- Avoiding office gossip   260
- Office romance   263

Chapter 13—Avoiding and Solving Problems   271
- How to deal with difficult co-workers   272
- Unacceptable workplace behaviour   280
- Discrimination and harassment in the workplace   281

Chapter 14—Networking, Small-talk, and Relationship Building   286
- How networking can help your career   287
- Networking within your organization   290
- Networking outside of your organization   291
- How to network in Canada   295
- How to make connections at networking events   300
- How to use small-talk to build relationships   303

Section 4: Achieving Success   315

Chapter 15—Managing Your Time and Being Productive   316
- Understanding how Canadians view time   317
- Planning your time and being productive   321
- How to create a work / life balance   336

Chapter 16—Business outside the Office   339
- The ins and outs of business travel   340
- Trade shows and conferences   348
- Parties, events, and dinners outside the office   351

Chapter 17—Meetings and Presentations   361
- How to make your meeting time count   362
- How to plan and organize a meeting   368
- How to give a presentation   375
- How to speak effectively   379

Words of Wisdom on Achieving Success   386

Glossary   392

Appendix   397

Index   398

Photo Credits   403

Key Features

Look for these features throughout the book. They provide tips and ideas to help you familiarize yourself with the Canadian workplace.

Look for these features throughout the book. They feature immigrants' stories to illustrate key points.

Foreword

As an Executive Director of a growing, highly diverse company, I have learned over the years that an employee's technical or "hard" skills are only one part of his or her success at work. Employees' ability to communicate effectively, build good working relationships with their colleagues and supervisors, and project a professional image are critical for their success in the workplace and their ability to move forward in their careers.

Our organization is one of a number across Canada that offers services to help prepare and place newcomers in the Canadian workplace. These services have often focused on teaching job search skills and linking newcomers with employers and placing them in meaningful employment. We know, however, that once newcomers find work, they often experience barriers to moving ahead in their careers. Like all employees who want to succeed at work, newcomers need to learn about the culture of their new workplaces, how to build relationships, and how to navigate their way up the career ladder.

This book is an invaluable guide for newcomers about to begin their first jobs in Canada, or for anyone involved in helping newcomers transition smoothly into their careers. It offers tips on such basics as how to write a business memo and how to leave an effective voice message, but also offers advice on more complex issues such as how to build professional networks in Canada and how to develop effective relationships with your managers and colleagues.

Finally, I would recommend this book as a resource for Canadian employers. As we see increasingly diverse workplaces across Canada, and as employers depend on the skills newcomers bring, companies need new and better ways to integrate immigrant employees into the workplace and to support this diversity. Successful businesses can use *You're Hired ... Now What?* to build strategies to help all their employees grow in their careers, succeed in their workplace, and fully contribute their skills to the success of the company and the Canadian economy overall.

Allison Pond
Executive Director
ACCES Employment

Introduction

Congratulations—you're hired! You are about to start working in Canada.

Starting a new job is a lot like moving to a foreign place. When you arrived in Canada, people's actions and habits may have surprised or puzzled you. You had to learn about the basics of living in Canada—everything from Canadian food and housing to surviving your first Canadian winter.

Now you are about to put all this together in the workplace. The business world has is own culture, which varies from industry to industry and from company to company.

This book is filled with information that will apply to any workplace. It will also give you strategies for things such as getting along with your co-workers and manger and speaking and writing business English. It's your job to apply these ideas to your specific workplace.

But first, let's think about baking a cake. You may be wondering, "What does baking a cake have to do with working in Canada?" Think of it this way: Oil and water are two ingredients of a cake. Each is valuable on its own. But if you pour oil into a glass of water the liquids don't mix. The oil floats on top of the water. However, if you add flour, sugar, chocolate, and other ingredients, mix them together and bake the whole thing in the oven, you get something delicious: cake!

The same idea applies to mixing cultures in the workplace. At first there may be clashes between people who see things differently—they don't naturally mix well. One person has a slow-moving manner, while another person is quick-acting. One person likes to discuss ideas for a while before making decisions, while another person prefers to make decisions quickly.

This book focuses on how to work in Canada. Many of the principals of living in Canada are based on our ideas about work—how much time we spend working, our view of the value of work, and what it means to succeed.

Why this book was written

Many books and courses tell you how to find a job. But few resources tell you how to *keep* the job, and succeed, after you are hired.

You may have already read *Arrival Survival Canada* and *How to Find a Job in Canada*, both of which should set you up for getting a job. Now you have the job, and you also have the challenge of understanding your Canadian workplace.

The most common question immigrants have about the Canadian workplace is, "How do I succeed?" This book answers that question.

What will you learn from this book?

When you are starting at a new company, you don't need lots of theory about how to succeed. You need practical tips that you can put into action. This book will help you …

- understand Canada's workplace culture, and how to work well in your job in Canada

- project a professional image in person, in writing, and on the telephone

- learn and use business language and workplace jargon

- get along well with your manager, co-workers, and clients

- use Canadian business etiquette to make a great first impression

- avoid problems with office politics and gossip

- network and build relationships within your company, with clients, and with others in your industry

- manage your time and be productive so you accomplish more

- speak with confidence at meetings, business events, and conferences

Who will benefit from this book?

Canadian immigrants who …

* have just been hired and are about to start a new job

* are looking for a job, and want to understand the Canadian workplace so they can succeed more quickly

* have been working for some time, and want to progress higher in their company

Managers and human resources professionals who …

* want to guide new immigrant employees and help them succeed

* would like to learn more about the work styles and thought processes of employees from different cultures

* are struggling with common cultural misunderstandings in the workplace

Once managers become sensitive to the challenges that Canadian immigrants face, they can head off many problems, harness employees' talent, and groom employees for leadership roles.

How is This Book Different?

This is the only book written specifically for Canadian immigrants that tells you how to succeed in Canada. You'll benefit from the following features:

* Real-life stories give you example to illustrate each concept.

* Canadian Business Concepts offer tips and ideas about common business practices in Canada

* Photos and illustrations provide visual reinforcement

* Clear, simple language makes the text easy to understand if English is not your first language

* Business Buzzwords help you understand common slang, jargon, and acronyms in the workplace

* Action plans at the end of chapters help you put your new knowledge into action

* Quotations from business leaders across Canada—many of them immigrants themselves who have succeeded in the Canadian workplace—give encouragement and solutions to many of your challenges

How to read this book

Employees

If you are about to start your first job in Canada, it's a good idea to read Section 1: Getting Started before you begin your job. It will give you an overview of the Canadian workplace and what to expect in your first weeks on the job.

After that, you don't have to read the whole book at once. Read one or two chapters at a time, or skip ahead to the chapters that are most important to you.

If you have been on the job for some time, feel free to skip around to the chapters that are most relevant to you. However, it's a good idea to read the first chapters as well, as they may fill in some gaps in your knowledge and understanding of the Canadian workplace.

Managers and human resources professionals

Reading Section 1: Getting Started will help you understand the main cultural challenges that your employees face. The whole book will give you a wealth of information that you can use to coach your employees to greater success.

You may also appreciate reading the hard-won wisdom of vice-presidents and mangers from large corporations—immigrants who have succeeded in the Canadian workplace.

To your success!

Lynda Goldman

Questions or comments? Join me at my blog,
www.YoureHiredNowWhat.Wordpress.com

Dedication

This book is dedicated to my loving and supportive family: my husband, John Berish, and my daughters, Tara and Andrea Berish who inspired me, and my parents Millicent and Max Goldman, who always encouraged me to achieve more than I ever thought I could!

Acknowledgements

I am very grateful to the many vice-presidents, managers, human resources professionals, and Canadian immigrants who took time out of their busy lives to share their stories and tips for success.

Special thanks go to: Shelley Brown, who gave me invaluable information from the human resources point of view, Sandra Thibaudeau, who provided excellent tips for the written communication sections, Teresa McGill, Margaret Yapp, and Lynn Palmer for your support, and Allison Pond for writing the foreword.

Thank you to the amazing team at Oxford University Press: Julie Wade, with whom I spent a great deal of time driving to every corner of Ontario, and Matt Adamson, Jason Tomassini, Cindy Angelini, Hayley Dalgleish, and Carrie Purcell. It's been a great joy working with all of you to produce this book, and the fun is just beginning.

I wish I had the time and space to separately acknowledge each person who contributed to this book. Please accept my gratitude for your stories and insights:

Naeem "Nick" Noorani, Marvi Yap, Baljit Chadha, Karen Wallis-Musselman, Jeannine Pereira, Lynn Lapierre, Catalina Duque, Sharon Wingfelder, Dessalen Wood, Judith Thompson, Loreli Buenaventura, Alan Kearns, Nicolas Fagnard, Sandra Bizier, Felix Quartey, Karen Bowen, Rakesh Kirtikar, Judith C. Hart, Thomas Manuel, Steve Applebaum, Jean-Rene Paquette, Rania Llewellyn, Gautam Nath, Tina Bakin, Jane Lewis, Adrian Cheung, Marco Della Rocca, Marc Lalande, Cory Garlough, Srini Iyenger, Haakon Saake, Jayne Edmonds, Deborah Bugeja, Norma Tombari, Michelle Caba, Paresh Vyas, Yasmin Meralli, Rhonda Scharf , Tej Singh Hazra, Nazia Bundhoo, Victoria Pazukha, Sheelagh Freeman, Clyde Robertson, Gillian Leithman, Gita Clarkson, Billy Wong

Section 1

Getting Started

How to Work Well in Canada

Beginning a new job in a new country is exciting and challenging. The work environment may be similar to, or very different from, what you are used to.

In This Chapter

- Canadian culture in the workplace
- Professional behaviour in Canada
- Sharing ideas and learning about Canada
- Canadian work values compared with values in other cultures
- How to work successfully in Canada

Canadian culture in the workplace

Culture is a word that applies to your own background or the backgrounds of others. The *Oxford ESL Dictionary* defines culture as "the customs, ideas, civilization, etc. of a particular society or group of people."

We all learn sets of behavioural rules from our families, our teachers, and society. These rules guide us in how we act toward each other in different situations. For important life events, such as birth, marriage, and death, each culture has whole sets of rules on how to act. There are rules about what to wear, what to eat, how to spend one's time, and what to say to one another.

Culture is like an iceberg. Only a small portion of any iceberg is visible above the water because most of the ice is hidden below the water's surface. Just like the tip of an iceberg, there are many aspects of a culture that we can easily recognize through the use of our five senses. These are things we see, hear, smell, feel, and taste. These easily observable parts of culture include the clothes we wear, the food we eat, and our art, sports, and recreation. They also influence how we act on the job.

But under the surface are many cultural influences that we don't observe right away. These may include such things as how we view time, the importance we place on work, and our attitude toward men and women in the workplace. These attitudes and ideas shape the way we interact and do our work.

Canada is home to a mix of Aboriginal people, English and French Canadians, and a rapidly growing population of immigrants from many countries. Canadians share in certain values with Americans, due to geography and the widespread influence of US culture, yet the two groups are distinctly different in other ways.

In *Arrival Survival Canada*, Naeem "Nick" Noorani writes, "Canadians are proud that their country embraces many cultures. It is, in fact, one of the most ethnically and racially diverse countries in the world … (a) mosaic that makes this land of about 33 million people truly multicultural.

"Canada, often called a 'nation of immigrants,' has always been a land of ethnic diversity, from as early as the 1880s when Chinese men came to work on the transnational railway connecting Canada's east and west. Some people say that Canada is a unique country that was created not through war and bloodshed, but through the creation of the railway. While it would be inaccurate and simplistic to suggest that its people have lived side by side in perfect harmony through the years, they have lived in relative peace.

"As the country grows through immigration, Canadians of every ethnicity and background are finding places for themselves and learning to enjoy and celebrate their diversity. Under the Canadian Multiculturalism Act, all are encouraged to practise their traditions, customs, and religious beliefs as long as they respect Canadian law."

Canadian culture and workplace customs may be new to you. The business world has its own set of rules on how we dress, what we say to each other, and how we act toward each other. Each company has a distinct culture as well. Companies can be formal or informal, fast-paced or leisurely, and future-oriented or traditional.

This chapter gives you an overview of Canadian business culture and ideas on how to fit in.

Professional behaviour in Canada

The *Oxford ESL Dictionary* defines *professionalism* as "the quality of showing great skill or care when you are doing a job." You are hired for your skills and knowledge, and your ability to do your job. However, the way you do your job is equally important—or even more important—to your success.

Here is an outline of some important concepts related to being professional in Canada. These concepts will be explored in more depth throughout this book.

- Present a professional image. Have good manners. Dress for your industry and company, so you inspire trust and look like you belong.

- Speak professionally and strive to communicate clearly.

- Act professionally. Be courteous and respectful, and have a positive attitude.

- Listen to people and try to understand what they need and want.

- Be reliable. Do what you say you will do, and do it on time. Respect people's schedules, and don't make anyone wait for you.

- Always do your best work and check the details.

- Make every effort to support your manager and to work well with your colleagues.

- Be honest and "above board." Don't spread gossip or say things that are untrue.

- Learn what your boss and your company expect of you, and aim to meet those goals.

- Take responsibility for what you do. If you make a mistake, apologize and do what you can to correct the situation.

Sharing ideas and learning about Canada

"You may appear different from the outside, with a different skin colour or different accent, but sometimes we immigrants tend to be more conscious of that 'difference' than the locals or people born here. Most people are more accepting than you think," says Marvi Yap, of AV Communications, who came to Canada from the Philippines nine years ago.

"Try to go beyond the colour of skin. Try to expand your circle of friends to people of other nationalities. Talk to people who look different from you and you will find life so much more interesting and refreshing. Canada is such a great place to be. You don't need to travel the world to meet so many different kinds of people. The world is Canada!"

Baljit Chadha, who came to Canada at age 21, offers this advice: "Be open to new ideas. Do what's necessary to get started. Your first years will be a learning experience. Don't sulk and complain. Keep a positive attitude. The working conditions in Canada may be different (from what you are used to), so you have to adapt. For example, in Asia, when the boss speaks, everyone steps behind. Here, everyone speaks equally."

Mr. Chadha's positive attitude helped him succeed; he is the president and founder of Balcorp Limited (an international trade and marketing firm), a well-known philanthropist, and a leader of the Sikh community in Canada.

In 2003, Chadha was appointed by Prime Minister Jean Chrétien to the Security Intelligence Review Committee as well as to the Queen's Privy Council for Canada.

When you start working in Canada, be open to your new environment. You came here for a reason, so try not to say negative things about your new country. If you constantly say things like, "Canada is so cold," or "Canada is too conservative," your co-workers may feel that you dislike your new home or workplace.

"As immigrants, it is important to keep our cultures alive," says Karen Wallis-Musselman, an HR Independent Consultant who was born in Caracas, Venezuela. She came to Canada in 2004. "Make sure you discuss any important cultural issues with your employer when you are hired. Remember you are in a different country and you have to abide by the laws of the country, without losing your cultural identity."

At work, speak English or French. It's fine to speak your native language to a co-worker at lunch if you are alone, but if other people join you, don't exclude them by speaking a language they don't understand.

Jeannine Pereira and Lynn Lapierre from Ernst & Young LLP agree. As Associate Directors, they work with professionals from many different backgrounds. "We recognize that every newcomer brings something unique to the workplace, and adds tremendous insight to our firm. At the same time, we encourage employees from different cultural backgrounds to learn about their new working environment," they say. "Don't stick with people from your background. Reach out to understand and find out about other people."

Be open, and share your culture while you learn about Canada. Here are some tips for starting a warm relationship in the Canadian workplace:

- Be open to learning about Canadian culture and other cultures, and also be open to helping people understand your culture.

- Socialize with everyone, not just with people from your country.

- Only bring food from your country to your workplace on special occasions. If you frequently bring food for your co-workers to sample, you'll gain a reputation of being "Mom" or "Dad" at the office, and everyone else will expect you to feed them.

- Share information about your holidays during casual conversations at lunch, not during office hours.

Canadian work values compared with values in other cultures

Here are some common (although not universal) basic principles of working in Canada, compared to principles of some other cultures.

Common Canadian Values	Contrasting Values of Some Other Cultures
Directness, honesty, openness: People should be open and honest and say what they think, but they should be polite and speak in a way that is considerate of other people's feelings.	**Indirectness / Increased directness**: In many Asian cultures, saving face is most important. People are taught to be diplomatic and put the feelings of others first. Honesty isn't necessarily the best policy. In Russia and some Eastern European countries, people are even more direct than in Canada. They see directness as a sign of honesty and respect, but can seem rude to people from less-direct cultures.
Equality: All people are equal. In the workplace, status is observed in a less-obvious way than in other cultures.	**Rank or status**: Roles are defined in terms of one person being subordinate or superior to another, as in Russia or China.
Self-direction: Employees are often given a task and expected to figure out how to do it. They should be willing to work hard and show initiative.	**Hierarchy**: Employees are told exactly what to do and how to do it. Cultures such as those in East Asia and South Asia have a steep pyramid. The boss or chief at the top gives detailed directives which employees are expected to implement.
Change: New ideas are often well-received. Many organizations change constantly.	**Tradition**: In some Asian cultures people are taught to respect their ancestors and observe the rituals, customs, and beliefs from their past.
Time flies: People must save time and be organized, using schedules and time management techniques. In business, it's important to be punctual.	**Time walks**: In many South American cultures and countries such as Indonesia, people take it easy and don't rush. They have more flexible hours and feel that what isn't done today will get done tomorrow.
Short-term outlook: Companies focus on short-term goals. They measure success on a quarter-by-quarter basis.	**Long-term outlook:** Companies sacrifice short-term gain for long-term goals. The Japanese auto industry, for example, has longer-term goals than the North American auto industry.

Common Canadian Values	Contrasting Values of Some Other Cultures
Individualism and privacy: Respect individual needs, personal property and privacy. For example, people do not discuss their salaries with co-workers.	**Group:** The group's needs are most important. Individual needs and property are sacrificed for the group. In the Chinese culture, for example, people tend to consult the group before making decisions. In group cultures, salaries are public knowledge.
Work: Many people define themselves by the type of work they do. They work hard and make work a priority, often giving up personal time for their jobs.	**Being:** People don't define themselves by their work. It's acceptable not to focus on work. In the Scandinavian countries, family life in considered more important than work.
Action and achievement: Action and accomplishment are highly valued. Being productive is a great asset.	**Relationships:** Relationships are more important than action and accomplishments. In the Middle East, business leaders take much longer to get to know each other than North Americans do before they conduct business together.
Self-improvement: People try to improve their own lives. Continued learning is encouraged; many companies offer seminars and workshops, and pay for employees' evening courses.	**Birthright or fate:** People are born into wealth or poverty as determined by fate. It is difficult to change their positions in society. This view is part of Indian culture, although it is changing in some places.
Material goods: Acquiring material possessions is important. (Whoever has the most toys, wins.)	**Spiritualism:** Spiritual and intellectual goals are more important than material goods.
Informality: People relate in a casual way, often using first names, and wear business-casual clothing. There are not many formal rituals.	**Formality:** People are polite with each other. They dress more conservatively, use formal titles and have many rituals. The British and some Europeans are more formal than North Americans

How to work successfully in the Canadian workplace

"It's important to understand the way business in conducted in Canada," says Sharon Wingfelder, Vice-President of Human Resources for Diversity at Canadian Imperial Bank of Commerce (CIBC). People come to Canada because they hear it's a great place, or know someone here. It's important to ask questions and learn the do's and don'ts of working in Canada."

Let's look at some of these values and how they contribute to success in the workplace.

Be direct and open

Yumi, from Japan, had been at her company in Vancouver for several months. Whenever her boss asked for her input on a project, Yumi always said, "This is just a suggestion, but ..." Her boss became frustrated and asked Yumi, "Can you give me some clear input? I need to get all the pros and cons out on the table so I can make the right decisions. You never tell me anything negative, but I know there are some problems with this project."

Neither Yumi nor her boss understood how cultural influences can affect the way people communicate in the workplace. To "get all the pros and cons out on the table" reflects a very Western way of thinking. It means that you say clearly all the good and bad aspects of something. Asians are taught to approach problems or challenges in a more indirect, subtle way.

There are many expressions in English about the importance of being direct:

- Get to the point.
- Don't beat around the bush.
- Let's get down to business.
- Don't talk in circles.
- Let's not waste time.

From an early age, North Americans are taught to speak up in school and say what they want or expect. They learn to be clear and direct, and to look people in the eye to show they are honest. They are taught that it's okay to disagree with people and to stand up for their rights in a professional, objective manner, without becoming overly emotional.

You may come from a culture where direct eye contact is considered threatening, and you may feel that it is more important to maintain a sense of harmony and balance than to confront people directly. If so, you might find communication in Canada to be confusing, and worry about creating conflicts with co-workers and managers.

People with direct communication styles focus on tasks and accomplishments, present facts and figures, and express their opinions and ideas. They use fewer words and say things as clearly as possible to avoid confusion or misinterpretation.

They are concerned with getting their meaning across and see communication as a way to exchange information.

People with indirect communication styles generally provide background information before they make their main point. In unpleasant situations in particular, they use extra words to soften the message and allow the listener to save face. For example, in many Asian countries, the word *yes* can have many different meanings, including "maybe," "I understand," or "not likely." The listener has to interpret the true meaning from the context, and through body language and facial expression.

...But not *too* direct

On a "directness" scale, Canadians are a bit toward the indirect side of the scale. Canadians have a more direct communication style than people from South Asian or Japanese cultures, but are less direct than people from the United States and some Eastern European countries.

People who come from a more direct culture may seem rude or unsophisticated because they make strong comments and judgments. They may offend clients or co-workers (who are used to less-direct communication) when they don't use subtleties in their communication.

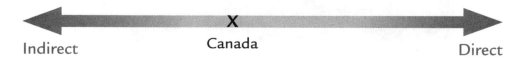

Indirect   **X** Canada   Direct

"I never realized that it's possible to hurt someone's feelings by saying something that is normal in your own culture," one of Teresa McGill's students told her. Teresa McGill is President of Gandy Associates, which provides English Communication Training. They work with technical professionals from many cultural backgrounds. She says, "Some people seem too direct, and some aren't direct enough. Other people notice and react to what they say, but they don't always tell them (that there may be a communication problem)."

McGill says that it's important to learn the language of influence so you can establish common ground with other people. She suggests memorizing key phrases so you are comfortable using them. This way, you'll be able to speak professionally even in stressful situations, such as working on a tight deadline. For example, one of McGill's students realized that he was speaking strongly to co-workers and getting a negative reaction. He practised and used the phrase, "I'm sure we can all agree that ..." and got better results.

Learn the nuances of Canadian business language

"Compare Canadian business language to a hamburger," suggests Dessalen Wood, Senior Director of Human Resources at Airborne Mobile. "The meat of the hamburger is the content—what you want to say. The bun and dressing make it tastier to eat. So the meat of your message could be, 'We have a problem' and the dressing would be, 'How can we resolve this together?'"

Canadians "sandwich" their messages with words and phrases to smooth the way. They use phrases that persuade people and make it easier to work together. This helps them get support, and avoids unnecessary conflict.

As Wood suggests, you need a bun around the hamburger to work well with people. For example, instead of saying, "You have to ..." use softening phrases such as the following:

- "We need to ..."
- "Is there anything I can do to help?"
- "How can we resolve this issue?"
- "Let's work together on this challenge."
- "I need your help in ..."

Be self-directed

Assad's new boss gave him a project to work on. Assad agreed, and went back to his desk. A week later his boss asked Assad to give him a progress report. Assad was confused, and said he hadn't done anything. His boss looked annoyed and asked, "Why not?" Assad replied, "You never told me how to do it."

What are your expectations at your Canadian job? Do you expect your boss to tell you exactly what to do? Or do you expect to take initiative and do the job on your own once it is assigned to you? Much of this depends on your cultural background and your beliefs about the workplace.

Communication conflicts occur when people from a hierarchal culture work with people from a self-directed culture, such as in Canada. In the hierarchal culture, the boss makes all the decisions and tells the employees what to do. The subordinates are paid to carry out the boss's directives.

The hierarchal style means that direction comes from above. Employees show respect and do not challenge people in power, because of an understanding of status and position. Employees take on specific roles and are limited in their behaviours. There are many guidelines and regulations for how people should act, and men and women often behave differently and are treated differently by their employers and co-workers.

Canada is relatively low in hierarchical structure, and many managers here act like coaches. They influence their team members and only give direction in a general way. The manager may decide what needs to be accomplished, and then let the employees figure out how to do the work. For example, a manager may say, "Prepare a presentation for the client," and allow the employee to take care of the details.

In contrast, a top-down manager in a hierarchal culture will want to check all the details of the presentation, and may even supply all of the information.

Employees in Canada are expected to be self-directed and are allowed to make many decisions on their own. They have flexibility in how they get the job done, and in their role on a team. Employees are expected to ask questions up front, and then make sure that the job gets completed.

Employees can—respectfully—challenge the opinions of the people in power, although this varies from company to company, and from one department to another. Men and women are treated basically in the same way, although there are still many instances where inequality exists.

Conflicts can happen when a Canadian employer assumes that an employee will solve a problem or make a decision on his own or with minimal instruction, as in the case of Assad. The employee from a hierarchal culture waits for further instruction, while the boss assumes the work is being done. The employee may think, "Isn't my boss being paid to make decisions and figure out how to do things? Why is he putting the responsibility on me? My job is to do what people tell me to do." In this situation, each person is expecting the other one to act, and nothing is being accomplished.

What should you do?

One of the greatest challenges for immigrants is figuring out who makes decisions in their workplace. If you come from a culture where managers tell employees what to do, good employees listen carefully to their managers' opinions and directives and follow these instructions to the letter.

Pay close attention to what is expected of you in Canada. Your manager may expect you to implement ideas with little direction. If you aren't sure how much responsibility to take on, ask your manager to explain what is expected of you and how much he wants you to report back on your progress.

Make sure you know what to do and when to have each task completed. Don't be afraid to ask questions. Good employees take the time to figure out what they need to do before they begin a new project. Don't forget that your manager will be the judge of your success on any task that he gives you.

Take individual responsibility

The Sorin Group manufactures medical devices. They have 250 employees, with over 90 percent coming from cultural backgrounds other than Canada. Judith Thompson, Senior Manager of Human Resources, explains that the company no longer gives public recognition for excellent performance.

"We've had people give extraordinary performances. Some have never failed once in delivering a perfect product. However, when we gave individuals public recognition, the recipients felt very uncomfortable and asked not to be recognized publicly. Now we recognize people's achievements in private and only give awards publicly when someone has worked for the company for five or ten years."

Individualism can be a striking difference for people from collective cultures. Westerners place high importance on individuality and personal success. In the past, some physicians told parents to let their babies cry so they would develop independence. Of course many parents didn't do this, but many still agree with the philosophy that individuals should independently develop their skills and find their own true path in life. Westerners are taught to value themselves as separate individuals with responsibility for their own destinies and actions.

Even more than Canadians, Americans are perhaps the leaders in the rugged, individualistic style of self-reliance. Typical American expressions include the following:

- Do your own thing. (Do whatever is important to you.)

- You can't depend on anyone but yourself.

- You made your bed, now lie in it. (You have to take the consequences for what you do).

- You'd better look out for yourself—no one else will.

- It's every man for himself (or woman for herself).

Canadian Business Concept: Canadians and Americans are among the most individualistic people in the world. In business, they reward employees for taking initiative and they often give public awards for personal achievement and individual leadership.

An example of individual cultures versus collective cultures can be observed in restaurants. Canadian restaurants offer many choices, and generally everyone at the table orders something different. In contrast, China is a collective culture. Chinese people order food for the whole table, and place it on a turntable so that everyone shares all the dishes. There is no sense of "my food" and "your food" as in Canada.

Other examples can be found in the values taught in Japanese, Chinese, and Malaysian cultures, which value the group over the individual. Children are taught that they are a part of a circle of relations, or a member of a group. They are rewarded for cooperating and conforming to group norms. A person's identity is not isolated, but is connected to his social network. In the Sorin Group, employees from group cultures did not want to be singled out, and felt disloyal when they were publicly recognized—even when they merited the recognition.

Show initiative

"A new professional in our department came from a culture where he didn't make eye contact or question clients directly. He had a great deal of knowledge, but he thought that he was showing respect by not speaking unless he was addressed. His clients, however, were waiting for him to take the lead and provide solutions to their problems. We coached him on leadership skills, so that he realized that his Canadian clients wanted to hear his ideas. He is now a partner in the firm," said Jeannine Pereira and Lynn Lapierre, Associate Directors of Ernst & Young LLP.

Lack of initiative is a common misperception that managers have of immigrants from cultures such as East Asia, South Asia, and Africa. People who come from a culture that is more hierarchal may be seen as lacking in initiative if they rarely speak out or challenge anyone, or don't offer their ideas or volunteer for projects.

Managers say that dealing with this unwillingness to speak up is like pulling teeth when employees sit silently in meetings and don't share their ideas.

In Canada, you will be encouraged to take initiative. It will put you on the path to leadership, and clients will appreciate when you ask questions and help them find solutions to their problems.

Canadian managers have little patience for open-ended questions such as "What should I do?" or "How do you want me to do this?" When you first start working at a company, you should ask your manager how he wants you to do things. After that, don't ask him the same questions every time you have a task to do. Try to do research on the Internet, or ask a colleague how something was done before. On the other hand, if you really need help, don't try to do something new without checking with your boss on how to do it. Managers don't want you to waste time reinventing the wheel.

You'll raise your esteem in your manager's eyes by going to him with solutions, not just questions, and by finding out how to get things done on your own.

Understand equality in the workplace

 Carlos was working in a team with several other Canadians. His boss explained what needed to be done, and asked the team members to divide up the work. Alice, another team member, took the initiative to organize the work, and together the team members decided who would do what.

At their next team meeting, Carlos was the only one who hadn't done his work. He had felt uncomfortable taking direction from a woman, and decided to wait until his male boss told him what to do.

Women's equality in the workplace has been a sensitive issue for many years in North America. Two generations ago, most Canadian women stayed home to take care of families. Today, most young women plan to spend at least part, if not all, of their adult lives working. In fact, now more than 50 percent of students studying to work in the legal and medical fields are female.

In Canada, women work in every segment of the job market. And, while overall there are still fewer women than men at the very top tiers of companies, there are more women leading companies than in the past. There are also many more women at middle- and senior-management levels.

"I'm used to seeing men in higher positions in Colombia," says Catalina Duque, a Graduate Leadership Program Associate at Royal Bank of Canada (RBC). "There are not many women in management. But in Canada there are more opportunities. At RBC, women are considered differently (than they are in Colombia). RBC really values your skills and helps you develop. I see lots of women in management positions, making high-level decisions."

If you are a male who feels uncomfortable taking direction from a female manager, an understanding of the changing workplace is important. Although some men continue to feel threatened by working with women, most men have accepted that woman are equal partners in the workplace, and these men have friendly working relationships with their female co-workers.

Canadian Business Concept: In Canada's changing workplace, there are more women leading companies and working at all levels of companies than ever before.

Female managers have the same expectations of their employees as their male counterparts do. Observing acceptable behaviours will help minimize embarrassment and conflict on the job. Here are some tips for men who work for women:

- As with any manager, let her take the lead in how formal or informal the working relationship will be.

- Allow your manager to dictate the timeframe and pace for getting work done.

- Treat your female manager with the same respect and consideration that you would treat a male manager. The rule is to treat everyone according to position within the company, not according to gender.

- Don't be condescending and assume women need your help. Never say, "Since you're a woman, you'll need help from a man."

- Never interpret friendliness from any women in the workplace as a romantic gesture. Remember that Canadians are less formal than those from some other cultures, and co-workers often engage in friendly discussion. It is normal for men and women to be friends.

Respect people's time—never be late

 Elizabeth had two new analysts in her department, Arti and Fajar from Indonesia. She wanted to welcome them to her team, and decided to host a dinner party at her home. She invited the ten people in her group to her house for 7 p.m. The eight Canadians arrived promptly. There was no sign of the two new team members. Elizabeth was upset and worried that Arti and Fajar were lost or that something had happened to them. Finally, at 8:15 the doorbell rang. The two analysts stood at the door, relaxed and smiling, completely oblivious to the annoyed looks from their teammates.

In Canada, time is important. We view time as a valuable, scarce resource. Canadians value promptness and take time and commitments seriously.

Many people outside of North America proceed at a more leisurely pace. In fact, Indonesians talk about *rubber time*. They are relaxed about time, and see time as plentiful. If something doesn't get done today, it will get done tomorrow.

Canadians do not understand people who don't respect time, and may become very irritated when people don't respect time commitments. If you are invited somewhere for 7 p.m., you are expected to arrive at 7 p.m. This is important for a dinner party, where the hosts may be cooking food that they expect to serve at a specific time. For a social event where people don't sit down to dinner, being 10 or 15 minutes late is alright, but being later than that is never acceptable. The exception is a very open invitation such as "drop by between 5 and 7 for drinks."

Canadians view time as linear, and they do one task after another. They place great importance on managing their time, reading books and attending workshops devoted to creating schedules, and coordinating and allocating time to various tasks. They track their time using calendars and software, and are always looking for ways to save time and do things more quickly. (See Chapter 15 for advice on how to do this.)

Understand Canada's work ethic

 When Sven first came to Canada, he was surprised to hear his co-workers complaining, "I work 60 or 70 hours a week." It didn't really sound like they were complaining, though. In fact, it sounded like they were boasting.

According to Everest College's Labour Day Poll, 55 percent of employed Canadians routinely spend nine or more hours a day working and commuting, and 35 percent say they work over the Labour Day weekend.

Many Canadians and Americans define themselves by what they do. They say, "I'm an accountant" or "I'm a nurse." In fact, people in other cultures are often surprised at how North Americans "live to work" and are ready to sacrifice anything for their jobs, often uprooting families to relocate for a better job. Canadians see work as central to life, not just part of life. They often put work ahead of family, friends, leisure time, and even their own health. In places such as Scandinavia, people "work to live." They leave the office at 5 p.m. and don't bring work home with them.

In the past, there were some differences in this aspect of work culture within Canada. In Toronto, people worked long hours and took few vacations. Montrealers had the reputation for being more European in sentiment, placing more importance on family and recreation than on work. This has changed, and Montreal is now closer to Toronto in its work ethic.

 Canadian Business Concept: Work is a high priority for most Canadians, and many people work overtime and on weekends to complete their work.

Recognize that job success is based on performance

Lily was hired to replace someone on sick leave. She wanted to work at this particular company, and was very happy to get a temporary job in the marketing department. When the person she was replacing returned from sick leave, the manager asked Lily if she wanted to replace someone in the shipping department for a few weeks. Lily was hoping to get a full-time job with the company, so she agreed, although she was not excited about working in shipping.

Lily quickly became very bored packing boxes, and she slacked off. She frequently arrived late and took extra long lunches and coffee breaks. She appeared uninterested in her job, and complained often that her back hurt.

When a new marketing job opened up, Lily eagerly applied. She was stunned to find out that someone from outside the company had been hired. The manager told Lily that her negative attitude and poor performance put her out of the running for any job at that company.

When you start a new job, the most important things you can do are to work hard and show initiative. Demonstrate that you are responsible and serious about your work. Do your best at every task you receive, even if you find it boring or it's not in your job description.

In Canada, people are hired with the understanding that to keep their jobs and get promoted, they have to perform their job functions well and get along with people.

In some countries, the only reason people lose their jobs is for criminal behaviour. In Canada, people cannot be fired legally without a reason, but people understand that no job is permanent. While there are many different circumstances that contribute to how long someone keeps a job, to a large part, success in the workplace depends on performing well.

Prove that you are dependable

In a new team of five people, Gail consistently arrived late at meetings. Several times during the course of the project, Gail was supposed to provide specific information for other team members. Instead of bringing the information, Gail brought excuses: she had too much work, she misunderstood what she was supposed to do ... the list was endless. Needless to say, team members started to talk about their frustration in working with Gail, and the team was not able to meet its goals. Gail's lack of professionalism had a negative impact on the whole team.

In business, time is money. People who are habitually late, or turn in sloppy work, cause the company to lose revenues. They also cause ongoing frustration to teammates who depend on them. In Canada, being unreliable is being disrespectful to team members.

When you fail to show up on time, other people on your team have to cover for you. This can make you unpopular and your career can suffer.

To gain respect, be reliable. Do what you say you will do. You will gain a reputation for being dependable. Your boss will become confident that you will be ready to work tomorrow and the next day, and that you'll get the job done properly.

How to show respect in the Canadian workplace

You may be wondering what Canadians do to show respect in the workplace. Here are some guidelines:

- Greet people briefly in the morning. People typically don't have elaborate or lengthy greetings.

- Remember people's names, and use them—but don't overdo it.

- Shake hands when you meet someone new. People don't typically shake hands every day.

- Be on time (never more than five minutes late, and always at least five minutes early for important meetings and events).

- Respect people's privacy—this includes not looking at papers on your co-workers' desks.

- Show interest in other people and help them when you can.

- Get your work done on time, or warn people if there will be a delay.

Writer Anais Nin says, "How we see things is more about how experience has shaped our lives than some absolute truth." We are all influenced by the behavioural rules we learned from family, school, and society early in life. When you come to a new country, you may find people behaving in ways that are different. Be open to learning about these new behaviours, and keep in mind that there isn't one way to do things, but many possible ways.

Business Buzzwords

- beat around the bush
- cover for someone
- do your own thing
- out of the running
- time flies
- time is money

Chapter 1 Action Plan

1. What have you observed about Canadian work values? Using the chart on pages 7 and 8 as a starting point, write down three observations you've had about the Canadian workplace. How similar or different are these values to your working experience in other countries?

   _____

   _____

   _____

2. What expressions do you hear in your workplace, such as *Get to the point* or *Let's not waste time*? Write down any expression you hear your manager or co-workers use.

   _____

   _____

   _____

3. How can you adapt to fit into the Canadian workplace more easily? List any changes to your language or behaviour that will help you fit in.

   _____

   _____

   _____

Understanding Your Workplace Culture

You've worked hard to land the job you want, and now you are getting started. They've chosen you!

In This Chapter

- Learning about your workplace culture
- Getting oriented to your workplace
- Finding out your rights and benefits
- Finding out the norms in your workplace

Learning about your workplace culture

You probably heaved a sigh of relief when you landed the job. From now until the end of the first month, you have to learn the ropes and make a positive first impression on your boss, co-workers, and clients. You want to show everyone that you can do the job, and that they made the right decision in hiring you.

You may be feeling nervous and uncertain about what is expected of you, even if you've been in a similar job before. Being in a new company means you are starting all over again. While this may sound intimidating, transitions into a new work situation are fairly easy when you know what to do.

Every workplace has a culture

When Mila began working at a technology company, she was surprised to get emails from the person in the cubicle next to her. In her previous job, people would chat in the corridor, or walk over to someone else's desk. At her new company, email was the main way to communicate.

Just as every country has its own culture, every workplace has its own culture or personality as well. A company's personality is made up of the people in the organization—both the employers and the employees. Each company has its special rituals, methods of communicating, and ways of doing business.

Every workplace has its accepted practices and unwritten rules, which you have to learn. For example, if you want to talk to your boss or to co-workers, do you just walk over to them for a chat? Do you send an email? Is there a special meeting request program to communicate about these matters? Does your manager come to your cubicle, or do you go to her office?

To do well in your company, you have to understand and appreciate the culture and values of the organization. You also have to recognize and participate in the formal and informal social networks in your organization.

Many big companies provide a great deal of support for new employees. Loreli Buenaventura, National Manager of Diversity, Equity, and Inclusion at KPMG says, "We have a Peer Coach program as part of our onboarding process, where we pair new employees with someone to answer questions and provide guidance in the first months.

"We also have the International Club that assists international hires and secondees (people who come to Canada from other KPMG firms for a period of time and then return to their home country), as they acclimatize to the Canadian business environment. The club provides support on such issues as international credentials, obtaining Canadian designations, Canadian business culture, and common questions about living and working in Canada. The club also matches new members with mentors and holds regular social networking events."

"'Help me understand,' is one of the key requests a newcomer can make," says Sharon Wingfelder, Vice-President of Human Resources for Diversity at CIBC. "Joining a large organization can be an overwhelming experience and can make you feel lonely until you get to know people and build a network. We help new employees even before they start work by providing a portal with information about the organization and its priorities, and a welcome video from the CEO who describes why they've made a great choice to join our organization.

"We launched an onboarding program to connect employees to the organization before they begin, help them understand how their roles contribute to the broader priorities and objectives of the organization, and ensure that logistical factors are in place by an employee's first day. By succeeding in these areas, employees can begin to feel connected to the organization faster.

"Even more important, we provide support. We make sure new employees have someone to lean on. They always have someone to go to with questions."

Scotiabank also has a novel way to help new employees from different cultures, as well as educational and business backgrounds, fit into the workplace, says Rania Llewellyn, Vice-President of Multicultural Banking. "We provide a mentorship toolkit to help employees find not just one mentor, but two mentors if they choose. For instance, one mentor comes from the same cultural background, to help people understand the Canadian workplace. The other mentor has been in the organization for a while, and is not new to Canada. This mentor helps new employees see how they are being perceived by others. Having a mentor is up to the employee, but Scotiabank strongly encourages it.

"Attending office, business, and social events is another method of finding out about your company's culture. This is a good way to quietly observe how your company operates."

If you work in a smaller company that does not match you up with a mentor, look for some friendly people who will take you under their wing. These people are your key to understanding and working with the rest of the employees.

Watch and listen to learn about your company's culture

 At Chen's first meeting at his new company, he was surprised at the behaviour he witnessed. As a team member gave a brief presentation on his project, the manager was slouched over in her chair, resting her head on her arm. One co-worker arrived wearing a tank top, a short skirt, and flip-flops. Another colleague was chewing gum and doodling in his notebook. The person to Chen's left was text messaging under the table.

Like Chen, you may come from a formal culture where there are specific ways of doing things. North American workplaces are generally informal. *Let's not stand on ceremony* is a saying that means "let's not be stuffy and formal." Canadians tend to be slightly more formal than Americans, but less strict about following protocol than the British.

You'll see evidence of this in dress codes that allow people to wear clothes that are not business-appropriate in other cultures. Canadians often sit in a relaxed manner during meetings and call each other by their first names.

This informality is noticeable in workplaces where many generations work together. The older generations tend to be formal, while the younger generations are increasingly informal. However, you will also notice that Canadians of all ages are very polite, and say more than their share of *please* and *thank you*.

When you begin your job, the most important thing you can do is to pay attention. Every company is different. Look and listen to what people say and how they act. Study every aspect of the company to figure out what level of formality is the office norm.

Watch how people in your company present themselves. Do they dress formally or casually? Ask your supervisor if your company has a dress code. Before your first day, discuss what to wear so you don't start off on the wrong foot.

Do people politely hold open the doors for each other? How do your co-workers greet each other every day? Do most people just say a casual "Hi"? How do your colleagues interact with managers, executives, and clients? Learn the unwritten rules of your workplace. Then begin to adapt your behaviour to your work environment.

Gathering critical information

Start gathering critical information about your company. This may be easier with large companies that have existed for many years and have extensive websites. Begin with the basics, such as your company's history, current products, and future vision. Find information about your company's mission statement, goals, values, and corporate image. Examine the website, recruiting materials, and annual report.

Is your company guided by cooperation or competition? Is it focused on new products or customer service? Is the company very concerned with its bottom line, or is it a family-focused business? Does it have a gym or daycare on the premises? This can demonstrate the company's values and the way it supports employees.

Ask what kind of training you will receive. Many companies provide extensive training before you are expected to work on your own. Make the most of this training period. For example, if you are in sales, start learning about the products on your own, even before the training begins. You'll impress the trainers with your thoroughness.

Find out about your industry. Who are the important players? These may include competitors, customers, or suppliers. What are the trends and forecasts for your industry and for your company? Understanding these trends is crucial—continue to stay on top of industry events during your entire stay at the company, not just in your first weeks.

Learning your company's rules

"Recognize the need to change and adapt," suggests Alan Kearns, author of *Career Joy*. "What works in one company doesn't work in another. This doesn't mean you have to change yourself, but you have to adapt to the circumstances. People who are unwilling to change won't survive."

Although companies are the same in many ways, each one has its own way of doing things. In your first weeks on the job, you will be finding out how the company operates. It will take time to understand what is unique about your company—until then, you may wish you had a GPS system to guide you!

Every company has its own set of rules, processes, and procedures. Some of the elements are easy to see. Other behaviours and processes are not as apparent at first.

At the first level, there are things you can see, such as the office building, the work processes, and the art or awards on the walls. At the next level are the values, which include the goals, strategies, and philosophies of the company. Hidden below is the third level, the underlying beliefs.

At the first level, for example, you can see that your company has a daycare centre or a gym. At the second level, this shows you that the company wants to make the workplace convenient and comfortable. Employees don't have to rush to pick up their children from daycares across town or travel to a gym. The third level, or underlying belief, is that employees who are in good health and know that their children are in good hands will feel less stressed and be more productive. This company values its employees' health, including their work / life balance.

Most companies are a combination of things that are great and things that are not ideal. Like people, companies are not perfect. As you get to know the company better, you will find things to appreciate and things you have to learn to live with.

Company pace

Each company has its own timelines and ways of operating. Some companies are slower to get a project off the ground, while others go quickly from idea to execution. You will learn about your company's pace and how it fits in to the industry.

Some industries have calendars that dictate when products are launched and marketed, or when services are required. For example, the fashion industry has specific seasons, while the accounting industry is in frenzy every April, when people file their income tax returns. Some companies always have a sense of urgency, with employees who feel that it's always crazy around their workplace.

Keep your eyes open to see how decisions are made, and what steps are involved in getting a new idea up and running.

Workplace language—what do these acronyms mean?

During your first weeks, you will find new uses of the English language that you never learned in ESL classes. Don't panic or reach for your dictionary. These are the acronyms that are specific to your company—combinations of letters that may have no meaning to anyone outside your organization.

The *Oxford ESL Dictionary* defines an *acronym* as "a short word that is made from the first letters of a group of words." For example, ESL is an acronym for English as a Second Language.

Some common acronyms that you may hear include the following:

Don't panic if you don't understand the acronyms your company uses.

- **HR:** Human Resources
- **CEO:** Chief Executive Officer
- **VP:** Vice President
- **IT:** Information Technology
- **PR:** Public Relations

As a new employee, you can ask questions about these terms without getting funny looks for not knowing them. And remember that new acronyms are created all the time, so be sure to ask for clarification.

Getting oriented to your workplace

"If your company runs an orientation session, go!" says Shelley Brown, President of Bromelin People Practices. "Many employees don't bother. This is a mistake. The orientation session is critical to integrating into the company. If you are given materials about the company in the first few days, be sure to read them. If you are not given information on the company's products, ask for it."

At the orientation session you will hear about the company's values and processes. At smaller companies the orientation may be less formal.

Most companies give you some orientation documents. These can vary from a new-hire folder to an employee handbook that outlines things such as performance reviews, compensation, company benefits, vacations, and dress codes. Study the package of materials to find out the company's rules and regulations. Treat it like your new best friend.

If you don't receive information about the company, ask for it. Not many people ask questions at orientation sessions. You'll make a good impression if you do, because it shows that you are interested.

Also, check the company's website for general policies, and to see if the company has been in the news recently. If the site has a PR (public relations) section, read the news releases.

Paperwork for human resources (HR)

You will receive paperwork from the HR department (or your employer, if your company does not have an HR department), including legal documents such as tax forms. It is important to fill out these documents right away. Without doing so, you cannot be put on the payroll. If you aren't sure what one of the documents is for, ask your manager or a colleague to help you.

You may also be asked to give your employer a specimen cheque. This is a blank cheque from your bank account. It is used for direct deposit, which means that your company will deposit your earnings directly into your account instead of handing you a paycheque.

Simply draw two lines through your cheque and write *Void* in the middle.

Return your documents to HR as soon as possible. Administrators appreciate when you complete paperwork quickly. They will see that you are responsible and efficient, and you'll earn brownie points with them. This can help you later on; when you need something from the administration, they will make life easier for you.

Fill out all of your forms completely, and don't forget to name a beneficiary. If you are unsure of who to name as your beneficiary, designate your estate. Filling out the forms completely will ensure that your benefit coverage and your pension contributions start immediately. The forms that require this information are company-paid life insurance, optional employee-paid group life insurance, pension enrolment forms, and group RRSP (Registered Retirement Savings Plan) contribution forms.

A **beneficiary** is the person who receives an individual's money or property when that individual dies. For example, people usually name beneficiaries in their wills.

A **will** is a legal document that outlines what will happen to someone's money and property after she dies.

An estate refers to all the money and property that a person owns, especially everything that is left when she dies.

A **pension** is the money you will receive when you retire. From every paycheque, your employer will deduct some money that will be contributed to your pension fund.

Canadian Business Concept: Find out about all the forms you have to sign, and what they mean. Ask your HR representative to explain them to you. It can make a big difference in the amount of money you collect when you retire or when you have an insurance claim.

Finding out your rights and benefits

Canadian Business Concept: A perk is something extra you get from your employer in addition to your salary. For example, international travel may be one of the perks of your job.

Time off

Now that you have the job, you can find out the perks, such as how much vacation time you have. Be sure to read and understand your company's vacation policy. Most companies give a standard two weeks per year, but policies on paid holidays, personal days, sick and bereavement leave, and short- and long-term disability vary from company to company.

Find out about the statutory holidays, or the days that you will either not have to work or be paid overtime. Some statutory holidays are only observed in certain provinces; the chart on the next page shows the ones that are generally observed nationally. If you work in an industry that gives round-the-clock services, such as a hospital or some essential services, find out the policies for overtime work and pay.

Civic holidays also vary from province to province. For example, most provinces have a civic day the first Monday in August. Quebec doesn't have this holiday, but is the only province that celebrates the statutory holiday Saint-Jean-Baptiste day on June 24. In Quebec, many businesses also close down during the last two weeks of July.

Some companies also limit the vacation time you can take during your first months of employment. It's a good idea not to ask for a vacation in the first few months. If you ask for time off too soon, it looks like you are more interested in the perks of the job than in the job itself.

Religious holidays are acknowledged by most Canadian workplaces in one way or another. Check your provincial guidelines, and speak to your manager about your company's policies. In some companies, employees exchange vacation days or sick days for faith holidays. In other companies, employees can take these days off without pay.

Statutory Holidays	2010	2011	2012	2013	2014
New Year's Day	Jan 1	Jan 1	Jan 1	Jan 1	Jan 1
Good Friday	April 2	April 22	April 6	March 29	April 18
Easter Monday	April 5	April 25	April 9	April 1	April 21
Victoria Day	May 24	May 23	May 21	May 20	May 19
Canada Day	July 1	July 1	July 1	July 1	July 1
Labour Day	Sept 6	Sept 5	Sept 3	Sept 2	Sept 1
Thanksgiving Day	Oct 11	Oct 10	Oct 8	Oct 14	Oct 13
Christmas	Dec 25	Dec 25	Dec 25	Dec 25	Dec 25
Boxing Day	Dec 26	Dec 26	Dec 26	Dec 26	Dec 26

Maternity or paternity leave is a period of time when parents are allowed to leave their jobs to give birth to or begin raising their babies. The parents continue to receive a large portion of their pay during this time; a small amount is deducted. Maternity or paternity leave can also be taken when someone adopts a baby. Maternity and paternity leave policies vary from company to company. Find out the details of your company's policy and how much time off you can expect.

Medical benefits

Canada has a medicare system that covers your basic medical care. However, dental services and some other health needs such as physiotherapy are not covered. Many companies have group health policies that cover everything from eyeglasses to massages. However, every policy is different, so read yours carefully. Some policies have a waiting period, so check to make sure your coverage has begun before you book an eye exam or physiotherapy appointment.

Companies may also require a pre-employment medical exam. Even if you don't want to go because you feel that your health is private, it is important to understand that you need this exam if you want your employer to provide coverage.

The insurance company wants to know if you have a pre-existing condition, because medical conditions that began before your employment will not be covered. As well, if you work in a warehouse and lift boxes, some companies require a medical exam to see if you can fulfill your duties. Additionally, some employers will need to check their employees' eyesight, to make sure the employee is able to safely drive a bus or perform other work that requires perfect vision.

Expense accounts

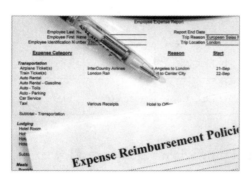

Getting reimbursed for your expenses involves more than just handing in receipts for anything you spend money on for the company.

You have to find out what you can expense, how to expense it (on paper or through a computer-based system), whether you should use a specific credit card for company expenses, and whether you are required to use certain vendors in order to be reimbursed.

When you travel or eat out on company time, don't choose the most expensive dinners and wines. Select items in the middle price range. Most companies have a daily limit—for example, $15 for lunch and $30 for dinner. Check on your company's policy before you spend your money, because if you spend more than the limit, you will have to pay the difference. Find out about any restrictions on expenses and learn what your per diem (daily allocation of money for meals and expenses) is. You may have to use your own credit card and then hand in your receipts for reimbursement.

Find out exactly what you will be reimbursed for, and don't submit anything that does not meet these requirements. As enticing as it sounds, don't pad your account with non-business expenses or take your spouse out to dinner when you return from a business trip. You may get away with it once or twice, but this practice can cost you substantially if the company finds out.

When you stay at a hotel, remember that anything you take from the mini-bar in your room comes out of your total for the day, and the prices add up quickly. Taking these items can also look bad because your boss may assume you are drinking the alcohol from the mini-bar. Instead, go down to the store in the hotel lobby, where the prices are almost always lower. Remember that many companies don't pay for alcohol. Some people also make the mistake of ordering a movie or two in their hotel room, but most companies will not reimburse for these.

Finding out the norms in your workplace

Nicolas Fagnard recently came to Canada from Belgium. He observed, "In Belgium you'd be considered rude if you didn't say good morning to everyone who works in your area—even if you're a manager. For example, one manager I knew used to arrive half an hour later than his employees, but he made sure to greet every single employee in the department every day (about 35 people) by shaking hands or kissing the women on their cheeks.

"In Canada, I noticed that people mostly greet each other when they have to ask them something, and it's pretty rare to shake hands with someone except for meeting them the first day of work or after the New Year's vacation.

"I also noticed that when people make small-talk about personal things at work, it only lasts a few minutes before they get back to work. In Belgium it can last an hour."

Of all the things we do at work every day, one of the most common is greeting people—including co-workers, managers, and clients. In many cultures, greetings are a way for people to connect and build relationships. People are often very surprised to see how brief Canadian greetings can be. Canadians often greet their managers or co-workers with a quick "Hi, how's it going?" or even just nodding their heads, smiling or waving their hands. They may ask a co-worker "Did you catch the game last night?" but then return to work quickly.

Every workplace has its own way of operating on a day-to-day basis. The following are some things to look for.

Greetings and small-talk

- How do people greet each other when they arrive in the morning and leave at the end of the day?

- When do people shake hands?

- How much office chit-chat occurs? How long does it last? What do people talk about?

Personal business

Watch carefully how employees deal with personal business during the workday. How many personal emails and phone calls are tolerated? How do people deal with personal and family issues?

Find out how you are expected to deal with personal and family issues, such as taking time off to care for a sick child, go to an appointment at the bank, sign paperwork to purchase a new car, or go to a doctor or dentist appointment. In most professional environments you can take an hour or two off and make it up by staying late. Most employers are compassionate when you have to attend a funeral, and don't ask you to make up the time.

The amount of time off that employees receive varies among provinces and employers. Look into how many unpaid days you can take off for family emergencies—such as looking after a sick child or parent—or for bereavement leave, marriage leave, or moving. Be sure to ask your manager for these details. If you ask your co-workers, you may not get accurate information.

Breaks

Observe how people take breaks at your office. Although breaks are required by law, every company has its own ways of operating. Some breaks are formal—for example, everyone may get a coffee break at a certain time. In other companies, you can take your break whenever you want it.

Observe your co-workers. If they invite you for a cup of coffee or a quick chat, join them. To be on the safe side, keep your breaks short, especially at the beginning of your employment. Refresh yourself and then return to your desk.

Lunch breaks are generally one hour, but every company is different. At some companies people eat at their desks. At others, people go to the cafeteria, or go out to eat. Follow what others do, but when you first begin, be extra careful to stick to your allotted time. Canadians are time-conscious, and taking even a few extra minutes can make a poor impression on your boss or co-workers.

"Take your breaks and lunch on time. At most companies, employees take different lunch hours so there is always somebody in the office. Make sure you ask what kind of facilities they have: kitchen with microwave oven, cafeteria, et cetera. Some companies have the policy of no food on your desk," says Karen Wallis-Musselman.

The end of the day

Find out how to end the day in your company culture. In environments where you punch a clock, everyone leaves at the same time. But in offices, you may have specific tasks to complete, such as printing end-of-the-day reports, speaking with your manager, or completing routine procedures that include clearing your desk.

Find out what people normally do. Do they leave on the dot, or stay an hour or more to complete their work? Aim to leave at the midpoint. When you begin, you may have to work longer hours to learn how to do your job. However, continuing to work extra hours can create problems. Some of your co-workers could start to resent you if they think you are making them look like slackers because they leave on time. They may feel they have to stay later to show their dedication as well.

Calling in sick

A few weeks after starting work, Paola woke up in the middle of the night with her throat feeling like sandpaper. She hoped to feel better in the morning so she wouldn't have to call in sick to work. She had a lot of work to do and she worried that her absence would reflect poorly on her.

In Canada, it seems as if people start catching colds as soon as the weather turns damp and cold in the fall. A sick employee generally isn't productive. Even worse, once someone in your office gets a cold, it will spread to others in the workplace. The flu is more serious, and can disable employees for many days and even weeks.

Every company has its own rules for when employees should call in sick. Some companies don't want employees spreading germs, and employees are encouraged to take off time for a bad cold. In other companies, you have to be seriously ill to take a day off. Find out your company's policies and workplace culture, and use your good judgment to make the final decision.

Canadian Business Concept: If you go to work with a cold, be sure to wash your hands frequently, and dispose of used tissues carefully in a wastepaper basket. If other people use your phone and computer, clean them with alcohol wipes to keep them free of germs. Don't shake hands with anyone, and don't be offended if people don't stand close to you—they don't want to get sick either.

When you are sick, call first thing in the morning, and speak to your supervisor (not a co-worker). Explain what is wrong, what you plan to do about it, and when you expect to be back at work. Remember that your company has to plan around your work and may need someone else to take over for you.

You should call in every day and let your employer know how you are doing—do not just call once and never call back again. For example, you can say, "I'm going to see the doctor today, and I expect to be back in two days."

Business Buzzwords

- bottom line
- brownie points
- off the ground
- onboarding
- pad your account

Chapter 2 Action Plan

1. Every industry and every company has its own culture. In your first few weeks on the job, gather information about your company's culture. Write three things you've observed about your company's culture.

   _____

   _____

   _____

2. Most companies have their own sets of acronyms that have no meaning to anyone outside the company. Write down any acronyms your company uses, and any other company-specific language that you hear.

   _____

   _____

   _____

3. Become familiar with your company's pace and observe the norms in your office.

   Write down ...

   a) what time most of your co-workers arrive and leave each day.

   _____

   b) what times most of your co-workers take breaks, and how long these breaks are. _____

   c) where people eat lunch, and how long they take. _____

   _____

Setting the Stage for Success

In the first few weeks at your new job, you will be getting established. You will meet with your manager, your teammates, and other people in your company. Now is the time to make a great first impression and start building relationships.

In This Chapter

- How to prepare for your first days on the job
- How to make a great first impression
- Meeting people and establishing good working relationships
- Setting up your workspace
- How to start off on the right foot
- Eight tips to get on track in the first two weeks

How to prepare for your first days on the job

The first day at a new job is always a surprise: new company, new employees, new computer systems, et cetera," says Karen Wallis-Musselman, an HR Independent Consultant born in Venezuela. She has been in Canada since 2004. She offers these tips for getting started: "Make sure to write down the correct name, address, and phone number of the company and put it in a visible place for you to see. Also write the name of your boss and colleagues that work in the same department. They don't expect you to know everything the first day, but showing interest makes a big difference."

In the first days at your new job, you will be getting to know your environment, the company, and your co-workers. You will also be starting to work on the tasks you were hired to do.

You'll have to find out where everything is located. It's a bit like being a detective. Whether you have someone orienting you, or you are on your own, here are some of the things you'll need to find out:

- Are you in a cubicle, an open space, or another environment?
- How easily can people hear your voice in other parts of your workplace?
- How does your computer work?
- What are the special rules and procedures for your computer system, including passwords and user IDs (identifications)?
- Do you have a list of internal phone numbers and email addresses?
- Who should you consult for computer help?
- Where is the cafeteria or lunchroom?
- If there is no cafeteria, do people bring their own lunches or go to local restaurants for lunch?
- Where are the photocopy machines, printers, and fax machines?
- Where can you get office supplies?
- Where are the washrooms?
- Where are the elevators and staircases?
- Where do you hang your coat and put your boots during winter?

Your manager will probably meet with you sometime during the first day to assign your work. You may be working on projects that are already underway, or you may have been hired to start a new project. If you are lucky, you may have some time to get to know your environment, the company, and your co-workers before you need to focus on major projects.

Learn what your manager wants from you

In your early days in the company, you need to understand exactly what your company wants from you. If your manager has not explained this to you, you should open the channels of communication.

Always ask for a job description, and find out whom you report to. You and your supervisors should have an open discussion about your job functions; there should never be any surprises. Find out who to go to if you have questions when your supervisor is not available.

Shelley Brown, President of Bromelin People Practices, suggests that in the first week of your job, you should ask your manager for a copy of his objectives so you know what he is trying to achieve. When you meet with him, ask these questions:

- What is my job description? (If there isn't one, volunteer to write one for your manager to review.)
- What are your objectives for me in the next 30 days, so I can align my tasks with your objectives? What are the priorities?
- Can we meet weekly for the first three months so that you can keep me informed about what I should do on my job, and so that I can update you on my progress?
- How often should I report to you on my progress?
- Will we have regular team meetings or department meetings?
- What is my role in meetings? Do I have responsibility for any agenda items?
- When we meet one-on-one, do you want me to draft the agenda?
- Who do you recommend that I meet with in the company during the first 30 days?
- When is the annual performance appraisal meeting?
- May I have a copy of the performance appraisal guidelines?
- Do you recommend any reading materials on the company's products or services?

"If you don't understand something, *ask*," says Karen Wallis-Musselman. "Trying to figure out what is expected from you is not enough. Write down what you need to do so you can come back and read it later."

If you still don't understand something, ask more questions. The problem may not be lack of communication, but miscommunication. In other words, your manager may have told you what he wants you to do, but you may not have understood what he wants or how you should do it.

This is part of the challenge of communicating with people from other cultures whose work styles and communication strategies may be vastly different.

How to make a great first impression

You only have seconds to make a positive first impression that can influence how people perceive you. This is because our minds are like computers. We instantly form an overall impression based on how someone looks and acts.

We unconsciously notice people's hair, grooming, posture, handshake, facial expression, clothing, scent, and much more. We also notice whether people are approachable. Do their clothes, style, and mannerisms make others feel comfortable? Are they welcoming?

You may be thinking, "That's not fair. People should get to know the real me." It may not be fair, but most of these evaluations are unconscious. People make quick judgments, and it can be difficult to change their minds.

Over time, people at your workplace will get to know you. But starting off on the right foot will go a long way toward making your first days and weeks more pleasant. Changing a negative impression is also much more difficult than making a positive one in the first place.

During your first days at a new job, you will meet many people who will be important to your success. Managing your first impression is important to your career at this company.

Preparing for day one

In the days before you begin your job, prepare by asking whether the company has a dress code. Think about how people were dressed when you went for your interview. This will give you an indication about how formally or informally to dress.

In some workplaces, you may have to wear a specific uniform or you may be given certain articles of clothing, such as a lab coat, to wear over your own clothes.

This means that you will not have to spend too much time figuring out how to dress appropriately for your workplace. However, you should still focus on presenting a polished, professional appearance at all times.

The suggestions here focus primarily on people working in an office setting, but many of the tips can easily be applied to any work situation.

Most companies are conservative. If you don't know your company's dress code, wear a neatly tailored suit on your first day. If you know that your company is very casual, wear a jacket and pants or skirt the first day— you can remove your jacket if you appear overdressed. Even if you are overdressed, no one will criticize you for this. In fact, your manager will feel proud to introduce you around the company. Dressing well shows respect for the people who hired you and projects a professional image.

This is the time to get a haircut if you need one, and perhaps get a manicure. Decide what you will wear ahead of time, and make sure your clothes are clean, pressed, and fit you well. You may need to get your jacket tailored to fit you or sent to the cleaners to be pressed. Make sure there are no buttons missing, or hems hanging down. Lay out your clothes the night before so you won't be searching for the right shirt or socks on your first day of work.

Shoes are among the first things that people notice. Wear dress (business) shoes, not sneakers. Women should wear classic but up-to-date shoes, not open-toed sandals. Check that your shoes are in good condition and not scuffed or worn down at the heels. If you don't have at least one pair of business shoes, now is the time to invest in a pair.

Keep your jewellery simple, and don't wear too much. A gold or silver necklace is appropriate for a woman, and a tasteful watch is appropriate for anyone.

If you don't know your company's dress code, wear a neatly tailored suit.

Give yourself plenty of time to prepare for your first day. Plan to wash and style your hair that day or the day before. Make sure your nails are clean and trimmed. The night before, get a good night's sleep so you are rested and alert.

On your first day, focus on good grooming. When you wake up, shower and put on deodorant, but don't wear too much perfume or scent. Brush your teeth and watch for any food odours or bad breath. Then put on your best business clothes—you'll present yourself with confidence and professionalism. (See Chapter 4 for more information on professional image.)

Meeting people and establishing good working relationships

"Treat everyone you meet with respect and courtesy," says Sandra Bizier, Account Manager with TD Commercial Banking. "People make a big mistake when they are only respectful to executives, and disregard the administrative assistants. For one thing, people can see that you act differently to people who can further your career. But more importantly, you don't know who in your company has influence. Administrative assistants have the executives' ears, and they know how the system works. Be especially polite to them. They may be the most important allies you have."

Once you have learned about your company and its place in the market, it's time to look more closely at the people in your company. Find out who's who before you grab the last brownie from the president at an office birthday party. Try to get a copy of the company's annual report, and look at the pictures of the company executives, or bigwigs. Check the company intranet to see if there are photos of company leaders.

If your company has an organization chart, ask for a copy to use as a quick reference. It's like a cheat sheet that will help you see the various departments, the heads of each department, the organizational chain, and who reports to whom. This will help you understand how the different departments of your company function, and where you and your team fit into the big picture.

How to connect with people

On Armand's first day on the job, a co-worker was assigned to introduce him to people on his team, to managers in different departments, and to his manager's administrative assistant. He was polite and respectful to everyone. His manager's administrative assistant reported to the manager that Armand had made a great first impression.

If you are working for a large company, the first few days of your job may be a whirlwind of meeting new people. You may be confused and not remember everyone's name. However, they are only meeting one new person—you! In their first few minutes of meeting you, they will form an impression of you that may last a long time. Here's what to do when you meet new people:

- When you meet someone, smile, make eye contact, and shake hands. (See Chapter 5 for tips on shaking hands and making eye contact when you meet people.)

- The person who introduces you will probably tell you the name of each new person you meet. Concentrate and try to remember each name. A good way to do this is to say the name three times during the conversation. For example, "It's nice to meet you, Scott. What kind of work do you do, Scott? Well, it's been a pleasure talking to you, Scott (when you part)." If you can't remember the name, don't worry. In the first few seconds of meeting someone, you may be nervous and not listen carefully to the name. As soon as you leave, ask your introducer for the name again and write it down.

- If you have time to talk for a few minutes, ask the person what he does for the company. Chat for a few minutes if he seems to have time, but take your cues from your introducer or the people you meet. If you sense that someone wants to end a conversation, you can say, "I'd better let you get back to work. It was nice to meet you, Scott."

Canadian Business Concept: Canadians shake hands firmly when they meet. If you aren't comfortable shaking hands, smile and nod, and say, "It's not my custom to shake hands, but I am very pleased to meet you."

Meeting people on your team

You may be working on a team or in a work group. What's the difference? A team has shared goals and accountability, while a group is just several people who report to the same person.

Being part of a team has many benefits. You'll find camaraderie and be able to share resources. A team that works well together makes everyone more successful. You'll build relationships, learn together, and accomplish more than if you work alone.

In your first weeks, don't hide in your office or cubicle. Get out and meet your team members or the people who work for the same manager. Since you are new, you have the perfect introduction: "Hi, I'm … I just started here." Meet as many of your co-workers as possible and start building working relationships with them. Don't expect that you will immediately become best friends with these people—this may not happen, or it will take time if it does. But strong working relationships will help you learn about the company and work productively from the beginning.

What if you are shy? You still need to learn social skills to be successful at work. If you find it hard to talk to new people, take small steps to meet people and be friendly. This doesn't mean you have to be very personal. Just talk about your past work experience and mention some facts about yourself: where you live, whether you are married or single, whether you have children or pets, and so on. In fact, it's more important to find out about others in your workplace than to talk about yourself.

A team that works well together makes everyone more successful.

Meeting people outside your team

People outside your department or team will be important to you as well. Companies are social systems that bring people together for the same purpose: selling your product or service. This creates an environment of interactions and relationships.

Even if these people work in different departments than you do now, you may work with them at some point. People change jobs and teams. You may also have to interact with people in different teams or departments more than with your own team. For example, if you are on a marketing team, with each team member supporting a different product, you may be interacting frequently with the engineers or sales representatives who focus on your product.

Get to know your neighbours. Building relationships is a big part of your job because it helps you get your work done more smoothly. Being part of a network is also a great source of information. You don't want to be the only one who doesn't know about the latest company or industry news. Your network will keep you in the loop.

Whether it's for Wednesday's bowling night, or Thursday's pizza lunch, make sure you join most of your team's social activities. Attend as many team dinners and lunches as you can, especially when you are new at the job.

Felix Quartey, a loans operations officer at CIBC says, "Take advantage of any mentoring opportunities your company offers. Go out for lunch with colleagues and participate in company events. For example, I joined in the indoor golf at CIBC, as well as the egg hunt at Easter, and I contribute to the charities the company supports. It's a way to meet new people and start friendships."

Setting up your workspace

Your new workplace will be your home away from home. You can create an environment that is comfortable, as well as functional and efficient.

To set up your workspace you will need a phone and an email account. You may also need an access badge. Most companies operate on servers and you will need an account and password. Ideally, this will all be set up by the time you arrive, but if not, you may have to find the IT department and organize your computer set-up on your own.

Find out where the printer, scanner, fax machine, and any other devices you will be using are located. They may be shared on another part of your floor.

Organize your desk and your computer. Adjust your computer monitor, chair, and keyboard to your physical proportions.

You can add a few personal touches, but keep it simple and efficient. Your office space or cubicle is a reflection of you. It's fine to put in a few personal touches, such as a small framed picture of your family or pet, or a plant to add a touch of nature to the indoor space. Don't go overboard and bring in large posters or stuffed animals. Keep your space professional.

Be careful about keeping food in your cubicle. Food can attract mice, but even more important, it can bring in odours that people may not welcome.

Organize your desk. Some people believe that they look busy and productive when their desk is piled high with papers. That may be true, but it also makes them look disorganized. Take the time to create systems in the beginning, so you will avoid paper overload when the work starts coming in.

To show that you are organized and efficient, do the following:

- Create filing systems for your papers and email. A co-worker who needs to take over a project should be able to find everything easily.

- Deal with email messages by filing the ones you need to keep and deleting the ones you no longer need.

- Keep an agenda or notebook on your desk, or a whiteboard nearby to write notes to yourself.

- Don't put sticky notes all over your office. Write information in your agenda.

- Keep all personal items, including paperwork, in a drawer that you can lock at night. You may have to share a cubicle with shift workers.

Note: Under Canada's privacy legislation, you have to keep all client information private and secure. Do not leave information on your desk—or anywhere that is easily accessible—overnight.

 Canadian Business Concept: Being efficient and organized will go a long way toward helping you succeed in Canada.

How to start off on the right foot

They are watching you

 It was Eva's first month in a job downtown. She wanted to take advantage of summer in the city, and invited a friend to meet her for lunch. The two friends got into an involved conversation, and Eva lost track of the time. She realized she had taken close to two hours instead of the one hour she was allotted. No one said anything that day, but months later, at her first performance review, her manager mentioned that he had seen her take long lunches. Even though Eva only took a long lunch once, it made a lasting negative impression.

Canada is very time-oriented. In many companies, employees have to sign in or punch a clock when they arrive and when they leave, so that management knows whether or not workers are putting in their eight hours a day.

Some managers are clock-watchers, others aren't as strict. But in your first few months on the job, your manager and co-workers will be watching you, so make sure you are on your best behaviour.

At busy times, you may want to eat lunch at your desk to save time from going out for lunch; people will notice that you are hard-working. If you go out, be sure you are back on time.

Many companies now offer a flexible working schedule. For example, you can work from 8:30 to 4:30, or from 9:00 to 5:00. In the corporate world, many employers still want employees to be at their desks and ready to work at a specific time. One company president admits that he stands at the window of his office and watches to see who drives into the parking lot at 8:59 a.m. Make sure you don't get caught in your company's attendance radar. Show up a few minutes early every day.

Some managers are clock-watchers

Once you are at work, make sure you look busy even when you're not. At the beginning of your employment you may not have very much to do. It may be too late to get involved in ongoing projects before you have proper training. But do not sit and twiddle your thumbs. Offer to help your manager or colleagues. If they give you something to do, make sure you do the job better than they expect you to. This is also a good time to read office procedures and manuals.

"If you finish your job and have some time, you can use it in a constructive way: helping a co-worker, cleaning your desk, filing, et cetera. Never sit there doing nothing, because people will notice," says Karen Wallis-Musselman.

If people ask you to do work that you feel is beneath your job description, be pleasant and accommodating. Everyone has to do these things from time to time, and it's a good way to learn how the business runs. You won't end up doing these tasks forever, because if your salary is higher than that of someone who does these simple tasks, your employer will want to make use of your skills elsewhere.

During your first weeks, use your free time to find out more about the company and industry. Highlight key points and show your manager what you've learned. Ask, "How can I help?"

When you start working alongside your new co-workers, resist the temptation to make suggestions on how to improve things. Do more listening than talking. No one wants to be told that they aren't doing things right.

"First observe, and then try to be seen as reliable, useful, and loyal. I think that's the best way to collaborate with people. This way you can contribute new ideas or ways of working without being seen as someone who's trying to change Canada's culture," suggests Nicolas Fagnard, from Belgium.

How to establish an office routine

In the first weeks of work it's important to establish a routine so you can manage your time well. This will help you get to work on time, and organize your day to get the most work done, with less stress.

It's important to find out what time everyone else starts. If you have flextime, you may be able to start between 8:00 and 9:00 a.m. The reality is that if everyone else starts work at 8:00, and you arrive at 9:00, people will notice that you are coming in at the last minute.

As well, lots of things are discussed in the early morning, and you'll miss out on the conversation. Aim to come in at the midpoint, or experiment to see what time most people actually arrive, and be sure to arrive at that time or earlier.

The next thing to do is figure out your morning routine. Once you know what time you want to arrive, develop a routine to get you there on time. If you rush in to the office at the last moment, you'll look disorganized and unprofessional.

Set your alarm so you wake up early enough to have breakfast, take care of children or pets, and put together your business wardrobe to look well-groomed and professional. Develop your morning routine by working backward.

- How much time do you need to get into your office and to your desk?

- How long does your trip take by public transit, or how long does it take you to drive to your workplace, including time to deal with traffic jams and parking? Don't forget that snow and rain can slow traffic and add significant time to your travels. Canadians are always checking the weather report to see what's coming down from the sky—such as snow, rain, or hailstones.

- How much time do you need to eat breakfast? How much time do you need to make sure your children or pets are fed?

- How much time do you need to shower, shave, put on makeup, do your hair, and get dressed?

- How many times do you press your alarm clock's snooze button before you actually get out of bed?

- How much sleep do you need? Most people need between seven and eight hours of sleep to be productive. What time do you have to get to bed to get enough sleep?

Working backward, you can see that while you may have estimated that you need only 45 minutes to get ready for work, you may actually need much longer to arrive at work focused and alert.

Use time management to plan the end of your workday as well. What do you need to complete at the end of the day in order to meet your work requirements and your personal obligations?

Preparing for Canadian weather

 Martin's new job was about 30 minutes away from his apartment. One day during his second week of work, it was snowing hard. The bus ride that was usually 30 minutes long took close to an hour. He rushed to his desk, thinking that everyone else would be late because of the snow. Surprisingly, his co-workers were in place at their desks, looking up at him as he entered.

Canadians are used to all kinds of weather. They listen to weather reports regularly, especially during winter.

Getting to work when the roads are covered with snow can be frustrating. If you take public transportation, give yourself double the amount of time it normally takes you to get to work. If the roads have not been cleared, they can be icy and everyone has to drive more slowly. There may be accidents causing roadblocks, and snowplows may be out spreading salt or sand, with these large vehicles further reducing traffic flow.

If you drive a car, be sure to wake up earlier than usual to remove snow or ice from your windshield. You'll have to clear your walkway or driveway as well. Allow lots of extra time for driving in snow, heavy rain, or on icy roads. In bad weather, traffic often slows to a crawl.

Canadian Business Concept: Many Canadians check the weather reports several times a day to make decisions about everything including whether to have a barbecue, how to dress their children, and how much time they need to get to work.

Eight tips to get on track in the first two weeks

Alex got a job as an estimator at a small plumbing company. He did not have direct industry experience but he had good technical, math, and analytical skills. He was very hard-working and exceeded his employer's expectations.

After two weeks his employer told him, "I have a hard time keeping up with you. You do everything well. You work quickly and learn quickly too. I am satisfied, but stressed at the same time."

It's good to do your job well, but you also have to understand the dynamics of your company. The early weeks in a new job are the time to figure out how your company functions and what your manager needs from you.

Here is a summary of ways to help you make the most of this time:

1. Present yourself professionally. Have a confident, mature manner. Stand up straight, keep your voice even, and be pleasant to the people you work with.

Dress well. On your first day of work you may notice that people vary widely in their interpretation of the dress code. Make sure you stay on the side of business professional dress. (See Chapter 4 for suggestions.) Don't overdress, but aim to dress similarly to the better-dressed people at your level in the company.

2. Find company resources. Find out about the resources, systems, and people at your job. Where is the fax machine? What computer systems are in use? Who do you call if your computer doesn't work? Where do you get office supplies? Once you learn the systems and the right people to call, you'll do your job more efficiently.

Always ask for the tools you need to do your job. Don't wait for your manager to give you everything. She may have forgotten what it's like on the first day or week of a new job.

3. Meet people and learn their names. Don't wait for someone to take you around and introduce you to everyone in the office. Take the initiative to reach out to people. Do your best to remember names when you are introduced. It's okay to keep a notebook with you and jot down names and titles. If you meet these people again and forget their names, simply ask them to remind you. They will understand.

If you are told any details about people, remember these as well. For example, if you find out that Sheila is originally from Saskatchewan, has been at the company for eight years, and has a ten-year-old daughter, keep this in mind and ask her about these things the next time you see her, so you can begin to build a relationship.

Also, get a list of telephone extensions and email addresses so you can reach people easily.

4. Take your work seriously. Find a goal to work toward, and start making sure you achieve it. Your manager should give you work to start on right away. If he doesn't, find some tasks and begin taking initiative.

Make sure you know whom you report to. You may be working on a project in one area while your supervisor is in another area. If you have any questions, go to your supervisor.

5. Start building relationships. Human beings are social animals, and the relationships you form can make a big difference in your success. In fact, people who have at least one good friend at work are more successful at their jobs.

Take advantage of any formal and informal opportunities to get to know your co-workers. Does everyone eat lunch together in the cafeteria or lunchroom? Join them rather than making personal calls on your lunch hour. Are your co-workers going out to celebrate someone's birthday? Most invitations are open to everyone in the department, so even if you aren't explicitly invited, assume you are included.

6. Follow office etiquette. You'll be working closely with your co-workers and supervisor. Use good manners in everything from cleaning up after yourself in the kitchen, to using email and cellphones properly. Be on time and respect people's time and space. Always be willing to help, even if it is not your job. Perception really is reality, so make a good impression during your first weeks. It will help you succeed in the long-run.

7. Ask for feedback. Some managers don't give much feedback because they are too busy, or they may give you feedback that is confusing to you. It's always nice to get positive feedback, but it's even more important to find out, as early as possible, what you should be doing differently.

8. Don't be hard on yourself. It's normal to feel a bit overwhelmed at first. There is so much to learn and so many people to meet. Remember that you made it through the interview process, so at least one person believes you deserve your position. Your co-workers understand that you will have a lot to learn before you make any significant contribution. However, don't keep this attitude for too long. Jump in and start contributing as soon as you can.

Business Buzzwords

- bigwig
- have the executives' ears
- in the loop
- on the right foot
- punch a clock
- twiddle your thumbs

Chapter 3 Action Plan

1. What is your job description? Write it here, along with the name of the person you report to, and your main job functions. If your manager didn't give you a job description, write your own and take it to your manager to discuss.

   Job description:

   _____

   _____

   Person you report to: _____

   Main job functions:

   _____

   _____

2. Who have you met? Write down the names of people on your team or in your work group, and anyone else you've met.

Team or work group	Other people at work

3. Find out about company resources. Write down any information about the individuals to contact about office systems and resources.

   Who do you call for computer information or help? _____

   Where do you get office supplies? _____

   Where are the fax machines and printers located? _____

   What passwords do you need? _____

Projecting a Professional Image

Every industry and company has its own dress code. If you are new on the job, you're probably wondering what to wear to work and how to look professional.

In This Chapter

- How to dress for success in Canada
- What to wear in your industry and company
- Business clothing for the Canadian climate
- How to look up-to-date
- What you should know about grooming
- What to wear for business occasions

How to dress for success in Canada

Jim was hired to work in a laboratory. He did excellent work, and he was well qualified. Jim wore a lab coat at work, so his clothes didn't show much. But his appearance was still sloppy. His hair was dirty and uncombed, and his shoes were scuffed and worn down at the heel. Sometimes he didn't wear socks. His posture was slouched and he looked messy. When it came time to promote someone, Jim was overlooked. He just didn't look like a manager.

Do looks matter in the workplace? The answer is yes. The way you present yourself can make the difference between being promoted and being left behind.

You may have heard the expression *Dress for the job you want, not for the job you have.* If you want to succeed, you have to dress like your manager, or like a higher-ranking employee. Your manager will see you as someone who is easy to promote.

Well-dressed and confident

Wrinkled and lacking confidence

It's also much easier to act professional when you look the part. When you wear a suit or jacket, you unconsciously stand up straighter. If you feel like a million bucks, you walk and talk with confidence. On the other hand, if you dress more casually, you tend to act more casually as well. You will not receive as much respect in meetings or from your manager.

As an immigrant to Canada, you may be wondering what to wear to be successful in the workplace. Here are some tips to get started. The rest of this chapter gives you more details on how to decide what to wear in your particular workplace.

- There is a wide range of acceptable clothing choices in the workplace. Each company and industry has its own dress code. Ask whether your company has a dress policy, and observe how the people around you dress.

- What you wear will depend on whether or not you meet the public.

- It's important to recognize that people do judge others based on physical appearance and clothing. This is human nature, and not particular to any one person or workplace.

- All employees have to adapt their clothing to the workplace. That's why we each have a business wardrobe and a weekend wardrobe.

- The Canadian workplace has become more casual. However, you can still dress conservatively and project a professional image. Follow the guidelines for the two levels of professional business dress in this chapter: formal and professional.

- If a particular type of clothing is important to you for cultural or religious reasons, discuss this with your manager or human resources department.

Felix Quartey, who works at CIBC, one of Canada's largest financial institutions, says, "I didn't realize how informally people dress here. On my first day of work I wore a suit and tie. I was surprised to see that no one wears a tie here. Most of my contact with clients is on the phone, so now I dress informally, the way my colleagues do."

What to wear in your industry and company

 Andrea was working in a fashion company where everyone wore trendy, casual clothes. She wore whatever she liked to work. Her usual work uniform consisted of jeans with a sweater or T-shirt. She often wore fashion boots in winter and flip-flops in summer.

When she changed jobs and began working at a recruiting company, she was told that jeans were not allowed, and that she had to wear business clothing. Suddenly Andrea realized she needed a business wardrobe. Her casual items didn't work in her new environment.

The way you dress for work depends on where you work and the type of job you do. Every industry has its own dress code. Within an industry, every company has its own guidelines for acceptable dress.

In conservative industries like law, finance, pharmaceuticals, and publishing, people dress more formally. People who deal with the public have to present a professional image so that they will be respected and trusted.

At the opposite end are high-tech companies, where people dress very casually, and trendy industries such as fashion and advertising, where people wear the latest styles.

People who work in health care, food services, or certain other industries may be issued a uniform to wear to work.

Most companies have dress codes that are somewhere in the middle. You are expected to dress professionally, but you don't have to wear a suit every day. You may have casual days on Fridays, but you should still look neat and well-groomed.

Larger companies often have dress policies that spell out what to wear. Smaller companies are often more casual and let you wear what you choose, within reason. No one should ever appear sloppy or grungy.

Canadian Business Concept: If you didn't receive a description of the dress code when you were hired, ask to see it before you begin, so you'll know what to wear on your first day of work.

People who meet the public are expected to dress more professionally than employees who work in a warehouse. And employees in large cities like Toronto and Montreal tend to dress more formally, and keep more up-to-date with fashion, than those who work in smaller towns.

There are three basic levels of dress in the business world: formal, professional (smart), and business casual.

Formal: the image of authority

Who should wear this?

This for people who work in conservative industries, such as in financial services, law, accounting, pharmaceuticals, and many large corporations.

When should you wear this?

If you work in a conservative environment, or if people higher up in your company dress this way, you should dress formally every day as well.

If you work in a more casual environment, you should dress formally for important meetings, when you are presenting to a group, or for conferences and special company events.

Think of the image of the business suit. We are conditioned to assume that a person wearing a suit is an authority figure. When you are presenting to a group or meeting clients in a formal setting, a dark business suit creates an image of power and authority.

Canadian Business Concept: Coco Chanel, the famous fashion designer, said, "Dress sharply and they'll remember the outfit; dress impeccably and they'll remember the woman (or man)."

What should you wear to look formal?

Dark business suit with white shirt

Dark suits: Wear a matched suit. For a woman, a jacket and skirt is a slightly more formal outfit than a jacket with pants, but a pantsuit is generally acceptable.

People associate business wear with dark colours. A suit in navy, charcoal grey, or black looks more formal and projects a higher level of authority than one in a lighter colour. Fabrics change with the seasons. In winter, people wear heavier wools, while in summer people wear suits in lightweight wool.

Contrasting colours: Wear a white or cream-coloured shirt with your dark suit. The greater the contrast of light and dark, the more powerful you appear.

Classic fabrics: Smoother, plainer wools and silks in solid colours give you a formal business look. The more bulky, textured, or patterned your fabric, the less formal you look.

The dark business suit is more formal that the lighter suit.

Clean, simple looks: Don't wear too many prints or patterns on shirts, blouses, or ties. The fewer details and colours you have, the more power you project.

Classic and conservative pieces: Buy timeless clothing that won't go out of style quickly. Invest in a classic suit, gold or silver jewellery, a watch with a leather or metal strap, and leather business shoes. You will wear all these items for a long time, so buy the best quality you can afford.

For women, this means wearing a business suit, a matched skirt and jacket, or pantsuit. Closed-toe shoes (no sandals), pantyhose, and conservative hairstyle, jewellery, and makeup complete the look.

Classic business shoes for men and women

Professional or smart business

Two suppliers were presenting a technical product to the marketing department of a large corporation. One professional was dressed in a business suit. His hair was neat and he was well-groomed. He stood tall and looked at the people in the room.

The other supplier, by stark contrast, was dressed casually in slacks and a shirt. His hair looked as if he had just gotten out of the shower, and he had a five o'clock shadow on his chin. He slouched in his chair and looked at his laptop when he wasn't presenting. Both men had good products and were very knowledgeable about them.

After the presentation, the marketing department decided to go with the first man. He projected more credibility by the way he was dressed and in how he presented himself.

If you work with the public, you want to look professional so people will trust you. You also want to look approachable. Some people call this a "smart business" look.

You can create a friendly, welcoming look by changing one or two elements of a formal outfit.

The man and the woman on the right are wearing professional (or smart) business wear. The woman in the middle is more formal.

Who should wear this?

This is the way most people dress in offices today, unless you work in a very conservative or very casual environment.

When should you wear this?

Dress this way every day, except for special events such as meetings or presentations, when you should dress more formally. If your office has casual Fridays, you can dress more casually on that day.

What should you wear to look professional?

Here are the essentials. You can make them more formal or more casual, depending on your accessories. As you build your wardrobe, you can add shirts and accessories with more colours and textures. Women can add a few jackets with more flare, as long as they are not too trendy for your environment.

 Canadian Business Concept: Dress for the job you want, not for the job you have.

Jackets: Have one or more jackets in business-appropriate colours (black, brown, charcoal, or navy) with pants or skirts to mix and match. Blazers are good investments because they never go out of style.

A wool sweater and cotton shirt are part of a smart business look.

Shirts: A few white or light-coloured shirts take you a long way. You can also wear darker colours such as grey or blue. Men can wear these with suits or with dress pants. Women can wear them with black, navy, or grey pants and a simple pearl or gold necklace, or with a pantsuit. When your budget is larger, you can add more colours to your wardrobe, in the form of shirts and accessories.

Sweaters: Choose sweaters made of fine wool so they are not too bulky. Business-appropriate colours such as navy or grey will match your pants or skirts.

Dress pants: These are business pants, usually made of wool or a wool blend. They are the staples of every person's working wardrobe. Invest in a few pairs of black or charcoal grey pants that fit you well. Then you can add a shirt and sweater or jacket, and you'll be ready for work.

Shoes: You can wear good leather shoes anywhere. Men's styles don't change often, so any investment will last you for years. Women will want a selection of low-heeled pumps and flats. For formal environments, stick to dark colours

with closed toes. In more casual environments, you can experiment with colours and textures—such as suede or exotic skins—for interest. Don't wear flip-flops to work. They are too casual for the workplace.

Structured handbag: Women need a smooth black, grey, or brown handbag with a structured frame to give their outfits a pulled-together, tailored look.

Business casual

You may be overjoyed to hear about casual Friday, or perhaps you wear casual clothes every day. But it's difficult to interpret what *business casual* means. Some of your co-workers may look as if they should be jogging in the park or walking their dog—their clothes are just a bit too casual for the workplace.

Who should wear this?

This is for anyone working in a very casual environment, such as in a high-tech company, a creative agency, or in a department where you don't meet the public.

When should you wear this?

Dress this way every day, or only on casual Fridays, depending on your company dress code.

What should you wear to look casual?

You can wear casual pants or skirts, with shirts and sweaters. Make sure everything is clean and pressed. Casual doesn't mean sloppy or dirty.

The biggest problem with casual wear is what **not** to wear. Here are some types of clothing that **do not** belong in the workplace.

Avoid wearing . . .

✗ sports clothing such as jogging suits, sweatshirts, or casual T-shirts

✗ beachwear such as shorts, tank tops, sandals, or flip-flops

✗ party clothing, including anything sheer, sequined, shiny, or revealing

✗ T-shirts or sweatshirts with slogans or off-colour remarks

✗ sexy clothing such as miniskirts, sheer sundresses, strappy stiletto sandals, or anything that is made of see-through lace or has spaghetti straps

✗ leisure clothing such as jeans, shorts, T-shirts, hats, or sneakers

✗ sloppy clothing that is wrinkled or baggy with too many layers

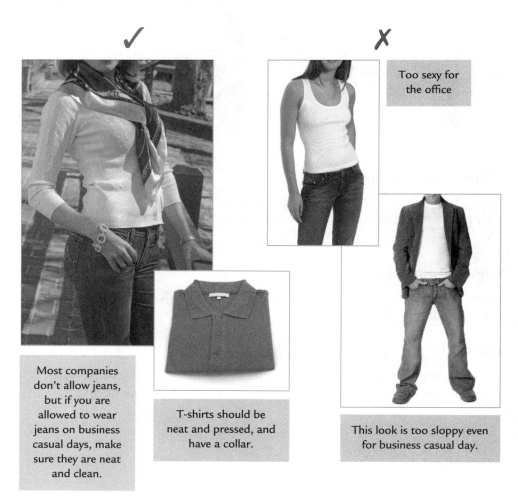

✓

✗

Too sexy for the office

Most companies don't allow jeans, but if you are allowed to wear jeans on business casual days, make sure they are neat and clean.

T-shirts should be neat and pressed, and have a collar.

This look is too sloppy even for business casual day.

Canadian Business Concept: The only time to wear a shirt with a logo or slogan would be when you wear your company's shirt, because you are promoting the company. It's unprofessional to wear shirts with slogans that promote other companies in your workplace. However, a tiny symbol or logo embroidered on a shirt is fine on business casual days—as long as the logo is not promoting your competitor's brand.

Remember that you want people to focus on your professional skills, not your body. If you wear anything extreme—very short, tight, low-cut or revealing, people may talk about your clothes rather than your work.

A good rule for casual Friday is that you should change just one or two items from your smart business look, or what you would wear to work on an average day.

How to decide what to wear to work

First, find out whether your workplace has a written dress code, and take the dress code with you when you shop. Remember that you are dressing to represent your company. Find out what you are expected to wear, so you impress your manager and customers.

Next, look at what other people in your office are wearing. Does your manager wear a suit every day, or is she dressed more casually?

Look at co-workers who you believe are successful. Try to adapt their style to your own body shape and personality without directly copying them.

Finally, listen carefully to comments people make about your clothes. If someone asks, "Why are you dressed up?" or "Are you going for a job interview?" you may be wearing party clothes or dressing in a way that is too formal for your office.

How to dress like your manager

Everyone feels most comfortable with people who are like them. An easy way to show that you want to be promoted is to dress at the same level of formality that your manager does.

If your male manager always comes to work with a suit and tie, with shoes shined, and face freshly shaved, you should dress formally as well. But if he wears khaki pants and a T-shirt, you can wear them too. No matter what you wear, make sure it is always clean and pressed.

If your female manager is always smartly dressed in the latest styles, pay extra attention to how you present yourself. Women should study the female manager's style more closely. Does your manager wear mostly skirt suits or pantsuits? Does she wear pantyhose or have bare legs in summer? Are her shoes pumps or flats?

Women who don't have a female executive to model themselves after should see what the male executives are wearing. If they wear suits and ties every day, you should dress formally in a suit or a jacket with a skirt or pants.

 Canadian Business Concept: Managers who pay attention to how **they** look will notice how **you** look as well.

How to dress to meet clients

If you meet with clients, you are representing your company. Most companies encourage employees to dress as well as, or better than, their clients.

Your manager will probably go with you on your first sales call. Observe carefully how she dresses, and in the future dress the same way. It's a good idea to ask her how to dress for the appointment beforehand.

What you should wear will depend on your industry. For information technology professionals, you may want to add a jacket to a neat shirt and pants. For financial professionals, you will be wearing a suit.

Make sure you are always prepared by keeping an extra "meet the client" jacket at the office for unexpected meetings. You will instantly upgrade your look. If you wear a uniform, make sure you have a clean one ready to wear when meeting customers.

If you still aren't sure what to wear to a client meeting, ask you manager. Or ask yourself: How will my customer or manager feel if I show up wearing this? If you think they may feel uncomfortable, why risk your career success? Dress the way you like on your own time. At the office, dress for the corporate environment.

Business clothing for the Canadian climate

 When Diwata first arrived in Montreal from the Philippines, she went shopping for winter clothes. She bought some fashionable high-heeled boots and a light fall coat to prepare for the first snowfall. The coat and boots were fine until the end of November, when it began to snow heavily. Diwata's boots leaked when she stepped into the slush, and she was freezing in her light coat. She realized that she wasn't really prepared for winter at all.

Many regions of Canada have sub-zero temperatures in winter, with lots of snow. With ice and slush to contend with, you need the proper boots to keep your feet from freezing.

Business wear in winter

Boots

Both men and women need a pair of warm, waterproof boots for everyday use. Most people keep a pair of shoes at their office and change out of their boots when they arrive.

Many women also have fashionable leather boots with small or higher heels. These are great for winter days that are dry (no wet snow or rain), or for going out in the evening. In fact, if you go to networking events or meetings in restaurants, you will need leather fashion boots to go with your skirt or business suit. You can buy tall boots to wear with skirts, and short boots to wear with pants.

Men can find winter boots to wear outside, then change out of at the office. For less-snowy days, you can also find slip-ons, or rubbers, that protect your business shoes when you go outside.

Coats

Coats are the first things people see most of the year in Canada. You will need a variety of coats and jackets for Canadians climates, including raincoats for spring, light summer jackets, and heavier winter wear.

Both men and women need a warm coat or jacket for winter. If you wear a suit to work, look for a wool coat that is stylish yet warm. Check the materials. A warm coat is mainly wool or a wool blend—the higher the wool content, the warmer the coat. The coat should also have a lining, usually made of a synthetic material.

Women's coat styles change with the fashions trends, but a classic coat in a neutral color such as black, navy, or grey will last for years. For a little flair, try red, dark green, blue, or burgundy.

Men's coats don't change in style very often, so invest in the best winter coat you can afford. It will last you for years.

Jackets

If you work in a casual environment, you can wear a warm jacket. You will see many styles of anorak, which is a classic Canadian jacket. It's a mid-length jacket with a zipper and hood. Pea jackets are also good shorter coats.

Raincoats

A good raincoat is very handy for summer and fall. A trench coat with a zip-out lining in a classic colour such as beige or tan will last for years. For spring and fall weather, you can also get a fall coat or jacket, which is lighter than a winter coat.

Here are some other items to complete your winter business wardrobe:

Scarves

Wool or acrylic scarves keep your neck warm and can add style to your winter coat.

Gloves

Leather gloves look professional with a wool coat. Black is the standard colour, but women can add a touch of flair with gloves in other colours. Wool gloves are fine for everyday use, but are more casual than leather.

Hats

If you spend time outside waiting for a bus, look for a fashionable hat that will also keep you warm. Many women don't like to wear hats, because it causes hat hair: the wool and the dry air combine to make your hair stand on end with static electricity. Some women prefer hoods on their winter coats, since these are easy to slip on and off and do less damage to your hair.

Business wear in summer

Summer in many parts of Canada can be very hot and humid. Most large offices are air conditioned. In fact, in many buildings the air conditioning is set to such a low temperature that some people feel chilled.

This is more of a problem for women, who tend to wear light fabrics, short sleeves, and sandals in summer. If you find that you are cold in your workplace, consider bringing a cover-up, such as a cardigan sweater or a light jacket to wear inside.

Where to shop for clothes

Larger Canadian cities like Vancouver, Toronto, and Montreal have a wide variety of stores and boutiques, but not all the clothing is office-appropriate. Here are some types of stores to check out. Buy the best quality you can afford—you will save money by not having to replace your clothing very often.

The examples below are just a few possibilities. Check what is available in your area.

Type of store	Advantages	Disadvantages	Examples
High-end stores	Sell top-quality, classic clothing that will last for many years	Can be expensive unless you buy items that are on sale	Holt Renfrew Harry Rosen (men only) Ogilvy
Department stores	Have wide variety of clothing and frequent sales	You need to find the right department in the store—not all clothing is suitable for business	The Bay Sears
Chain stores	Sell career clothes at more affordable prices than the high-end stores	You need to find the right stores to suit your style	Banana Republic Gap Mexx Le Chateau Laura Tristan
Economical stores	Offer clothing at low prices	You have to be sure to check each item for fit and quality	Zellers Wal-Mart Winners
Boutiques	Provide personal service and unique items	You have to find a store that carries the type of clothing you are looking for	Varies from place to place
Trendy stores	Offer trendy, high-fashion clothing at low prices	Clothing may not be as well made; it may go out of style more quickly	H&M Zara
Second-hand shops	Often have good quality clothes at a fraction of the original price	You have to check what is available often, as items can be sold quickly	Varies from place to place

Before buying a new item of clothing, ask yourself the following questions:

- Is it appropriate for my job?
- Is it appropriate for this climate (according to the season)?
- Does it fit well?
- Does it make me look my best?
- Is it well made, and will it last?
- Does it look up-to-date, but not extreme?
- What message am I sending with this outfit?

How to look great on a budget

Every fall, fashion magazines such as *Vogue, Harper's Bazaar*, and *In Style* feature hundreds of pages of new styles. Canadian magazines such as *Chatelaine, LOULOU*, and *Flare* also have fashion pages with items available in Canada.

Strangely enough, fall items start appearing in the stores in July, once the main summer shopping season is over. And summer items start appearing in the stores as early as March, once the winter stock is gone.

What does this mean for you? It means that winter clothes usually start going on sale at the end of November. In December, you can find many items on sale. January and February are great times to pick up good quality clothing at 50 to 70 percent off.

Summer clothes start going on sale in June, just when the weather really heats up in many parts of Canada. So you can get great summer fashions at a discount by the time you need them. There's no need to buy very much at full price!

As well, many stores get new stock every few weeks. For example, at some stores you may find great work clothes, but at high prices. If you return every few weeks, you could find that the clothing you liked has gone on sale. Department stores also have great sales on a regular basis.

The best way to buy clothing on sale is to watch for flyers in your newspaper and check the dates of the advertised sales. You can also browse your favourite stores on a regular basis and wait for the items you like to be discounted. Finally, many stores will send you advance notices of their sales by email or postcard if you sign up for this service.

Career killers and career boosters

 Becca made a good impression at her job interview, but when she showed up for her first day of work in August, she looked completely different. It was a hot day, so she wore a sleeveless top that revealed a large tattoo on her shoulder. She had on several clanging bracelets and long chandelier earrings. Her tank top and flip-flops looked more suited to a beach party than to a large office.

Whether you dress formally or informally, it's easy to look professional by paying attention to the details of what you wear. Our eyes are drawn to anything unusual or out of order. People will focus on whatever is capturing their attention.

Career killers

When dressing for the workplace, your goals should be to avoid distractions and to keep people's attention on your face so they listen to you. Here are some clothing mistakes that can rob you of credibility and, in the extreme, can be career killers.

✗ Wearing clothing that doesn't suit the occasion: dressing too casually for a client meeting, or too formally for a team meeting.

✗ Wearing clothing that doesn't fit properly and makes you appear sloppy.

✗ Wearing clothing that is too sexy for the workplace, such as shirts that reveal your navel, or pants that sit so low that skin shows when you bend over.

✗ Wearing anything extreme—loud neon colours, distracting patterns, over-the-top hairstyles or accessories, strong perfume, extra-long nails, or bright red nail polish (which is more for evening wear than day wear)—in conservative environments.

✗ Having poor grooming habits, including going to work with a five o'clock shadow, stale breath, or ragged fingernails.

✗ Wearing too much jewellery, jangling earrings, or clanging bracelets.

✗ Exposing body piercings or tattoos. Most companies don't appreciate body art. Keep it covered, or remove visible piercings, unless you work for an extremely casual company. Take your cues from people higher up in your organization. If they don't have any visible body art, you shouldn't either. Males in particular should remove earrings in conservative environments.

✗ Men not wearing socks, or wearing athletic socks with business clothes. Wear dress socks that match your pants and cover your ankles.

✗ Men wearing sneakers with a suit. This makes your whole outfit look casual. Don't wear sandals either, unless you work in an extremely casual environment where you don't meet customers.

✗ Women over-accessorizing. Don't wear multiples of anything, such as bracelets or rings. Save this for the weekend.

Career boosters

When you are well put-together, people perceive you as being professional. Their eyes will be drawn to your face rather than to individual items of your clothing. This encourages eye-to-eye contact and helps you build business relationships and career success. Pay attention to these details to boost your professional image.

✓ Always look neat. You don't have to spend a lot of money to look good. Just make sure you choose clothes that fit you property and keep them clean and pressed. Make sure the sleeves are at the right length, and hem your jackets, coats, and pants to fit you.

✓ Purchase quality clothing. Invest in one good quality jacket or suit instead of buying several trendy outfits. You'll save money in the long-run because your jacket or suit will cost less per wear. To check the quality, look at the label and feel the fabric. A suit that is 100-percent wool looks better and lasts longer than a suit made of polyester or a blend of materials. Cotton or silk shirts look and feel better than acrylic blends.

✓ Wear work-appropriate colours. Colour plays a big part in your professional image. Stick to traditional career colours such as navy, grey, and black as the basics of your wardrobe. Add ice blue, lilac, soft pink, and ivory for shirts and blouses, and red, green, or royal blue for extra colour. Avoid loud colours such as orange or hot pink, and wild prints, except within very creative environments.

✓ Accessorize well. Your belt, pen, and briefcase can add to your professional image. Choose the best quality you can afford.

✓ Keep your shoes clean. Shoes get noticed. Make sure yours are polished and in good condition. It shows people that you pay attention to details.

✓ Have an emergency outfit. Keep a jacket (and tie, for men) available in your office or car. If you are dressed casually and suddenly have to meet a client or your manager, you can slip on the jacket and upgrade your look instantly.

✓ Keep it simple. If you want to look well put-together, keep your business look simple. You will always look professional if you wear clean, classic lines and business colours. This works well even with casual clothes.

✓ Create a focal point. Choose one piece of jewellery as a focal point. For women, tasteful earrings or a necklace projects a polished image. If you have too many bracelets or rings, or long dangling earrings, people get distracted and don't look at your face.

How to look up-to-date

Gia was 23 and starting her first job in Canada. She wanted to fit in, and bought new clothes for her office job. But her hairstyle hadn't changed since she was six years old, and her glasses were more than ten years old. She wanted to be treated like an adult, but she felt like a little girl.

One day her glasses broke, and she asked a colleague where to get new ones. The optician she visited suggested some modern frames that made Gia look grown-up and professional. Gia was delighted, and decided to get a new haircut as well. When she arrived at work, everyone was surprised at her transformation, and Gia gained new confidence at work.

To fit in to your workplace in Canada, it's important to look up-to-date. This doesn't mean you have to wear all the latest styles. Many new styles are not suited to the workplace, or only look good on 18-year-old movie stars.

However, if your clothing is out of style, you look like you are not aware of social trends. Here are the most important things to make sure you keep up-to-date:

Hairstyle

If you've had the same hairstyle for many years and you aren't sure of how to wear your hair in Canada, observe the people in your office who are conscious of fashion. These are people who keep up-to-date with style changes but still look professional. Ask them for suggestions on finding a good hairstylist. You can start with a compliment, such as, "I love your hairstyle. May I ask if you know of a good hairdresser that I can go to?"

Also, check some fashion magazines and look at the advertisements that come with your local newspaper. The hairstyles will be up-to-date. Look for a photo of a simple hairstyle that would work with your type of hair, and take the photo to the hairdresser.

Glasses

Your glasses are the first thing people see because they are on your face, and people look at faces first. If your glasses are out of style, people will notice immediately.

Styles, shapes, and colours of frames change often, and subtle changes make the difference between a current look and a dated look. If your glasses are large when everyone is wearing small glasses, or if you have plastic frames when the trend is to have metal frames, you will look out of date.

Ask a friend or co-worker with good taste to help you choose frames, or go to one of the larger optometrists in your area and ask for a consultation. Explain that you are starting a new job and are not sure what shape of frame looks best on you. You can usually get expert help at no cost.

Another option is to hire an image consultant. You can get leads from a good quality clothing store or search the Internet to find one. It's worth the investment. When you know you look your best, you'll be confident and poised.

What you should know about grooming

Basic cleanliness is essential for looking and feeling fresh at all times. No matter how well you are dressed, if you are not well groomed, you will sabotage your image and your chances for business success.

If you ask people what turns them off the most when they meet someone new, most people list dirty hair or fingernails, body odour, bad breath, and stained clothing. Being well groomed is a big part of your business image.

If you work long hours or travel a lot, it can be hard to keep track of details such as getting your clothes cleaned. And after a long hard day at the office, people may not realize that they don't smell as fresh as they could. But their co-workers will notice.

Here are some basic things that can go wrong:

Breath

Have you ever stepped away from someone who had bad breath? This seems to happen more often in the morning, if people skip breakfast and go to work with stale breath. Cigarettes, spicy foods, and even coffee can contribute to bad breath. That's why we see so many commercials for breath mints, breath sprays, gum, and breath-freshening toothpastes. But these things only mask the odour. Bad breath stems from two places: the mouth or the stomach.

Be sure to see your dentist regularly. Brush your teeth for two minutes after each meal and floss at least once a day. Food that is stuck in your teeth leads to bacteria, which cause bad breath. Brush your tongue as well.

Don't smoke. Eat healthy foods, such as fruits and vegetables, and drink water. Avoid having too much fast food, or food with strong odours such as garlic, onions, and spicy foods.

Keep breath strips or a small bottle of mouthwash handy. (Don't chew gum at work. It looks unprofessional.) Keep mints and floss in your pocket, desk, or purse. They are smaller and easier to use than a toothbrush and toothpaste.

 Canadian Business Concept: If someone offers you a mint, take it!

Body odour

 Sanjay was new to Canada, and was living on his own for the first time. He was proud to be working in a large software company. Sanjay was well qualified for his job, and his manager was pleased with his work. However, after a few days Sanjay noticed that people were cutting their conversations with him short, and they didn't approach him in the lunchroom. He did not understand their behaviour.

Luckily, he had an understanding manager who explained to Sanjay that he had body odour. Sanjay was surprised. After all, he showered every day. His manager explained that showering was not enough. Although Sanjay was clean, he often wore the same shirt to work for several days because he didn't know where to get his clothes cleaned. His manager gave him some tips on where to find a dry cleaner, and the problem got resolved.

Everyone sweats, but not everyone smells bad. Perspiration doesn't smell, but when it mixes with bacteria on skin or on clothing, it can create a stinky, sweaty odour. As well, food odours can penetrate hair and clothing. To Canadians, body odour is one of the most offensive smells, and it can cause problems in the workplace.

Avoiding workplace problems

This is a sensitive subject because people feel uncomfortable telling a co-worker that she has body odour. People will simply avoid such co-workers, or end discussions with them quickly. This can have a big impact on your job. If you come from a culture where people are comfortable with body smells, you may not understand why people are avoiding you.

If you are living on your own for the first time, here's what to do:

- Find a good dry cleaner in your neighbourhood and take your shirts there after each wearing. You don't need to clean your pants every time you wear them, but you should have a few pairs of work pants, and clean them after five or six wearings.

- For a less costly alternative, wash your shirts on your own, either at home or at your local laundromat.

- Buy at least five work shirts—you will have one for each day of the week, and you'll only need to wash them on the weekend.

- Learn to iron. It will make your shirts crisp and fresh, and it's not all that hard to do!

- If you don't want to iron, buy wash-and-wear shirts so you don't have to iron them. Make sure to hang them up as soon as you take them out of the washing machine, so they don't wrinkle. Check the label: it will usually say *no iron* or *wash-and-wear*.

(See Chapter 5 for more information on how smell is perceived.)

Feet

Ewww! Have you ever suddenly gotten hit by a strong smell, and then noticed that your neighbour in the next cubicle just slipped off her shoes? There's nothing quite like that smell!

The mixture of perspiration and bacteria, all stuffed into the warm, closed environment of your shoes, can cook up a powerful odour. To avoid foot odour, wash feet every day during your bath or shower and dry them well. Put on clean socks every day, and don't wear the same shoes every day. Alternate shoes, letting each pair air out between uses.

A good way to absorb odours is to stuff your shoes with newspapers or scented dryer sheets when you're not wearing them. Don't stick your shoes into the back of your closet. Let the air circulate.

Nails

Dirty, chipped, broken nails are instant turnoffs. Extra long nails and bright red nail polish don't fit a corporate environment. Make sure your nails are filed. Keep them short and clean. If your nails are in bad shape, get a manicure—this applies to men, too. You don't have to use nail polish, just get your nails properly shaped. You'll be able to take care of them yourself after that.

Dandruff

If your expensive suit is dotted with dandruff, you'll look scruffy and unprofessional. Check your local pharmacy for special dandruff shampoos. If that doesn't work, make an appointment with your family doctor or a dermatologist.

Perfumes, lotions, and aftershave

Don't wear strong smelling perfumes or lotions to work. The smell carries easily into the next cubicle. Many companies now have scent-free policies because so many people are allergic to the chemicals in these products. In addition, some people just don't like to smell strong perfume all day.

Look for unscented deodorant, aftershave, and body lotion, and save your perfume or cologne for after-hours.

Hair

Make sure your hair is styled for business, and keep it clean. Find a hairdresser you like, and schedule regular haircuts. (See page 78 for styling tips.)

Canadian Business Concept: Carry tissues with you. In a cold climate, your nose may run when you come inside. If you eat spicy food in a restaurant, a tissue can save the day—you never want to use a linen napkin to wipe your nose.

What to wear for business occasions

You've just been invited to a business event. What should you wear?

Cocktail parties

For men, this means a suit. For women, a cocktail dress usually means a short dress, which is often black. In fact, the black dress is so popular that there's a nickname for it. It's called the LBD, or the Little Black Dress. It's popular because you can add glamorous accessories such as jewellery or stiletto heels to give it your signature style. Other options for cocktail parties are a dressy pantsuit or a beautiful skirt and top.

Office holiday party

What you wear will depend on where the party takes place. In most cases, you'll want to show yourself off at your most glamorous. It's fine to add some sparkles, but dress appropriately. This is not the time for women to wear their lowest-cut, shortest, or most revealing party dresses, or for men to go completely casual. Don't wear suggestive clothing. If you wouldn't wear it to the office, you shouldn't wear it to the office party.

Company picnics and casual events

If you are invited to the manager's house or a co-worker's barbecue, you can dress casually, but be sure to dress well. Women can wear a sundress or a skirt and summer top. Men can wear neat shorts or pants with a cotton summer shirt or golf shirt. The shirt should have a collar. Don't wear a T-shirt without a collar, short shorts, a halter top, or anything see-through, tight, or revealing. Remember, the people at the barbecue are still your co-workers.

(See more about business events in Chapter 16.)

Business Buzzwords

- look (or feel) like a million bucks
- business casual dress
- smart business dress
- spell out
- off-colour

Chapter 4 Action Plan

1. The way you present yourself on the job can make a difference in whether you are promoted or left behind. Observe what your manager and the better-dressed people in your company wear. Write down the styles of dress you see (for example, formal, professional, or business casual) and any specific business items you see people wearing (for example, suit, jacket, tie, dress shoes).

   Manager: _____

   _____

   Co-workers: _____

   _____

2. Most employees have to buy some business clothes to fit in to their new workplace. List the clothing purchases you would like to make. What other changes would you like to make, such as getting new glasses or a new hairstyle?

   Clothing: _____

   _____

   Other changes: _____

   _____

3. Check the sections on Career killers and Career boosters, on pages 76 and 77. Are there any changes you can make to boost your career?

   _____

   _____

   _____

Section 2

Communicating on the Job

Actions Speak Louder Than Words

In the business world we communicate in many ways, such as by talking and by writing emails and memos. We also communicate non-verbally, using body language.

In This Chapter

- Non-verbal communication in the Canadian workplace
- Understanding people's gestures and postures
- How to use body language to connect with people
- How to use body language to look like a leader
- Body language that makes a great first impression

Non-verbal communication in the Canadian workplace

Amirul, from Southeast Asia, was meeting with his new manager for the first time. His manager was sitting very casually, with an arm draped over the side of a chair. Partway through the meeting, the manager leaned back and crossed his leg, so that the bottom of his shoe was facing Amirul. Amirul was offended. He felt that his new manager didn't respect him, and wondered if he had made the wrong decision in accepting the job.

Have you ever been made uncomfortable by someone touching your shoulder or arm in a business situation? Do you wonder if you should shake hands or just nod and smile when you meet someone? Have you ever stepped closer to a co-worker and caused him to step back?

These are all examples of the effects of body language, or non-verbal communication, in the workplace. With non-verbal communication we send messages through eye contact, gestures, facial expressions, touch, smell, and interpersonal distance.

Amirul was offended because in his country, showing the bottom of your shoe is a sign of disrespect. However, in Canada, it is nothing more than a casual gesture.

People from different cultures have different ways of acting and of interpreting body language. These silent signals can be confusing. This chapter explains body language, or non-verbal communication, in the Canadian workplace.

Interpersonal space

Maria, from Venezuela, was discussing a project with her colleague Christina. Maria wanted to have a warm, friendly relationship, so she moved closer to Christina and touched her lightly on the arm. Christina involuntarily stepped back. Maria stepped closer again and Christina stepped further back. Within a few minutes, Christina was backed up against a desk and Maria was confused and hurt.

The physical distance between people is very much influenced by culture. The space between people is called interpersonal space. This involves how closely two people stand to one another. Territorial space is the arrangement we make with furniture such as chairs in our offices or other environments.

Most immigrants to Canada come from countries that are more densely populated than Canada, and so they are accustomed to less personal space. Canada is a large country, and Canadians are used to large open spaces. This difference can lead to tension during an otherwise pleasant interaction because Canadians may feel crowded when people stand closer to them than they are used to.

We all have our individual comfort zones, or "space bubbles," and we only allow certain people inside these bubbles. Here are the zones for Canadians:

Zone	Amount of Space	When Does This Apply?
Intimate	Less than 45 cm (18 inches)	Interacting with family or close friends
Personal	45 cm to 120 cm (18 inches to 4 feet)	Giving instructions or working with others
Social	120 cm to 3.5 m (4 - 12 feet)	Most business situations, such as meetings or discussions
Public	More than 3.5 m (12 feet)	Giving a speech

Generally, North Americans and Europeans stand about one metre (three feet), or an arm's length, apart. South Americans and people from India tend to stand closer than most Canadians do.

Canadian business people generally stand an arm's length from each other. The handshake is the only time most people touch in business.

Be aware that coming too close to others may intimidate or threaten them. In addition, you may be from a culture in which you have not dealt with women in managerial positions and you may not be sure how close or far to stand from them.

Here's how to tell whether you are making someone feel uncomfortable: watch to see whether someone moves backward when you move toward him, or if he uses furniture to create a space between the two of you, such as moving behind a desk. He may just want a little more elbow room. Try to stop yourself from stepping forward. Give him some breathing space so he feels more at ease with you. In Canada, people move into another person's space to shake hands, and then they step away.

Canadians generally face each other when they talk. In some other cultures people prefer a side-by-side arrangement, which helps them avoid direct eye contact. Canadians expect to have direct eye contact in business dealings. If this practice is not part of your culture, it is important to try to face people and make more eye contact. (See the section on Eye contact on pages 100 and 101).

Territorial space

We get information about business people through the location of their offices and the arrangement of their furniture, such as chairs and tables. The office environment sends non-verbal messages about who is in power and how people should interact.

People of higher status usually have private offices that have a lot of space. They tend to have more windows and their offices tend to be located on higher floors than those of their employees. The president of the company may have a corner office, or the best view of the city. The president's or owner's desk may face a large window, or be positioned in front of imposing pictures on the wall. With an expensive chair, this creates a throne-like effect.

High-ranking executives have their territory protected by doors and secretaries, with both acting as barriers to access. They often have large wooden desks and high-backed leather chairs with arms. This gives an image of power and authority.

Managers may have smaller offices than executives, with or without windows. Some managers want to create a more casual atmosphere, to encourage people to work together. To model this exchange of ideas, they may have their desks located in the same area as the people who work for them.

People at other levels in the company may have an open arrangement of workspaces in a common area, or they may have their space divided into cubicles. They generally share a communal kitchen where they can get coffee or tea and store lunches in a fridge.

When visiting the offices of managers or executives, be sure to respect the managers' territory and space. Never put your personal belongings—such as briefcase, purse, or papers—on their desks. Don't sit down until they indicate where you should sit; take your cues from the person whose office you are in.

Touch

Jason, from Ontario, was attending a national sales meeting. After three days of training with colleagues from across the country, he was confused when Lucie, a female colleague from Quebec, gave him a kiss on both cheeks. At first he thought she might be interested in dating him. Then he noticed that Lucie kissed everyone in the group.

For most Canadians, the appropriate amount of touch is limited to shaking hands when meeting someone and when parting company. Many people from Quebec have a different attitude, in that they hug and kiss in business settings more often. In fact, it is quite common for business people to greet each other with a kiss on each cheek or part with a hug at the end of a meeting. However, this is not universal, so take your cues from the individuals you meet.

At your place of business, hierarchy is involved in determining who may make physical contact with others in the workplace. The general understanding is that people of higher status can touch people of lower status or those who are younger. The president of a company or a manager should initiate a handshake with an employee, and may even touch an employee on the shoulder or arm, but employees normally do not touch the boss or president.

However, a male manager or president must be careful of touching a female employee, as it could be interpreted as sexual harassment. Most people are careful not to touch someone of the opposite sex in the workplace except to shake hands.

Canada is not a high-touch society. If you come from Italy, Greece, or South America, where people touch each other more frequently, be careful that you do not touch your co-workers too often or touch people who are uncomfortable with physical contact in the workplace.

It may be second nature for you to connect by touching a friend on the arm, but you may be making your Canadian colleagues feel uncomfortable. Observe how often people in your workplace touch each other, and hold yourself back from touching people if they seem uncomfortable or don't reciprocate the contact.

 Canadian Business Concept: Shaking hands is the only time most Canadians allow strangers to enter their intimate personal space and have physical contact. After the handshake, people step back out of the intimate zone.

Smell—a sensitive subject

Smell is a powerful tool of communication, and the way people respond to a scent is very personal. Just as some people salivate at the aromas of freshly brewed coffee or pungent cheese, other people are repelled by them. And we can be instantly transported back in time by the aroma of a food we had when we were young.

In the same way, bodily smells that seem wonderful to one person can seem disgusting to another. Scent is so powerful that we often make judgments about people based on the way they smell before we even say, "Hello."

Canadians place high importance on personal hygiene. It is normal for Canadians to shower daily, to wash their hair frequently, to brush their teeth after every meal or at least twice a day, and to apply deodorant and change their clothes daily.

If you observe advertisements on television and in magazines, you will notice many products designed to remove body odours, including body washes and soaps, toothpastes and mouthwashes, deodorants, laundry detergents, perfumes, and colognes. It is considered acceptable to smell like mint (in toothpaste or mouthwash), or like flowers or fruits (in shampoos and soaps), or like the outdoors (in laundry detergents).

People from many other cultures are not as particular about eliminating smells as Canadians are. In some cultures, body odour is considered natural and people do not feel the need to mask it. Individuals from France and Iran often use strong perfumes and colognes without worrying that the scents might bother some co-workers. Today, many Canadian offices are perfume-free and people are asked not to wear any scent because it causes allergic reactions for some people.

Canadians respond negatively to the smell of smoke.

Most westerners respond negatively to what they consider bad smells such as perspiration, sour breath, or clothes that smell stale. Smoke and pungent foods like garlic can stick to clothing and cause a negative reaction from co-workers. This can have a big impact on working relationships because people may avoid working with someone whose odour they consider offensive.

Refer back to Chapter 4 for tips on avoiding body odour and keeping your work clothes fresh. Take note that if you cook with strong-smelling spices, the smell can linger and you may have to launder your clothes more often.

Food at the office

Food is another area where unwelcome smells can cause problems. If you pack a lunch for work, be careful not to bring foods that have strong odours, such as sardines, curries, and garlic. If you eat at your desk or in a communal kitchen, your co-workers will not appreciate the smells that remain after lunch.

Foods that are warmed in the microwave will give off an odour. Save your delicious curries and garlic pasta for dinner at home. Sandwiches, salads, yogourts, and fruits are all good choices for the workplace.

Understanding people's gestures and postures

Tom, from China, was in a training session for a new product at his job in Vancouver. After the session, the trainer asked Tom if he had understood everything. Tom nodded, because he didn't want to imply that the trainer hadn't explained herself well. In fact, Tom hadn't understood several points, but didn't want to cause offence by asking questions.

People everywhere use their bodies to communicate messages. We look at people's faces first to read their emotions.

Our faces show a range of expressions and give instant
information about our thoughts and feelings.

Facial expressions are almost universal. There are at least six facial
expressions that seem to be found everywhere in the world: Happiness,
sadness, surprise, fear, anger, and disgust. These expressions communicate
very strong feelings. In many cases people choose their words carefully, but
facial expressions reveal their true feelings.

In some countries, people show their emotions freely. In other countries,
people are taught to keep a straight face and not reveal their emotions.
For example, in China, it is considered
bad manners to frown, because it can
cause other people embarrassment. This
is why Tom didn't reveal his lack of
understanding.

A face-to-face conversation

We use our head, arms, hands, shoulders,
and even legs and feet to make gestures
and emphasize what we are saying.
Posture and gestures mean different
things in different cultures, and they can
easily be misinterpreted.

Here are descriptions of some common body language signals to help you understand and connect better with Canadians and other cultures in your workplace.

Canadians generally face each other while speaking, and make direct eye contact for at least 50 percent of the time. This may vary from what is done in your culture. In some Asian cultures, people prefer a side by-side arrangement and don't make much direct eye contact.

Canadians have relaxed postures and mannerisms, including slouching in their chairs. They may cross their legs during meetings, and may remain seated when someone enters the room. This differs from some more formal cultures, where people stand as a sign of respect when an older person or one of higher rank enters or leaves the room.

We can describe body language as *open* or *closed*. People display closed body language when they feel threatened or uncomfortable. They withdraw or hide their bodies by using various stances and physical shields for protection. They project the feeling that they are unfriendly and do not want to connect.

In closed body language, people put up barriers between themselves and others. The woman is hugging a book for protection.

In open body language, people face each other and make eye contact.

Keys to body language

- Open body language invites interaction. People face each other and make eye contact. In Canada, you should become comfortable with open body language in order to communicate well with others.

- In Canada, nodding the head generally means, "I agree with you." It can also signal, "I hear you."

- Tilting the head to the side shows interest, active listening, and concern.

- Holding your head up indicates confidence. Looking down gives the impression that you are shy, tired, or uninterested.

- Shrugging the shoulders with a palms-up gesture indicates that the person doesn't know or care, or is bored or uninterested.

- People who are angry or defensive often lean forward, make direct eye contact, and point their fingers.

- An open palm suggests honesty and sincerity. A closed fist can be considered menacing, and hands on the hips can be seen as defiant.

- Canadians look at people's faces for signs, such as a smile or nod, to see if they are interested or following the conversation. If you don't show any emotion on your face, Canadians may feel uncomfortable, and not know whether they are relating to you.

- We look at people's faces to find out their moods and feelings. When your face and words don't match, you send a mixed message. For example, if someone asks how you are feeling and you answer "fine" but look sad and downcast, people get a confusing message. When your verbal and non-verbal language don't match, people believe what they see rather than the words you say.

Shrugging the shoulders indicates indifference or uncertainty.

Confrontational body language: leaning forward, pointing fingers

- It is important to show the right amount of emotion on your face. If you come from a culture that displays all your emotions, you may be perceived as being out of control or aggressive. On the other hand, if you don't let any emotion register on your face, Canadians may think that you have little interest in the conversation. Try to stay in the middle, and display appropriate emotions for the workplace.

Habits and mannerisms that annoy people

Dan was in an early-morning business meeting. He was tired and yawned continually. He also looked at his watch several times. At the end of the meeting his manager called him aside and asked what was wrong. Dan was surprised. He hadn't realized that his actions were sending such strong signals about how tired and bored he was.

We all have unconscious habits and mannerisms that annoy people or cause negative reactions. We generally don't realize when our mannerisms show that we are anxious, bored, confused, impatient, or preoccupied.

To appear calm and relaxed, avoid these gestures.

Do not . . .

- ✗ scratch yourself continually
- ✗ bite or lick your lips
- ✗ play with your hair, moustache, or beard
- ✗ pick your teeth or fingernails
- ✗ tap your feet
- ✗ adjust your glasses continually
- ✗ click your pen
- ✗ drum or tap your fingers on the desk
- ✗ spit
- ✗ clear your throat repeatedly
- ✗ sigh out of boredom
- ✗ play with objects such as a pen or paper clip
- ✗ glance at your watch constantly

Preoccupied

Impatient

How to use body language to connect with people

Stan, from the Philippines, went to a job interview. His handshake was very soft, and he didn't make much eye contact in order to show respect to the owner of the company. The owner decided not to hire Stan because of the poor impression he made. Stan didn't show the confidence that other job candidates showed by making direct eye contact and having a firm handshake.

In Canada, there are three important parts of a greeting: the handshake, the smile, and eye contact. The essential parts of each are described here.

The handshake

The handshake is a unique occasion because it is the only time that Canadians allow strangers to enter intimate personal space and have physical contact. (The exception is in Quebec. See the section on Touch on page 90.)

To Canadians, a firm handshake shows that you are confident, sincere, and friendly. You'll make a great first impression by being the first to extend your hand.

A good handshake: clasp hands web-to-web

If you come from a culture where a weak handshake is normal, it is important to try to make your handshake firmer. Here's how to do it:

- Extend your hand straight and clasp the other person's hand firmly and comfortably. The webs between your thumbs and forefingers should meet.

- Shake firmly once or twice and then let go. Don't keep pumping up and down.

- Don't turn your hand up or down, or clasp people's fingers. Canadians view this as a soft, weak handshake.

A poor handshake: Don't turn your hand or clasp the other person's fingers

- Adjust your handshake to the person you are meeting. Don't overpower a woman who has a delicate hand, but still give a firm handshake.

Who shakes hands?

Canada is not hierarchal when it comes to handshakes. Men shake hands with men and with women, and women shake hands with each other in a business setting.

People in senior positions should offer their hands first, but it is perfectly fine for anyone to offer their hand. It shows respect and professionalism.

You should shake hands when …

- you are introduced to someone
- you say goodbye to someone
- you meet someone you haven't seen for some time
- a meeting is beginning or ending
- you feel it is appropriate

When you meet someone, extend your hand, step forward, smile, and say something like, "I'm pleased to meet you, (name of person)."

What if you aren't comfortable shaking hands, because of your faith or for other reasons? As mentioned in Chapter 3, you can smile and nod, and say, "It's not my custom to shake hands, but I am very pleased to meet you."

You may also find that some people are reluctant to shake hands in winter, when colds and the flu are circulating. These individuals may tell you they have a cold or are coming down with something. Many people appreciate this consideration because they don't want to get sick themselves.

What if you are sick? In general it is fine to tell someone why you are not shaking hands, but it may be awkward to tell an important client that you are not feeling well. In this case, try to wash your hands very well before your meeting. You can also keep a small bottle of sanitizing gel or cloths (available in most drugstores) in your briefcase or purse to clean your hands before you meet people.

Smiling

Jin, from Korea, didn't understand why people were always asking him if he was angry or upset, even when he was feeling good. Jin didn't smile much during work hours because he felt that business was serious. Koreans perceive people who smile a great deal to be shallow. At his job in Canada, he was puzzled to see people smiling at him in meetings, and felt very uncomfortable.

People of all cultures are taught to control facial expressions and mask emotions in situations where they are not appropriate. For example, in Canada we understand that we should not cry in a business meeting or openly yawn during a boring presentation.

To Canadians, a smile indicates happiness, but in other cultures smiling may cover a range of emotions:

- Asians smile when they are embarrassed, or to conceal discomfort.
- Koreans perceive business people who smile to be insincere.
- Germans only smile "when there is something to smile about."
- The people of Thailand smile a great deal.

Canadians perceive a person who smiles to be sincere, warm, caring, and likeable. This does not mean you should go around smiling broadly all the time! If fact, too much smiling might lead co-workers to think you are strange. It's important to smile in the appropriate circumstances.

Here's how and when to smile in Canada:

- When someone smiles at you, you should return the smile.

- When you meet someone for the first time, make eye contact and smile warmly and sincerely. You should be thinking, "I'm really happy to meet this person!"

- A broad, open-mouthed smile, especially with lots of teeth showing, can seem insincere because it is easy to "put on" or fake.

- A warm, genuine smile involves the muscles of the mouth, jaw, and eyes. It is easy to contract the muscles of the mouth, but not as easy to engage the eyes. In a relaxed smile, the lips are closed or parted slightly. Have a warm, steady gaze, and allow your eyes to crinkle at the corners.

Eye contact

Lee was new in the department and wanted to make a good impression. When her manager talked to her, she lowered her eyes to show respect. Unfortunately, her manager didn't understand Lee's body language, and thought that Lee was shy and insecure. As a result, the manager was reluctant to give Lee a new assignment with an important client.

In Canada, the United States, Great Britain, and parts of Europe, direct eye contact is important to building relationships. Eye contact is considered a sign of respect and attentiveness. People who avoid eye contact may be considered insecure, unfriendly, dishonest, untrustworthy, or lacking in self-confidence.

In other cultures, people don't make much eye contact. In Asian cultures, people lower their eyes as a sign of respect, and feel that prolonged eye contact shows bad manners. In the Middle East, however, eye contact can be so intense that it exceeds the comfort zone for most people in Canada.

Aim to maintain eye contact about 60 to 70 percent of the time. This eye contact should not be steady, though. Look at the other person's eyes for a second or two, then move your eyes away for a few seconds. Keep your attention on the person's face by looking at his nose, chin, or forehead. You can alternate between direct eye contact and looking away, as long as you keep your attention around the face.

Be sensitive to individual differences. Some people are uncomfortable with eye contact because of personality, cultural background, or mood. A shy person may feel overwhelmed by eye contact that is considered normal by other people. You should never stare at someone.

Avoid sunglasses or tinted glasses indoors, as they interfere with eye contact. We feel uncomfortable when we can't see someone's eyes, because we don't know where the person is looking.

How to use body language to look like a leader

What your hands reveal

People's hands often reveal their true feelings. When someone is nervous or upset, he may rub or wring his hands together, or clasp and unclasp them.

Hiding your hands in your pockets or behind your back gives the impression that you are secretive or have a hidden agenda. Show your hands to help build trust.

Hand gestures have different meanings in different cultures. For example, using the thumb and forefinger to make a circle means "okay" in Canada and the US. In Brazil, it's an insult. This same gesture means "money" in Japan and in France it means "zero."

In Canada, the common gesture of an upturned thumb up means "okay," or that everything is fine, and a thumb turned down means that things are not good. However, these are considered rude gestures in some countries.

Steepling is a common gesture in business. The name comes from the shape the hands make, which looks like a church steeple. This action is interpreted as a sign of confidence, or suggests that the person is making a decision. Sales people often look for this sign!

Posture

Have you noticed people who seem to have charisma, or "presence"? Chances are they have great posture—they stand and walk tall.

Good posture makes a strong impression because people notice it from across the room. It involves the whole body and is associated with self-confidence and leadership ability.

Poor posture—with slumped shoulders and lowered head—is associated with lack of self-confidence, poor leadership skills, and low interest. Moreover, people with poor posture are also perceived to pay less attention to detail and may be considered to be less reliable and capable.

Good posture is almost magical because it can make anyone appear more self-confident. It is a particularly valuable tool for anyone who is shorter than average height, has a high or weak voice, or can't afford a top-quality wardrobe. In fact, good posture gives you many of the benefits of a new suit, without the cost!

What is good posture? Stand straight but not rigid. Balance your weight evenly on both feet. Relax your shoulders, but don't let them droop. Keep your chest up and your stomach in. Your head should be erect and your chin up, but in a comfortable manner. Your arms should hang naturally and comfortably at your side, with your fingers slightly curled.

When you walk, move purposefully to show that you are confident, professional, and relaxed. Keep an even pace and a deliberate stride. Don't drag or shuffle your feet.

 **Canadian Business Concept:** Good posture works like magic, because it makes everyone appear more self-confident. Even if you don't feel confident, by simply pulling yourself up, you will appear to be more in charge.

Sit up straight

People who stand up straight are often surprised by how much they slump while sitting. Drooping shoulders are the most visible posture problem. Don't sink into your chair. It makes you disappear, both physically and psychologically.

To make a good impression, sit with your spine erect, but not too stiff. Lean slightly forward, and keep your hands in a comfortable position, ready to gesture.

Body language that makes a great first impression

Warm smiles and open body language invite interaction

In business, you can learn to use body language to make a great first impression to connect with people. Here is a summary of the key steps:

- Use open body language to invite interaction.

- Have a firm handshake. Smile and make eye contact when you shake hands.

- Maintain eye contact by looking at the other person's face (without overdoing it).

- Have a warm, genuine smile.

- Show people you are paying attention by keeping your body relatively still, leaning forward slightly, and nodding when appropriate.

- Observe other people's body language to understand them better. Do not invade their space, or touch people who don't like to be touched.

- Become aware of your own body language to communicate better with others.

Business Buzzwords

- breathing space
- closed body language
- comfort zone
- elbow room
- open body language
- silent signals

Chapter 5 Action Plan

1. Observe people's body language in your workplace.

    - When do people shake hands?
    - How close do people stand to each other?
    - How often do they smile?
    - How often do people touch each other?
    - How much eye contact do people make?
    - What kind of scent (or lack of scent) do you notice?

    Write down three ways you can change your body language to fit in to the Canadian workplace more successfully.

    a) _____

    b) _____

    c) _____

2. Practise making eye contact, smiling, and offering a firm handshake if these things are not part of your culture.

3. Observe the leaders at your company: managers, vice-presidents, the president, or CEO. How do they project leadership through their body language? _____

    _____

    Write down one change you can make to your body language that will project leadership skills.

    _____

Business Talk on the Job

Business has its own specialized language, filled with acronyms, jargon, and specific conversational patterns.

In This Chapter

- Canadian communication styles
- Canadian conversation patterns
- Business buzzwords
- How to talk with your manager
- How to talk with co-workers
- Using the right words
- How to improve your speaking ability

Canadian communication styles

Communicating a message seems straightforward: You just talk to each other, eh? Well, it's not always that easy. Often when we have problems and conflicts, they are due to a failure to communicate.

Canadian Business Concept: "Eh" is a particularly Canadian way of ending a sentence when you are asking for agreement. Similarly, Americans often say, "huh?" at the end of a sentence.

To communicate, one person sends a message by speaking, writing, or using body language. The other person receives the message and interprets it. It's like a code, where people agree that the word *table* means the piece of furniture where we eat.

The most common way we send messages is by speaking. Particular combinations of sounds can represent complex ideas. In addition, most languages have expressions and jargon that are difficult to understand even when you know the language well. Business has its own codes and conventions which break down further into specialized language for different industries.

Learning English as a second language is challenging. Did you know that English has over 200,000 words in common use, as opposed to French, which has 100,000? Did you know that English is the only language with books of synonyms? A simple word like *fly* can have many definitions, including "travel in an airplane," "an insect," or "part of a pair of pants." And the word *high* has 20 different meanings. No wonder English is confusing!

English also has many variations between British English, Australian English, Indian English, Caribbean English, and even between Canadian and American English. Even if you know the language well, business language, or the jargon of your industry, may still be confusing.

If English is not your first language, and especially if you come from a culture where saving face is highly valued, you may respond to situations where you don't understand something by pretending you do understand.

This is normal, but it will cause problems in your workplace. If you don't understand something, it's fine to say, "Please explain that again in a different way. I want to make sure I understand." You can also say, "What I understand is … Is that what you are saying?"

In Canada, no means no, and yes means yes

 "In my culture, we have a habit of saying 'yes' to acknowledge that we heard someone," says Paresh Vyas, Consulting Architect with IBM, who is a Kenyan of South Asian descent. "One day a customer asked me if we were going to deploy a particular technology. I answered 'yes, yes' but that this technology was not included in our price. The customer said, 'You are leading us along.' We joked about it afterwards, but the small difference in our ways of speaking had big implications. You have to be very cautious about what you say and how you say it!"

Canadians use direct communication. In direct communication, the actual words used are the most important part of the communication. Direct communicators use facts and information when they communicate, and they expect you to do the same.

In indirect communication the context is most important. People with indirect communication styles focus not just on the words that are used, but on how they are used. They pay attention to the setting and relationships between people.

Indirect communicators don't want to risk offending anyone by expressing opinions that may cause negative feelings. A major goal of indirect communication is to save face, or avoid embarrassment. Communicating indirectly is a way to avoid angering, shaming, or embarrassing others.

In indirect cultures, speakers may say what other people want to hear instead of what they really believe. They may feel that being direct could lead to conflict, so they discreetly avoid controversial issues. They express concerns tactfully, and count on the listeners to interpret the meaning. To avoid conflict they may smile and say, "No problem!" when what they really mean is, "No way! Big problem!"

For example, in Japan there are at least 15 different ways to say "no" without actually saying the word. This is because the Japanese consider it rude to say directly, "I disagree with you" or "You're wrong."

Study how people interact in your workplace. Notice how direct or indirect people are in their communication styles. If other people express their real opinions in the workplace, you should too. If your manager asks your opinion on something pertaining to your work, he really wants to know your thoughts, even if they are different from his.

When your manager or a co-worker asks you to do something, be careful not to agree unless you are sure you can complete the task. Agreeing to do something because you are worried about offending the person who asks you will backfire, because in Canada, if you agree to do something, people expect you to do it. If you don't follow through, they will be angry or upset and, more importantly, they will not trust you in the future.

It's better to say, "I'm not sure how to do that" or "I'm having a challenge with this customer" than to smile and say, "Everything is fine" when it's not. The problem will get worse, and you will look as if you aren't doing your job well.

Polite conversations verses heated discussions

 Victor loved to discuss politics. When he arrived in Canada, he made a strong political statement, hoping to involve Robert, his Canadian colleague, in a lively discussion. Rather than openly disagreeing with Victor, Robert said, "Well, some people may see it that way. Everyone is entitled to his opinion. We'll have to agree to disagree on this point." Victor replied, "Is that all you have to say on the subject?" He was disappointed that Robert didn't want to engage in conversation about this controversial topic.

Cultural styles can create a great deal of misunderstanding. People from some cultures, such as the Russian, Italian, Spanish, Greek, South American, Arab, and African ones, have conversational styles that are called "high involvement." People may enjoy a heated argument, and may think that people who don't want to discuss controversial subjects are not interested. In fact, Russians, Arabs, and Mediterraneans are notorious for passionately arguing about their ideas to the point of pounding their fists on the table. Their conversations are characterized by a lot of talking. They speak loudly and quickly, interrupt people, and expect to be interrupted.

At the other end of the scale, most Southeast Asians prefer to keep their emotions in check when discussing or presenting an idea. They speak softly, refrain from interrupting, and listen and respond respectfully to their conversation partners.

Most Canadians are somewhere in the middle. As with North Americans in general, Canadians have a fairly direct style of speaking, but are generally less interested in getting involved in heated arguments that will upset people. Of course this is very individual, and you will find many Canadians who love to jump into a political or social debate!

Canadian conversation patterns
Ritual conversations and office talk

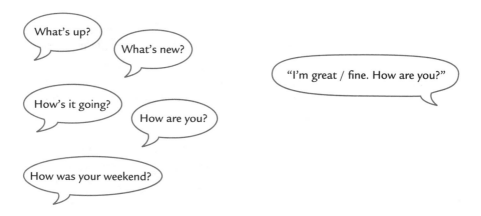

Canadians have many ritual conversations. When they pass someone they know, they say, "How's it going?" or "What's up?" When they meet someone they haven't seen recently they ask, "What's new?" or "How are you?"

Some new Canadians are surprised to learn that these are cultural rituals, with little meaning attached. You are not expected to give details about your health or personal information. The standard answer is, "I'm fine (or great). How are you?"

When co-workers ask you, "How was your weekend?" or "What did you do last night?" they are being friendly. It's fine to give some details about your weekend. You can talk about a movie or restaurant you went to, or a game you saw on TV. Always be sensitive to the fact that they may not have time for a long conversation. Monitor their body language to see if they want to end the conversation.

Until you know the person well, it's better to keep your answer short and positive. Be careful not to talk about personal problems such as illness or family situations unless you are close to the person. This would make most co-workers feel uncomfortable.

Canadian Business Concept: Canadians have many ritual conversations that don't require detailed answers. The language used may be more formal in a business setting, such as "How are you?" and more casual in other environments, such as "What's up?" or "How's it going?"

Talk and silence

How much you talk is cultural as well. Americans are known for talking a lot and speaking loudly. Canadians are not quite as loud, but they still speak fairly directly.

In some cultures, silence is considered a sign of respect, but in North America, when someone does not speak up, other people may become uncomfortable and frustrated. Silence is uncomfortable for people from western cultures. If you stop talking, most Canadians will start talking to fill the void in about four seconds. If you are used to long silences, Canadians may feel you have nothing to add to the discussion, and may not speak to you as frequently.

Verbal dueling

Listen to people in your workplace the day after a hockey game has been on TV. You'll hear people shouting in a loud, friendly manner about who will win the next game. You may hear this kind of discussion when your group is trying to decide on a new ad campaign and people have different opinions about which route to take.

This kind of verbal fighting is energetic and friendly, but it's not personal. Even if people insult each other, it's generally said in fun, with no hard feelings afterwards.

Conversation styles

Every culture has rules about who talks when, and for how long.

Playing Ping-Pong

Canadians use a specific conversation pattern. Some people describe this as being like a Ping-Pong game. One person—the first speaker—has the ball and hits it to the other person. The second person speaks, and returns the ball. If anyone doesn't return the ball, the conversation stops.

Conversations typically follow this pattern: first, the greeting and opening; next, the discussion of the topic; and finally, the closing and parting. Just as in Ping-Pong, Canadians take turns speaking. One person speaks for a few moments and the other person listens. Then the other person speaks while the first person listens.

When people know each other well, or get excited about a topic, they may jump in and interrupt each other, but people who do this too much are considered rude. Canadians do not like being cut off continually.

When you speak with Canadians, make an extra effort to take turns speaking. Be sure to ask enough questions to keep the conversation going. Ask the other person's opinion, and don't interrupt too often. On the other hand, you have to do your part and continue the conversation. Keep the Ping-Pong game in mind!

Interrupting

Canadians are often impatient with conversation styles that are different from their own, because these styles are unfamiliar to them.

In some cultures people speak for extended periods of time. Canadians become irritated if one person speaks for too long, and consider it bad manners to hog the floor. In Canadian conversation, everyone wants to have a chance to participate.

If you are used to talking for a long time, be sure to give other people a chance to speak. If you normally jump in and interrupt people, be conscious of your speech patterns. If you don't allow people to express their thoughts and opinions, they may be less interested in conversing with you in the future.

On the other hand, if you are the quiet type, you may have to learn to break into the conversation. You will have to interrupt some people or else you'll never get a word in edgewise. If you don't contribute to the conversation, people will think you have nothing to say or that you don't care.

As we discussed earlier, Canadians tend to get straight to the point and say what they think. In other cultures, people like to take their time and circle around the point, or become sidetracked before they eventually get to the point. They may insert stories to illustrate their idea, or go off in different directions before eventually getting to the point.

Needless to say, when the two styles mix in the workplace, there can be clashes. People with either style can be frustrated and confused by those with the other style. Canadians may be upset by what they see as wasted time, wondering when the speaker will finally get to the point. People from other cultures may feel insulted by Canadians who seem pushy and don't appreciate their subtlety.

Talking about yourself

Canadians do not consider it important to develop long-term relationships with people before doing business together, and are not likely to tell business contacts a great deal about themselves personally.

In other cultures, people want to get to know potential business partners well before they do business, and often feel very frustrated when Canadians don't disclose personal information.

Men's and women's conversation styles

Individuals vary greatly in their communication styles, but women have traditionally been less direct than men in expressing criticism or differing opinions. Yet women may be more direct in talking about emotional issues.

In today's workplace, women have learned to compete and communicate with men in a more direct manner. However, there is now much more recognition of the contributions that women make to the workplace: they tend to collaborate more and they are sensitive to personal issues.

Giving and asking for feedback

You know when people don't understand you because the conversation stops or they ask a question. But you don't always know when people *mis*understand you. They might give you a strange look, which you may or may not notice, but the conversation can go on … under the wrong assumptions.

If you aren't sure whether your message has been communicated clearly, ask questions to get feedback. Here are two types of questions you can ask:

Closed questions

Closed questions start with *do* (Do you …? / Did you …?) and can often be answered with one word: *yes*, *no*, or *uh-huh*. They are usually not good questions to ask, because you don't get much information from the answers.

Examples:
- **Do** you want to go ahead with this project?
- **Did** you finish the report?
- **Does** the system work properly?

Open questions

Open questions lead to more information. They start with *who, what, when, where, how,* or *why*. They encourage people to express themselves and provide information.

Examples:
- **Who** will handle this project?
- **What** do you think of my outline for the report?
- **When** will we launch the next phase of the marketing plan?
- **Where** do you think we should make the cuts in the budget?
- **Why** are we including XYZ on the agenda for tomorrow's meeting?
- **How** will we implement this initiative?

 Canadian Business Concept: *Uh-huh* and *uh-uh* sound very similar, but mean different things. According to the *Oxford ESL Dictionary*, *uh-huh* means agreement or understanding, while *uh-uh* means "no" or disagreement.

Business Buzzwords

 Elias was at Pearson Airport waiting for a flight to Montreal. Sitting next to him was a man dressed in a business suit, talking loudly on his cellphone. Elias couldn't help but overhear the man's one-sided conversation: "Let me run this by you ... This project is a strike-out. I can't get to first base with that guy ... he doesn't want to play ball. I can't even get  a ballpark estimate ... He's really playing hardball, but we'll have to step up to the plate if we want to hit this one out of the ballpark."

Elias was completely confused. Were they discussing business or baseball?

If you listen to anyone discussing business in North America, you are likely to hear a mixture of sports terms and military expressions.

Here are just a few common examples and their meanings. You will probably hear many more.

Business Expression	Meaning
Run this by you	Discuss it
Game plan / Battle plan	Overall strategy
Strike out	Lack of success
I can't get to first base with him.	I'm not making any progress dealing with him.
Let's touch base	Let's talk / speak to each other
Play ball	Go along with what everyone else wants
Right off the bat	From the beginning / immediately
Step up / Step up to the plate	Take responsibility for something
Level the playing field / Level the field	Make things equal
Ballpark figure	Rough estimate
Play hardball	Get tough / Do not compromise
Came out of left field	Was unexpected
Slam dunk	Complete and easy success
The whole nine yards	Everything
Lateralled	Move to a new position that's the same as your old position but with a new title
Goaltending	Protecting your business
Throw in the towel	Give up
Go to the mat	Do everything you can
Zero-sum game	Situation in which one person's gain or loss is balanced by the gains and losses of others

Listen carefully at any business meeting, event, or presentation, and you'll hear the latest business buzzwords. These terms are a kind of shorthand that people use to describe common business issues. Some words suddenly become popular, and you start hearing them everywhere. They may become a permanent part of the English language, or they may be used for a long or short time before new words replace them. Below are a few examples.

Business Buzzword	Meaning
Bottom line / At the end of the day / When all is said and done	Outcome / Profit
Brain dump	Too much information all at once
Customer-centric	Focused on customer needs
Deliverables	What you will do for or deliver to a customer
Drop-dead date	Final date when something must be done
Etched in stone	Definite / Unable to be changed
Fall-back position	What you will do if your first plan fails
Get your ducks in a row	Be organized
In the pipeline	In progress / In development
On the same page	In agreement / Understanding each other
Paradigm	Clear example
Parameter	Boundaries
Pencilled in	Able to be changed
Swamped / Having a lot on your plate	Very busy, a lot or too much work to do
Think outside the box	Think creatively
Value-added	Having some feature added to a product, often making it more expensive

Euphemisms

Some things are unpleasant to talk about, so we substitute or find new words for them. Some substitutions, or euphemisms, are listed below.

Euphemism	Meaning
Glow	Sweat, perspire
Washroom / Restroom / Ladies' room / Men's room / Bathroom / The loo (British) / Lavatory / WC (British)	Toilet
Pass / Pass away	Die
Golden agers / Seniors	Old people

Business also has its euphemisms. As a more pleasant way of talking about laying people off because there's no work, we use terms like *letting go*, *downsizing*, or *outplacing*. *Staff reduction* is a euphemism for mass layoffs.

Repurposing is a euphemism for giving someone a different job—usually of lower status, as in, "We feel that your talents are wasted as a salesperson, so we're going to repurpose you to security guard."

How to talk with your manager

Managers are often pressed for time. If you mumble and search for the right words, your manager may speak to you less frequently.

When speaking with your manager, use positive, powerful language. Employees who are committed and enthusiastic about their work are more likely to succeed, but you also have to make sure your manager knows how you feel. Choose language that helps you get the message across.

Words to use with your manager

able
accept
accomplish
achieve
appreciate
aware
better, best
can, capable
care
careful, cautious
committed
confident
consider
continue
contribute
create
dedicated
delighted
enjoy
enthusiastic
experience
expertise
fair
future
generous
goals
help, helpful
hope
ideas
imagine, imagination
improve
innovate
learn
manage
motivate, motivated
negotiate
objective
performance

plan, planning
positive
possibility
potential
prepared
pride, proud
priorities
productive
profitable
propose
reasonable
resolve
resourceful
responsible
retain
revitalize
reward

service
solve
strategy
strength
studied
support
talent
tested
thanks, thankful
think
thrilled
time
untiring
value, valuable
willing
wisdom
workable

Yes, our team is capable of achieving this goal. We're prepared to propose a workable solution that management will be thrilled with!

Phrases to use with your manager

Able to make decisions
Achieve goals
Best for the company / team
Best use of resources
Best suited
Big possibilities
Big picture
By all means (of course)
Commitment to (productivity /
    department / company)
Count on me (You can count on me)
Cut costs
Do a credible job
Expand territory
Gain experience
Get your input
Give full credit to (name of person)
Give this a trial
Good point
Greatest admiration
Happy to try it your way
I appreciate / look forward to
I gave a great deal of thought to …

I know you'll be pleased with …
I'll work on this immediately
I'm pleased
Improve productivity
Improve the bottom line
Increase market share
I need your take / advice on this
In the future
I think you'll find
Make better use of
Minimize risk
More flexible / efficient
Move forward
Open up possibilities
Our department / company
Play to my strengths
Resolve problems
Sink my teeth into (get involved)
Take the ball and run with it
Team player
Thank you for the opportunity
This is helpful
Try something new
Well-founded
Win-win situation
With great pleasure
You can rely on me
You will appreciate

You can count on me to improve the bottom line. Thank you for the opportunity to sink my teeth into this project.

Words to avoid using with your manager

afraid
bad
blame
bored
can't / cannot
catastrophe
crisis
delay
destroyed
disaster
doubt
dumb
embarrassing
exploded
failed
fault
fear
final
forgot
foul-up
hopeless / helpless
impossible
inadequate
incapable
late
mess
misjudged
mismanaged
mistake
nervous
non-negotiable
overloaded
panic
quit
refuse
reject
ridiculous
risk

silly
stuck
tedious
unappreciated
underpaid

undeserved
unfair
unworkable

I'm stuck with an unfair workload and I'm in a panic. I can't handle it.

Phrases to avoid using with your manager

Afraid to do it
Beyond me
Beyond repair
Big mistake
Big trouble
Blew it
Bombed out
Can't ask me to do that
Can't be done / fixed
Can't do that
Doesn't thrill me
Don't blame me
Don't want to do that
Doubt it will work

Fatal error
Get off my case
Give me a break
Give me a shot at …
Haven't got the
    experience
Huge problem
I can't afford to
I can't do any more
I can't do anything
    about this
I demand
I don't deserve this
I forgot to …

I insist
I'll have to quit
I'm fed up
I'm late
I'm only human
I'm overworked
It slipped past me
I've had it
Just one of those things
No future
No opportunity
Not my problem
Out of the question
Screwed up
This is unfair
Unreasonable demand
Waste of time
Won't work that way
Worn out
You don't appreciate me
You expect too much
You have no choice
You have to

Give me a break—that was Josh's fault. It's not my problem.

How to talk with co-workers

"I'm not interested in small-talk. I don't care about people's home life or family. I'm just here to do a job." This was the attitude of one of Karen Bowen's students. Bowen is Program Coordinator at Gandy Associates, which provides English Communication Training.

Unfortunately, this man had closed body language and an unhappy expression on his face. Bowen says, "We encouraged him to try to connect with people, as an exercise. He agreed, and started asking co-workers about their families and interests. Within a short time, he told us that he was much more comfortable in his job, and said 'Making small-talk changed my life.'"

Making small-talk with co-workers is important for building relationships at work. Having good relationships is vital to doing well at your job, and to enjoying your job. It will also help you acclimatize to the office culture.

Marvi Yap, who came to Canada nine years ago from the Philippines says, "When you keep to yourself, people think you are not interested in them, and they leave you alone. They are sizing you up, but they don't know if they should approach you."

You have to make the first move by giving your co-workers a cue. It's easy to smile and have a nice demeanor. Start by talking to one person. As you feel more comfortable, approach a group. Before you know it, you'll be one of them.

Make it a goal to meet one new person each day. Ask a simple question, such as, "Where's the coffee machine?" or "What time is lunch?" Or you can ask something like, "How was your Easter weekend?" and express interest in what they say. "When you open up, people become friendly and interested in you," Marvi Yap says.

Rakesh Kirtikar, Senior Manager of Multicultural and Local Marketing at Scotiabank says, "I've found that Canadians are very friendly. In the workplace, they are open to listening to you, and to giving you advice and direction. Many people are aware of the fact that you are new to Canada, and are very forgiving if you don't understand the cultural environment at first."

Take advantage of the time spent sitting in the cafeteria, waiting for a meeting to begin, or hanging out in the copier room, to exchange ideas with others. You can discuss anything from the weather to the company's upcoming trade show. Just be sure to avoid private information or hurtful gossip.

As you get to know people, you'll discover the go-to people in your company. These are the people to speak to if you have questions about the company, and they can be a very valuable resource. Be careful, however. You should always check with your immediate supervisor to make sure the information you get is correct.

By making an effort to talk to your co-workers, you'll also find out more about their personalities—their interests, hobbies, and families. This will help you feel more comfortable, and you'll start to feel that you fit in. You'll also learn which co-workers you may want to avoid, such as individuals with reputations for being mean or deceitful.

Here are some tips on how to make small-talk with co-workers so that you can start building positive relationships:

- If you're standing beside a co-worker as you wait for the elevator to arrive or for a meeting to begin, see if she is receptive before you start a conversation. If she seems distracted, she may have something else on her mind and not want to make small talk at that moment.

- Even if the person is friendly when you start chatting, keep the conversation professional, and don't talk for too long. Be sensitive to body language signals, such as looking at a watch or moving slowly away, which shows you that the person wants to end the conversation.

- If you don't know what to say, you can always start with simple topics such as the weather, the latest sporting event, or something in the news. (See Chapter 14 for tips on small-talk.)

- Don't try to dominate the conversation, or start all your sentences with *I*. Ask people's opinions, and show genuine interest in their ideas.

- If someone else arrives, try to include him in your conversation. You many need to change topics. Make him feel welcome. Don't give the impression that he interrupted an important conversation.

- To end the conversation, try to leave after *you* have spoken so you don't create the impression that the other person said something that drove you away. You can say, "Well, I have to get back to work now. This was interesting. Let's talk again soon."

Using the right words

The company's president entered the conference room and stood at the head of the table. All eyes were on her. She said, "We've had a terrible fourth quarter. This is unacceptable. You need to work harder to turn this around."

Everyone in the room was demoralized. The words were clear and direct, but they produced anxiety and stress. They didn't solve the problem. In fact, they made the situation worse. Productivity sank to a new low.

Imagine what the reaction would have been if she had said, "We've had a low fourth quarter, but I'm confident that we can turn this around. Thank you for your hard work in difficult times. Let's all pull together to make this company stronger."

The words we use can be powerful and positive, and inspire people to action. They can also be negative and destructive, and produce anger and frustration.

In Canada, we use direct communication, but that doesn't mean we should be blunt. In the workplace, we always have to choose our words carefully and find a balance between being honest and being positive.

Words that attack

Some words and phrases trigger negative reactions. People who are angry or upset may use strong words that accuse or seem to attack other people. Once the words are spoken, it's impossible to take them back.

Phrases such as, "You're kidding me" or "That's stupid" are sure to trigger a bad reaction from the listener. Here are other words that create negative reactions:

absurd	idiotic	nuts	rude
brain-dead	inconsiderate	off your rocker	selfish
crazy	irresponsible	pitiful	senseless
foolish	nonsense	ridiculous	

If you don't understand something, you should ask questions. But you have to choose your words carefully. Instead of bluntly asking, "Why did you do that?" you can use phrases that help you understand. Be careful about beginning questions with *why*, which can make people feel threatened.

To avoid making people feel uncomfortable, focus on correcting the problem rather than blaming someone. Use a tone that is solution-oriented rather than accusatory. Instead of "Did you break the photocopier?" ask, "What happened to the photocopier?" Here are other types of questions to ask:

- **What** went wrong here?
- **What** is a good way to …?
- **What** are some solutions for …?
- **What** are your thoughts on . . .?
- **How** can we avoid such costly misunderstandings?
- **Where** could your team cut costs in future?
- **When** can the report be ready?
- **Who** could you go to for advice on that problem?
- **When** could we implement this program?

Words to use when you're angry or upset

If you feel angry or upset, you have to express it, but it's important to use the right words so you don't make enemies.

Avoid beginning sentences with *you*, which can make someone feel attacked. Instead, focus on the problem instead of the person.

Instead of: You missed important details in your report.
Try: Some important details are missing in this report.

Instead of: You forgot to send out the memo.
Try: People need the information in that memo before the meeting. Could you please send it out right away?

Instead of: You should have read the instructions first.
Try: I think you'll find useful information in the instruction manual.

Instead of: You keep interrupting me.
Try: John, I'll be interested in your input when I finish explaining my idea.

Instead of: Why didn't you tell me you needed help?
Try: Please ask me for help if something isn't clear. My door is always open.

Instead of: That's not going to work.
Try: That's an interesting observation. My experience is …

Good speakers are good listeners

 Whenever Tony speaks with Ben, a co-worker, Ben seems to be in a hurry. He's always looking at papers on his desk, or at his watch, or over Tony's shoulder. As soon as Tony stops talking, Ben changes the subject. Tony can't relate to Ben at all.

If you've ever tried to talk to someone who doesn't listen, you know that it's impossible to have a meaningful conversation. In business, listening to your manager, clients, and co-workers is one of the most important skills you can have. Managers can tell how well you've been listening by the quality of the questions you ask. With clients, listening carefully can make all the difference in getting the sale and doing the job well.

Hearing is a passive activity, but *active listening* is a process that is hard work. Although we may want to listen effectively, it isn't always easy because we aren't taught this skill in school. However, listening well is a gift you give to others and it is a fundamental skill for business.

Why is listening well so difficult? Because we have distractions in our environment that make it difficult to focus on what's being said. Phones ringing, people interrupting us, and mental or physical fatigue can all make listening difficult. To overcome these barriers, you first have to identify them. Then you can develop strategies for dealing with them, since most of the time you can't make these barriers go away.

Here are some tips for active listening:

- Clear your mind. We are often distracted from listening because we are thinking about what else we have to do. A good way to solve this problem is to write down anything you have to do before you enter a meeting. Once it is written down, your mind will be clear to focus on the speaker.

- Concentrate. Pay close attention to what the speaker is saying. Try to be patient with people who speak slowly or falter in getting their message across.

- Paraphrase. To check whether you have understood the person, paraphrase what the speaker said. This means that you repeat part of what the person says, in your own words: "If I understand you correctly, you are saying …" "So what you're saying is … Is that correct?"

- Be patient. Don't interrupt the speaker. Someone who pauses may just be gathering her thoughts. If you cut her off, she will think you are rude, and you may miss some valuable information.

- Ask questions. If you don't understand someone, ask for a second explanation. If you come from a culture where people don't ask questions for fear of causing embarrassment, it's important to realize that in Canada, asking questions is considered a sign of interest and respect. People are happy that you listened carefully enough to consider what they said. Questions show that you listened and are involved. Your supervisor doesn't want you to pretend you understood something that you don't understand.

How to improve your speaking ability

By now you've seen how important language is in the workplace. Here are some tips to improve your speaking ability.

Pay attention

Pay attention to the words your manager and executives in your company use. You may hear many of the words from this chapter.

When you hear a word that you don't know, write it in a notebook, and describe how the word was used. What was the story or context in which you hear the word? Look it up, and then use it in a similar situation.

Online dictionaries can be very handy for finding the meaning and pronunciation of new words.

The *Oxford ESL Dictionary* gives you simple explanations of many business words. The *Oxford Advanced Learner's Thesaurus* is an excellent source of synonyms, and the *Oxford Business English Dictionary* is a handy resource of business terminology and buzzwords.

Read business magazines and books

Read journals and publications specific to your industry. These are good places to pick up specific vocabulary. Also read the Canadian version of *Time Magazine* and general business magazines such as *Canadian Business*.

Read a few popular business books, including all-time bestsellers such as *The 7 Habits of Highly Effective People* by Steven Covey. You can also ask your manager if she recommends any business books. She will be impressed when you speak with authority about trends in business.

For fun and enjoyment, read some fiction as well. Reading popular fiction will give you something to talk about at the office, and will improve your communication skills.

Look for talent

Listen to the people in your department or your company. Who has a way with words? These are people who express themselves well and hold their co-workers' attention easily. Talk to these people when you can, and see if you can pick up some of their patterns of speaking or vocabulary.

Take ESL classes

Judith Thompson, Senior Manager of Human Resources at the Sorin Group, says that many newcomers to Canada have good verbal skills, but have difficulty with reading and writing. This is particularly important when employees have to read policy and procedure manuals. The Sorin Group offers ESL courses to employees, but not all companies are as supportive. Thompson strongly recommends that you keep taking ESL courses until you are at a Canadian Language Benchmark of level 5 or 6.

Canadian Business Concept: Improving your language skills is one of the best investments you can make in your career in Canada. "Every single job deals with customers, clients, documents, and paperwork and every employee must communicate well," says Karen Wallis-Musselman, an independent HR consultant.

Business Buzzwords

- get a word in edgewise
- get to the point
- go-to person
- hog the floor
- play to one's strengths
- shorthand
- sink my teeth into
- way with words
- win-win strategy

Chapter 6 Action Plan

1. Canadians have many ritual questions and expressions, such as "How are you?" Write down three expressions hear at your office, and the most common answers.

   a) _____

   b) _____

   c) _____

2. Observe people's conversation patterns. Do you talk more than other people, or less? Do you interrupt people frequently, or do they interrupt you? What adjustments can you make, so that you play conversation Ping-Pong?

   _____

   _____

3. Listen for business buzzwords, such as sports and military terms. List any buzzwords your co-workers or managers use, and their meanings. If you don't understand the buzzwords, ask someone.

Buzzword	Meaning

Telephone Tips

Most business communication involves the telephone, at least to some extent.

In This Chapter

- How to be effective on the telephone
- How to begin and end business calls
- How to talk with receptionists
- How to answer the phone for business calls
- Telephone courtesies
- How to leave effective voice messages
- Cellphone protocol

How to be effective on the telephone

In Canada, the telephone is a business lifeline. A great deal of business takes place during phone calls. We use phone calls to introduce ourselves, give and get information, set up appointments, and follow up on previous contacts. In some cases, phone calls are the only contact we have with a particular person.

However, using the telephone may be one of your most difficult communication tasks—especially if English is not your first language—because you have to understand the telephone-specific language that people use. You also need to learn how to leave effective voice messages.

Here are some challenges people face when using the telephone:

Lack of visuals: You can't see other people's expressions or body language, and they can't see yours.

Language: Specific phrases, idioms, and expressions are used on the telephone.

Hectic pace: People are often in a rush and talk quickly.

Impersonal nature: You may find it difficult to leave a clear voice message, or frustrating to be unable to reach the person you want to speak to.

Here is a sample business telephone conversation:

Receptionist:	Hello, ABC Group. How may I help you?
John:	This is John Smith. Can I have extension 3514, please?
Receptionist:	Of course. Please hold on a minute and I'll put you through …
Brenda (assistant):	Janet White's office, Brenda speaking.
John:	This is John Smith calling, is Janet in?
Brenda:	I'm afraid she's out at the moment. Can I take a message?
John:	Yes, could you please ask her to call me at (613) 442-9987? I need to speak to her about the Rogers file.
Brenda:	Could you repeat the number please?
John:	Yes, that's (613) 442-9987, and my name is John Smith.
Brenda:	Thank you Mr. Smith, I'll make sure Janet gets this message.
John:	Thank you. Good-bye.

Let's look at some of the typical phrases people use on the phone.

Introducing yourself	This is John Smith. John speaking.
Asking who is on the telephone	Can I ask who is calling, please? Who's calling please?
Asking for someone	May I have extension 6643 please? (extensions are internal numbers at a company) Can I please speak to … (*May I* is more formal than *can I* or *could I*) Is Janet in? (informal way to ask, *Is Janet in the office?*)
Phrases a receptionist uses	**When connecting you to someone:** I'll put you through. (to *put someone through* means to connect them) Please hold for a moment. Can you hold the line, please? Can you hold on a moment, please? **When the person you've asked for is not available:** Ms White isn't in. / Ms White is out at the moment. I'm afraid Ms White is not available at the moment. The line is busy (the person is on the phone). Would you like to hold? **When asking if you would like to leave a message:** Can (could / may) I take a message? Could (can / may) I tell her who is calling? Would you like to leave a message? Would you like her voicemail?

How to speak well on the phone

Do people often ask you to repeat what you just said? You may be mumbling, not enunciating clearly or speaking too quickly. A good telephone voice is clear and loud enough for people to hear, without sounding harsh or shrill. Here are some tips for speaking well on the phone.

Speed

Pay attention to how quickly or slowly you talk. If people constantly interrupt you, you may be speaking too slowly. Or you may be speaking so quickly they can't understand what you are saying.

Loudness

Don't shout into the phone, but don't speak so softly that people on the other end can't hear you. Hold the mouthpiece about a centimetre from your lips so people can hear you well.

Clarity

When you say your name and your company's name, speak clearly and distinctly. Separate the words into tiny phrases.

"Hello. This is ABC Company, Tina Wong speaking."
"Shipping department, Ben Smith speaking."

Friendliness

Remember that you may say the same words many times a day, but each caller only hears you once. Always be friendly and courteous when you answer the phone.

Energy

Put energy into your voice. A good trick is to stand up during an important call. When you are sitting, your diaphragm is compressed. When you stand up and move around, you breathe more freely. You also have more energy, which comes across in your voice.

Smile

Another trick is to smile when you speak. It is almost impossible to have a negative tone when you are smiling. The person you speak to won't see the smile, but your voice will sound friendly, and the warmth that comes from a smile will carry across the phone line.

Show appreciation

Thank you is the most powerful phrase in the English language. Always say *please* when asking for something, and end your call with some form of thanks.

"Thank you for calling."
"Thank you for your patience."

How to begin and end business calls

How to prepare for a call and begin the call

Here are tips for preparing for and beginning the call:

Know the reason for your call

Prepare by writing down important points to discuss. Writing things down helps you stay focused. You will be less likely to get sidetracked or forget important items.

Prepare the materials you will need

Near the phone, you should have a pen and paper, your calendar (for setting appointments), and any information from previous contacts with the person you are calling. This way you can avoid putting anyone on hold while you search for facts or figures.

Identify yourself

Unless the person knows you well, give your full name and company name: "This is Marcie Brooks from XYZ Company. I'd like to speak with Jim Smith." Say your name slowly and clearly. Pause between your first and your last name.

Introduce yourself again

If you reach a receptionist, give your name. When you are transferred to the person you are calling, introduce yourself again.

Be brief and stick to your point

If you are on friendly terms with the person, it's fine to ask how he has been, but monitor his voice. If he sounds hurried, get to the point quickly, or ask when would be a good time to call back.

Explain why you called

Quickly tell the person why you called, and ask whether it's a convenient time to talk. If you are told it is a good time, state the purpose of your call and approximately how long it will take.

> "Mr. Smith, I'd like to ask you three questions about the marketing proposal. It should take about five minutes. Is that okay with you?"

Don't begin talking quickly before you find out whether the person has time to talk. He may be on the way to a meeting, or working on a deadline, and not be able to speak at that moment.

If he says he's busy, ask when you can call back

Don't ask the other person to call you, as this makes him do all the work. Also, he may call you when you aren't ready to take notes.

Canadian Business Concept: Don't begin talking before asking whether the person has time to talk. This is one of the biggest errors that people make on the phone.

Take notes

During the call, write down the points you discuss. This is a good way to be efficient and attentive to detail, and helps avoid having to make repeat phone calls to find out the same information.

Be prepared for voicemail

There is a good chance that you will reach voicemail. Be prepared with a brief message detailing who you are, why you are calling, and how the other person can reach you. (See page 142 for details on what to say.)

Know what to do if you are accidentally disconnected

You should call back since you placed the call and know how to reach the other person.

How to end a call

Ending a call well is just as important as beginning it. Your goal is to make a positive impression and make sure everyone knows what to do next.

Summarize the call

At the end of the call, briefly restate what you discussed to make sure each of you understands the next steps.

> "Let's go over what we decided to do."
> "To summarize, I will send you the document tomorrow, and we will discuss it on Wednesday, the 29th."

Use the past tense

Speak in the past tense to signal that the conversation is over.

> "As we discussed today … "
> "It was good to speak with you."
> "That was all the information I needed, thank you."

Thank the other person and be positive

Always say thank you and be positive at the end of the call.

> "Thank you for calling."
> "Thank you for your help. I've enjoyed talking with you."
> "Thank you for taking the time to speak with me. You've been very helpful."

Say good-bye

Even if you're in a rush, say good-bye. It's polite to wait for the other person to reciprocate and let him hang up first.

How to talk with receptionists

When you reach a receptionist, begin by giving your name. You will sound professional because the receptionist won't have to ask who you are.

Always be courteous and patient. The receptionist may be very busy with many incoming calls. She's doing her best so don't get annoyed if you are put on hold or accidentally cut off.

If you reach a receptionist who puts you on hold, it is acceptable to hang up if no one answers after three minutes. More likely than keeping you on hold, the receptionist will ask you if you would like to leave a voicemail message.

How to answer the phone for business calls

Anita, the vice-president's administrative assistant, was asked by her manager to contact several hotels to book space for an upcoming meeting. She called one of the major hotels in the area. After being bounced around to three different people, being put on hold twice, and then being told there was no space available for the dates she had in mind, she vowed never to waste her time calling that hotel again.

Roughly 70 percent of us make buying decisions based on how we are treated during our initial phone call with a company. A caller who isn't answered promptly, or isn't spoken to courteously, may never call back! A prompt reply and the words "Thank you for calling" go a long way toward making a customer feel valued.

When you answer the phone at work, you are representing your company. You should always answer calls promptly and courteously. Check with your manager on what you should say when you answer the phone.

Here are some tips for answering the phone at work:

- Answer calls within three rings, whenever possible.

- Use a friendly but professional greeting, giving your full name: "Hello, Jane Smith speaking" or "Hello, this is Jane Smith."

- If you work in a large company, you may also want to say the name of your department: "Accounting, Jane Smith speaking."

- If someone calls you when it's not convenient for you to talk, explain your situation and ask when you can return the call. Make sure you keep your word by calling when you say you will!

- When you hear the voice of someone you know, put a little extra energy and warmth into your voice. Make the person feel really special.

How to get people to slow down

Business people tend to speak quickly, especially on the phone. If you can't understand what they are saying, don't let them continue. Ask them immediately to speak more slowly. The following are some ways to get them to slow down.

- Say, "I'm sorry, can you please speak a little more slowly?"

- Say, "I'm sorry, but my first language isn't English. Can you please speak a little more slowly?"

- Speak more slowly yourself—people will often slow down to mirror you.

- Keep paper and a pen on your desk so you can take notes. Say, "Let me make sure I got this. You said …" and write it down as you say it.

- Always repeat names and phone numbers. If you don't know the other person's name, ask him to spell it for you. It's better to check than to make a mistake.

Don't say you understand if you don't. Remember that the speaker wants to make sure you understood the message correctly. Most people are thinking about their own work, and may not realize that English isn't your first language. But most Canadians understand that you are trying your best, and will slow down to help you.

Telephone courtesies

Srini Iyengar, Director of Multicultural Markets for the GTA Division of BMO Bank of Montreal, offers these telephone tips: At the office, don't have phone conversations in a language that no one around you can understand. Your co-workers will think you are talking about them. Also, never leave a client's personal information on a voice message—you never know who will retrieve the message. Speak to the client directly.

Here are more telephone courtesies for the workplace:

- Make appointments for important calls, the same way you make appointments for meetings in person. Being on someone's calendar for 3:00 p.m. on Thursday gives you as much importance as meeting them face-to-face. This way you don't run the risk of interrupting someone at a busy time. You can both schedule 10 or 15 minutes on your calendars to make sure you have enough time.

- Don't interrupt your co-workers when they are on the phone. If you walk into an office and someone is on the phone, be discreet. Step out of the office until the conversation is over. This seems obvious, yet many people fail to do it.

- Don't work on other tasks when you're on the phone. The person you are talking to may hear you clicking on your keyboard or eating your lunch, and will realize he is not getting your full attention.

- The person you are speaking to should always feel he is your top priority. If your phone rings during a business appointment, or while you're talking to someone on another line, let the call go to your voicemail. When meeting with co-workers, if you are expecting a call from your manager, let your co-workers know in advance that you have to answer an important call.

- Don't put people on hold unless it's absolutely necessary. If you do, ask their permission first. People may not have time to wait. Ask, "May I put you on hold for a moment while I find that information for you?"

- If you put someone on hold, don't leave him there for long without giving him an update or a chance to call back later. Always apologize for keeping him waiting: "I appreciate your patience and apologize for the delay."

- Return phone calls within one business day, whenever possible. Return calls from your manager as soon as you receive the message. People get frustrated and irritated when you don't return calls.

- Update your voice message every day to help people know when you are available, and when you won't be returning calls immediately because you are out of the office.

Telephone conversation do's and don'ts

The words you use on the phone have a big impact on how well you communicate. If your first language isn't English, you may wonder what to say on the phone. Here are some do's and don'ts.

Don't say	Do say
Who is this?	Who is calling please? May I ask who is calling?
What's your name? Who did you say you were?	I'm sorry, but I didn't get your name.
What do you need? What do you want?	How can I help you?
I can't hear you. Speak up, please.	I'm sorry, I can't hear you. Can you please speak a little louder?
She's out to lunch. She's in the washroom. She's on a break. She's busy. She's on the phone.	I'm sorry, Ms. Smith isn't available at the moment. May I have her call you back? She is in the office but away from her desk. May I help you?
I wasn't the person you talked to before.	I'm sorry, you must have spoken with someone else. How can I help you?
You have to call our accounting department.	That information is available at our accounting department. May I connect you?
That's not my department.	I'm sorry, I can't help you with that. May I connect you with our marketing department or have someone call you back?
He's not here. Call back later.	He's not available at the moment. May I have him call you back?
She doesn't work here anymore.	I'm sorry, she is no longer here. How can I help you?
He's playing golf today. He's sick today.	He is out of the office today. May I have him call you back tomorrow?
This is Sam. What do you need?	This is Sam. How can I help you?

How to leave effective voice messages

Nikhil arrived back in his office to check his voice message, and heard the following: "Oh, hi, this is Frank. I was thinking about …" The message rambled on for five minutes without ever getting to the point. Nikhil was frustrated with the waste of time, and never answered the caller because he couldn't figure out what he was expected to do.

Although voicemail is used by everyone, many people don't use it properly. They either don't leave enough information, or they leave too much information that is not clear and focused. You should plan your voice message before every call, so that your message will move the conversation forward.

Here are some things you should not do when leaving a message:

✗ Don't call and say, "This is Frank," and expect the person you are calling to know who you are. Always leave your full name.

✗ Don't leave a vague message such as, "Please call me back." Always give enough information to explain the purpose of your call.

✗ Don't call people over and over again without leaving a message. Many people have systems that identify the caller's name. They will see that you are calling incessantly, and will be annoyed.

✗ Don't leave a voice message for the same person more often than once every two or three days. The person may be out of the office or unable to deal with your concern right away. You can alternate between a voicemail message one day, and an email message the next day, since different people respond to different communication methods. But don't overdo it.

Before you make a call, think about these things:

• What is your main message? In business, you should be calling for a specific reason, not just to chat.

• What do you want your listener to know or do? Should this person call you back or send you something?

• Are you leaving information to update a previous conversation? A clear message may resolve your problem without the need for another phone call.

When calling, follow these steps:

1. State your name clearly. If it's difficult to pronounce, or if the person doesn't know you, spell it out.
2. State the date and time of your call.
3. Summarize your message. Write it out before you call, so you will be clear and you won't forget anything important.
4. If possible, leave instructions about how you can be reached—the more specific the better.

Here is an example of a telephone message:

Hello. This is Yumi Takahashi in marketing. It's Wednesday, April 15, at 1 p.m.

I'm calling for three reasons. I need to know the time of the meeting on Friday, who I should contact about product X, and which reports you need.

Please call me back at (514) 383-2255 any time today.

Again, it's Yumi Takahashi, at (514) 383-2255. I look forward to hearing from you.

How to leave your name and number

"Hi, it's Assad. Call me at (214) 335-3987, extension 42312."

Did you get that? Or were there too many numbers spoken too quickly? If you have to replay Assad's message several times to catch the number, you might just skip it and go on to the next message.

We know our own numbers, so we may not realize how quickly we say them. With area codes and extension numbers added to the list, it can be difficult to hear all the numbers and write them down.

When you say your number, imagine the person writing it. Say each digit separately: "3-9-8-7" rather than "39 87." Pause after each group of numerals.

Signal what's coming up next, then repeat it. For example, say, "Hi, it's Assad Farah. I'd like to speak to you about the ABC file, so please call me back today, if possible. Here's my number. It's area code 214. The number is 335-3987. My extension is 42312. Let me repeat that. It's area code 214 (pause) 335-3987. My extension is 42312."

Even if you are sure the person you are calling knows how to contact you, always leave your return number, including the area code. Your listener may be on the road and not have access to his phone directory. This is a small courtesy that saves time and makes it easy for people to call you back. Always leaving a return number will increase the chances of people returning your calls.

In addition to making sure the person you are calling clearly understands your phone number, always leave your last name as well. The listener may know other people with your first name.

What to record in your outgoing voice message

- Hello. You have reached Karen Black's voicemail. For Tuesday, June 4, I'm in the office. Please leave a message and I'll get back to you by the end of the business day.

- Hello. This is Fernando Esparza's voicemail. For Friday, March 5, I'm out of the office on business. Please leave me a message, and I'll get back to you on Monday. Enjoy your weekend.

- Hello, you've reached Luella Aguilar's voicemail. For the week of May 24, I am out of the office. For urgent matters, please contact Doug Wong at (403) 333-8383, or leave me a message and I'll get back to you within two business days. Again, that's Doug Wong at (403) 333-8383.

Your outgoing voice message should be warm and welcoming, and it should let people know whether they've reached a voice message or a real person. Sometimes it's difficult to tell.

Plan and practise a message that is friendly, concise, and informative. People need to know when you are likely to return their calls.

Begin with a sincere, brief greeting. Then tell callers what to do next. For example, say, "Please leave me a message and I'll call you back within one business day." Or, "I'm away from the office. Please contact Joe Green at (604) 333-8197."

Update your message daily, and include the date in your message. This tells your callers that you check your messages every day, and it gives them confidence to leave a message. The best time to update your message is in the evening, at the close of your business day—at this time, you can record the following day's message.

If you are usually on the road, you can record one message for the week.

If possible, give callers another option besides leaving a message. Say, "Dial zero to speak to the receptionist," or refer them to another person to contact about urgent matters.

Canadian Business Concept: When you leave a message, be sure it moves your conversation forward. Don't just ask someone to call you back. You may end up playing telephone tag endlessly.

Cellphone protocol

It was Friday afternoon, and Dina was about to drive a customer to the airport after a two-day meeting. She was expecting a call from her assistant, so when her cellphone rang, she answered it. It was her husband on the line. He was calling to give her details about a romantic weekend he had planned. After listening for a few minutes, Dina suddenly realized that the volume on her phone was so loud that the customer could hear everything, and was looking embarrassed. By this time, Dina was embarrassed as well.

We are so conditioned to answer the phone every time it rings, chimes, or beeps, that we sometimes put our professionalism, and even our safety, in jeopardy by answering calls while driving.

Your cellphone is as much a part of your business uniform as your briefcase, so it's important to use it well. Since people talk on cellphones in a louder voice than they would normally use, we occasionally hear details of other people's lives that we'd rather not hear. Be careful of how loudly you speak on your cellphone in public.

Cellphones are wonderful for returning quick calls, or for being reached while you're out of the office. They are not ideal for negotiations or sensitive conversations, where you can be cut off at a crucial moment. It's difficult to have important conversations when there is noise in the background or the reception isn't perfect.

How to use cellphones in the workplace

Employees often use a personal cellphone at work to call and check on their kids at home, or to arrange to meet friends for dinner. Most employers know that when you are talking on your cellphone, you are taking care of personal business. Most managers are okay with this, as long as you don't overdo it. They know that employees have personal lives and that making sure your kids are safe will allow you to concentrate on your work.

However, remember that every time your manager sees you on your cellphone, she knows that you are taking care of personal business on company time. Studies show that many managers think employees spend too much time on non-business related activities, such as emailing, text messaging, and using cellphones. So think twice before you grab your cellphone for a personal conversation at work.

Another worry for employers is that with today's increasingly sophisticated technologies, you may be doing more with your cellphone than just talking. It's easy to photograph or download company documents or confidential information, such as client mailing lists.

As well, your co-workers can hear you talking on your cellphone. If you ask them for help to complete a project by the deadline, they will resent you when they remember the long conversation with a friend they heard you having earlier.

Most people are simply not aware of how their cellphone behaviour comes across to others. Your cellphone etiquette is not just a reflection of you, but also of your employer. Here are some tips for better cellphone use:

Set limits

If you regularly receive phone calls from your mother or best friend at work, explain that you can only talk for five minutes, and that you will call back in the evening. Tell them not to resort to emailing you instead.

Turn it off

If you work in a cubicle, turn your ringer off, or at least put it on vibrate so you don't disturb the people working around you. As well as being a courtesy to your co-workers, this will prevent you from alerting your manager that you are receiving personal phone calls.

Take only important calls

At a meeting or business dinner, turn off your cellphone. The only time to make an exception would be when you are expecting vital information; for example, when someone in your family is in the hospital. If you answer your cellphone during a meeting, you are sending the message that you aren't concentrating fully on your job. Give your complete attention to the person you are with. Let your calls go to voicemail.

Keep the ring tone professional

With the large variety of tones and chimes available today, the latest song on the charts is not appropriate for the workplace.

Find a quiet, private place

If you are in a crowded area and hear your cellphone ring, move to a quieter area to talk. Otherwise, you will have to shout to be heard, and you will end up broadcasting your conversation to everyone near you. At your desk it is fine to use your cellphone during your breaks, but make sure you don't disturb people who are working.

Don't use your cellphone in the washroom

Hearing the sound of a toilet flushing isn't pleasant for the person on the other end. And you never know who else is in the washroom, listening to your conversation.

Tell them you're on a cellphone

If you make a business call from your cellphone, let the other person know that you may be interrupted or cut off. Arrange to call back on a land line as soon as possible.

Avoid cell yell

People tend to talk more loudly on a cellphone. If you don't want your entire department to hear about your personal life, don't broadcast the details by yelling into your cellphone.

Never discuss sensitive information

Don't discuss sensitive information about your company on a cellphone, especially in a crowded place like an airport terminal. It will be almost impossible for people sitting beside you to block out your conversation. Companies today are highly competitive, and they don't want their employees giving information away.

Check your messages regularly

Do this even when you are in the office.

Put safety first

Don't talk on your cellphone while driving. This is very dangerous. If you must talk on the phone, use a headset.

 Canadian Business Concept: In many parts if Canada, it is now illegal to use cellphones while driving, although many provinces allow you to use your phone if it is hands-free and has an earpiece.

Business Buzzwords

- cell yell
- do's and don'ts
- put someone through
- telephone tag

Chapter 7 Action Plan

1. Write an outgoing voicemail message that you can leave on your telephone system when you can't answer your phone. Check back to page 144 for ideas on what information to include.

   _____

   _____

   _____

2. Who do you call frequently? (This could be a specific customer, your manager, a co-worker, et cetera.) Imagine that you are calling this person, and you reach her voicemail. Write a clear message that you could use, telling her what you'd like to happen next. For example, will you call her back later? Do you need some specific information? Would you like her to call you back about something? Check back to page 142 for the steps to follow.

   _____

   _____

   _____

3. Write down a way to begin a business telephone call and to end a business call. What should you say?

   Beginning a call: _____

   Ending a call: _____

Business Writing that Gets Results

From emails to memos, written communication connects you with your clients, manager, and co-workers.

In This Chapter

- Five easy steps to business writing
- How to write an email
- How to write a business memo
- How to write a fax
- How to write a business letter
- How to write a thank-you note
- How to write clearly and professionally

Five easy steps to business writing

 Andy was staring at his blank computer screen. He had to write a memo to his manager, but the words escaped him. He heard the clock ticking loudly, and decided he needed another cup of coffee. "Maybe I'll just let it go until tomorrow," he muttered as he headed toward the office kitchen.

Many people regularly feel this way. When they have to write a memo or a report, they stare at the blank computer screen and feel overwhelmed by the process. They do anything to avoid writing because they don't know how to begin the process.

In today's business world, it's important to communicate well. People are under tremendous time pressure. If you know how to write a report with proper style, send a memo that gets action, and use email professionally, you will stand out from the crowd. In fact, many human resources professionals note that writing ability helps you get ahead in the job.

You don't have to be a professional writer to write a clear business email, memo, or report. Even if English isn't your first language, you can still communicate your message well. You just have to take time to structure your writing and revise it after the first draft.

Before you write

Before you write anything, ask yourself these two questions:

1. Do I need to write?
Is an email or memo the best way to convey my information? Could a telephone call clear things up more quickly? Or do I need a face-to-face meeting to accomplish more?

2. Is there a standard format to use?
Read company memos and other written materials, such as the minutes of meetings, to get a feel for the corporate culture and format. Analyze the structure and wording, and the language and tone. Try to make your writing fit in with that style.

Most companies have standard memo and fax forms. Ask for copies of previous correspondence and follow the format.

Five steps to business writing

Business communication always has a purpose. It is either to give information, to request action, or to persuade someone to do something.

Keep your business correspondence simple and factual. Avoid unnecessary information and get to your point quickly.

Here is a formula to apply to everything you write, from a simple email, memo, or fax, to a longer letter or even a report.

Step 1: Analyze your audience and define your purpose.

Before you start typing, ask yourself

a) Who will read this?
b) What will this be about?
c) Why should the reader want to read it? (What's the benefit for the reader?)
d) What action do I want the reader to take?

Step 2: Write a clear statement explaining why you are writing.

Step 3: Provide the information your reader needs to carry out your request. If you have more than one point to make, group your ideas into categories, and use headings for each section.

Step 4: Suggest an action—either one you will take, or one you want the reader to take. Make dates and deadlines clear in the message.

Step 5: Edit your work. Check the tone. Is it too formal or too informal for your audience? Then check the spelling and grammar.

Here's an example of how this works in a memo:

Memorandum

Date: December 5, 2015
To: Jane Jones *(Who will read this?)*
From: John Smith JS
Subject: New Business Casual Dress Code for Fridays
          (What will this be about?)

The new dress code will begin January 10. *(Clear statement explaining why you are writing)* As of that date, all employees will be allowed to wear business casual dress on Fridays. *(What action do I want the reader to take?)* This dress code will make everyone more comfortable at the end of the work week. *(What's the benefit for the reader?)*

The most important change is that jackets are not required. Employees can wear casual shirts and pants or skirts, but not jeans. Shirts must have collars. No T-shirts are allowed, except for the company shirts. *(Provide the information your reader needs to carry out your request.)*

You will receive a copy of the new guidelines next week.

Action requested: Please have your department read the new guidelines by January 7. *(Suggested action)*

Note: Since a memo doesn't have a signature line like a letter has, many writers put their initials next to their names on the *From* line, or sign or initial the bottom of the memo. Find out your company's preference, and follow it.

How to write an email

Vincent and Natalie were co-workers who got along well. One evening, they went out for drinks and found that they really liked each other. The next day, Vincent sent Natalie an email, asking her out for dinner. Unfortunately, Vincent didn't realize there was another Natalie in the company—a manager in another division. Her name came up when he pressed *N* in the company's email directory, and she received the message. Vincent was now in trouble for sending personal messages during work hours and, worse, for trying to date a co-worker, which is frowned upon in his company. He also gave everyone in the office something to gossip about.

Email is a powerful communication tool. It is so much a part of our lives that we think sending an email is just like talking on the phone. We send birthday wishes to a friend or fire off a few jokes to co-workers.

What's the harm? There's plenty. Email is a business tool. When you are at work, if you take 15 minutes to make arrangements to get together with your friends, or catch up on gossip, you're using company time and resources for personal use. This means lost productivity for the company—and possibly legal issues.

Remember that emails can be stored indefinitely on any computer. Your friend can forward your emails to any number of people, who can then copy them and send them to more people. You're not just sending a joke to your friend—you may be sending an offensive message all around the world. Not only can this compromise your job, but it could cause your company to be sued.

Emails can be quick and easy to send, but they are powerful and can take on a life of their own.

The right way to send email at work

Writing an action-oriented email is a critical business skill. However, like any communication tool, it is vital to know how and when to use email. Read your company's policy on email, which will explain what you can and cannot send. Keep in mind that once something has been written and emailed, it cannot be taken back, and it could come back to haunt you one day. Be careful of what you write.

The following are some do's and don'ts to help you decide when to use email.

Do use email in the workplace for ...

✓ quickly communicating specific ideas

✓ sending reasonably short messages (up to about 20 lines on a computer screen)

✓ handling routine business

✓ sending information to employees or clients on a distribution list

✓ reducing telephone and meeting time by sending information in advance

✓ communicating non-confidential messages

Don't use email for ...

✗ immediate action: If you send email for anything that needs immediate attention—such as a same-day notice about an unexpected meeting—you may not reach everyone. Use the telephone instead.

✗ important information: Never assume that because you sent an email, you communicated your message. There is a good chance that people either won't read the email within the timeframe you expect them to, or will not be in a position to act when they read it, and will forget about it.

✗ in-depth discussion: If an email will generate a string of four or more replies, a phone call or face-to-face meeting can often resolve things much more quickly.

✗ bad or sensitive news: Never deliver bad news or give negative feedback to someone by email. Some news should be delivered in person. Body language and facial expressions are important in interpreting a message, and email is cold and impersonal. Using email can generate bad feelings that may be impossible to reverse. Handle sensitive issues in person.

✗ people who don't use email: Don't communicate with people who seldom use email themselves. They may not check their email for days at a time. Call instead.

✗ angry or sarcastic messages: Messages that you send in anger will live on long after you've cooled down. Write your angry message on a piece of paper, then tear it up and throw it away. It's much safer.

✗ telling others they did something wrong: If you are telling someone you are unhappy about something, do it privately and in person. An email can inflame the situation. Be especially careful never to copy (CC) other people or say something like this in a "reply to all."

Netiquette

Raya was in the habit of sending the following email to her manager: "IT IS DONE!" For seven years, her manager never told her that he thought she was an aggressive person. Unfortunately, Raya didn't know that sending an email message in all capitals is considered rude in Canada. It is just like shouting in someone's face.

Raya (not her real name) was a student of Karen Bowen, Program Coordinator at Gandy Associations, which provides English Communication Training. Bowen taught this woman, and all her students, about email etiquette. "In Canada, people often won't tell you when they find something impolite. They just assume that you know." Bowen suggests that you find someone in your workplace or professional life to be your mentor—this person can help you understand when your written or spoken communication is too aggressive, or not strong enough for the Canadian workplace.

Netiquette, or *net etiquette*, refers to acceptable behaviour on the Internet. Everyone appreciates good manners, both in person and in cyberspace, so be sure to observe netiquette when sending emails.

Here are some best practices for using email in the workplace:

• Keep it strictly business. Anything you send can become public property. It can be forwarded, saved, and printed by people who were never intended to see it. Never send anything that will reflect badly on you or anyone else.

• Write about only one idea. Every email should have one main idea, and should fit onto one computer screen. Keep your message short, clear, and well organized. Use a subject line that reflects your main message and gives your reader enough information to retrieve it later if needed. (See page 158 for tips on how to write subject lines.)

- Don't send confidential information. Remember that any emails you send at work are company property. Many companies electronically monitor their employees by checking the employees' email usage, Internet usage, phone call records, and computer files. Also, anything written is permanent, accessible, and can be used in court. Because email messages can be forwarded or accessed by others easily, use a different method to send highly confidential information.

- Avoid jokes and offensive comments. Anything obscene, libellous, or racist never belongs in a company email. Something off-colour that you find humorous may not tickle the funny bone of your managers, and may even be grounds for dismissal.

- Don't type in all CAPS. It's perceived as YELLING! However, don't write with only lowercase letters, which is difficult for people to read.

- Keep your message cool. Avoid multiple exclamation points and emoticons, which can be interpreted as emotional language and are not professional.

- Check your writing. Don't send out a sloppy, unedited email. While the odd spelling mistake is overlooked, don't force your reader to figure out what you are saying. Remember that your emails reflect your professionalism. Take the extra time to check your message for typos or omitted words.

- Use clear language. Stay away from acronyms that some people may not understand. Don't use informal shortcuts—such as *LOL* (Laughing Out Loud)—that are considered unprofessional and may not be understood by others.

- Always use your company email address for business email. Don't send messages from your personal account.

 Canadian Business Concept: Be careful what you send by email. It can be monitored. Keep it strictly businesslike and professional.

How to write a subject line

The subject line is the most important part of your message. It is often the basis for your message being read—or deleted. Here are some tips for writing subject lines that will make sure your message is opened.

- Don't leave the subject line blank. Your reader will have trouble deciding whether or not to open the message, and will have difficulty filing and retrieving it later.

- Put your most important information in the subject line and include an action verb.

  Instead of   Article for review
  Write   Please comment on CMI article by 3:00 p.m. Monday

- Be specific. Include a date, as your readers may not be in the office the day you expect them to reply.

  Instead of   Tomorrow's meeting
  Write   Agenda for meeting November 12, 2:00 p.m.

- Be clear. Use short, uncluttered subject lines. Minimize unnecessary words.

  Instead of   We are having problems locating the missing documents
                    for tomorrow's meeting
  Write   Missing documents for August 15 meeting—help needed

- Make it complete. Make sure your subject line includes enough information for the reader to refer to later, once the message has been filed.

  Instead of   Follow up
  Write   Follow up to Sept. 21 meeting with John Smith

- Don't send silly, useless, or confusing subject lines.

  Instead of   Hi / Hello / FYI (For Your Information)
  Write   FYI—Information you asked for re: November conference

- Change the subject line to reflect new topics discussed in a string of emails. If you expand on a topic but need to reference information from before, add the new topic to the subject line.

- Use abbreviations if you are certain your readers will understand your meaning. For example, *mgr, acct, conf, admin,* and *info* are fine if they are used regularly within your company, or with your clients.

How to begin and end your emails

Email is increasingly informal, and many emails today begin with "Hi." "Hello" and "Dear" are also used, depending on the formality of the message and the relationship you have with your reader.

Usually, you can rely on common sense to tell you how to address the reader with respect. Here are a few guidelines:

- If you are responding to an email, simply follow the level of formality the sender used. If she wrote "Hi," you can begin this way as well.

- When you initiate email contact, choose an opening based on your relationship with the reader and the seriousness of the message.

- International emailing is more formal than emailing within Canada. Keep a formal tone until your reader becomes more informal.

- Abbreviate titles: Mr., Ms, Mrs.
  Don't use two titles that mean the same thing: Dr. Paul Smith, MD
  Spell out professional titles, except MD. For example: Vice-President, not VP

- In your conclusion, write "thank you," offer help, or request an action by a certain date.

- Don't use formal business clichés such as, "Do not hesitate to contact me," or "Should you have any further questions ..." These expressions are overly formal and stilted. Don't write anything you would never say in person.

Here are some conclusions to use:

- Please let me know if you need more information.

- I'm available to answer your questions at: (phone number)

- Thank you again for contacting me. I will call you next Wednesday to see if I can answer any other questions.

How to sign your emails

Make it easy for people to reach you. Develop an automatic email signature that includes your phone number and email address. It can also include your cellphone number, and your mailing address if you are likely to receive documents by regular mail.

This will save people from having to search for your business card or look up your company on the Internet if they want to reach you.

Here is an example of an email signature:

Jane Smith
Quality control
ABC Company
Tel: 516-xxx-xxxx ext. 123
1-800-xxx-xxxx
Fax: 516-xxx-xxxx
Jane@abc.com

Program this electronic signature so it appears in your reply email as well as in your first email to someone. This saves your readers from having to scroll down to the first email to search for your phone number if they want to call you.

How to set the right tone for your email

Email messages can be formal, conversational, or friendly, depending on who you are writing to. The key point is that business email is still more similar to a letter than to a text message.

Remember the "hamburger" described on page 11? Business emails also need a little padding to keep their tone cordial and to avoid misunderstandings. Interpreting one-line messages is very difficult, while accidentally offending someone is very easy.

To avoid short messages that can be interpreted the wrong way, take an extra moment to add some padding around your hamburger.

Instead of Send the file right away.
Write Please send the file as soon as possible. I need it right away, thanks.

Instead of Why didn't you send me the spreadsheet?
Write I need the spreadsheet by 10:00 a.m. today. Can you please send it right away? Thank you.

Instead of You're kidding me!
Write I'm surprised about ...

Take an extra few seconds to write *please* and *thanks*. These words can go a long way toward smoothing a tense situation.

(See the section Using the right words, on page 125 in Chapter 6 for more way to say things without causing offence.)

 Canadian Business Concept: Don't send terse, one-line emails that can be misinterpreted. Use softening expressions.

Here are three examples of emails with different tones:

Formal

Subject	ACE Conference Meeting Agenda
From	ScottW@xyzcorp.ca
Date	October 3
To	jjones@abccorp.ca

Dear Ms Jones,

Our next meeting to plan the ACE conference will take place at the Sunshine Hotel on October 17 at 7:00 p.m.

The main topics to discuss are:
• Team development and roles
• Training plans for this initiative
• New-hire tasks

We look forward to seeing you there. Please let me know if you would like any further information.

Sincerely,

Scott Wells,
Project Manager

1 800 666-4241

Tips for writing a formal email
- Address the reader by title (*Mr., Ms, Dr.*)
- Use formal, respectful language
- Avoid contractions (use *you would* instead of *you'd*)
- Use objective words and specific terminology
- Close with your name and title

Conversational

Subject	ACE Conference Meeting Agenda
From	ScottW@xyzcorp.ca
Date	October 3
To	jjones@abccorp.ca

Hi Jane,

Our next meeting for the ACE conference will be at the Sunshine Hotel on October 17 at 7:00 p.m.

The main topics for discussion are:
- Team development and roles
- Training plans for this initiative
- New-hire tasks

We look forward to seeing you there. Please let me know if you need any more information.

Regards,

Scott,
Project Manager

1 800 666-4241

Tips for writing a conversational email
- Greet the reader informally by first name
- Use a friendly but professional tone
- Use some contractions and personal pronouns
- Close with a brief and friendly salutation (*regards*) and your first name only

Friendly

Subject	ACE Conference Meeting Agenda
From	ScottW@xyzcorp.ca
Date	October 3
To	jjones@abccorp.ca

Hi Jane,

Get ready for a great meeting! See you at the Sunshine Hotel on October 17 at 7:00 p.m.

Be ready to discuss:
- Team development and roles
- Training plans for this initiative
- New-hire tasks

Can't wait to see you there. Give me a shout if you need any more info.

Cheers,

Scott

1 800 666-4241

Tips for writing a friendly email
- Greet the reader casually (*Hi*)
- Use contractions (*can't* instead of *cannot*)
- Use appropriate humour, with some jargon and slang (*give me a shout*)
- Close with a casual salutation (*cheers*) and your first name only

Canadian Business Concept: Think about how you would talk to the person if you were face-to-face. This will help you decide on the right level of formality for your email message.

Before you press *send*: how to edit your email

Wait! Before your press *send*, take a moment to proofread your message so you don't embarrass yourself by including typos or incorrect information.

Make sure to write the message, and *then* add the recipient's name. Most people address their email as the first step. But people often press the *send* button by mistake, before they have finished composing their message. This can lead to embarrassing situations when you send a message that is incomplete or poorly written. To avoid this possibility, only add the email address after you have finished writing and proofreading your message.

Compose important or longer messages in a word-processing document. It will save you the time of rewriting your email if your system goes down before you finish writing, and you'll have another record of the message in case you need it later. This also makes it easier to print and proofread your message. You can then paste it into your email before sending it.

Here is a checklist to complete prior to sending any email messages.

✓ **Subject line:** Is it clear and concise, yet informative enough to compel the reader to open the email?

✓ **Content:** Does the opening sentence or short paragraph outline the main idea and the call to action?

✓ **Design:** Is the email easy to read, with short paragraphs, bullet points, and lists?

✓ **Tone:** Are you addressing the reader with the most appropriate level of formality?

✓ **Language:** Is it clear and natural? Does it avoid "business speak" and only use technical jargon when you are communicating with another professional in your field?

✓ **Writing:** Did you proofread for grammar errors? Did you check your spelling?

✓ Ready? Now press *Send*!

How to manage and organize your email

Are you receiving too many emails? You're not alone. This is one of the biggest sources of "information overload" we experience today. You may even be contributing to information overload for other people at your company without realizing it.

Keep in mind that it takes a person a few seconds to open and read each email. Then the receiver must decide if she should respond, save the email, or delete it. This all adds up to a lot of time, and people who are inundated with emails don't appreciate receiving information that they don't need.

Here are some ways to manage the emails you send and receive. By putting some of these ideas into practice, you can help educate your co-workers on how to manage their emails better as well.

Respect people's time

Send emails only when necessary and only to the people who need to read them. Don't contribute to email overload by sending unnecessary emails. Many people don't like to receive emailed jokes or chain letters.

Don't reply to all

There's no need to reply to everyone just to say, "I agree" to one person. Don't include everyone unless everyone needs to know.

Don't CC everyone

Don't send copies of an email to everyone you can think of, just because you don't want to leave anyone out. Make sure that everyone who gets the email needs it. If you do send an email to too many recipients, the *reply to all* function can allow people to start generating endless loops of unnecessary emails.

Be careful about forwarding

If you aren't sure whether the original sender would want you to forward the message, don't send it.

Don't mark a message as urgent unless it is

The person receiving the email will be upset if her time is wasted reading an email that doesn't need to be read immediately.

Don't expect an answer right away

An email message may be delivered quickly, but your recipient may not read it right away, or may need time to consider your message before deciding how to respond.

Do respond within 24 hours

Check your email every day, and try to respond to each message within 24 hours, even if it's just to say you'll get back to the sender later.

Include the message thread

Keep the original message for a record of your conversation. However, when sending a new message (unrelated to the earlier conversation) to the same person, start a new thread with a new subject line. This will help people retrieve any individual conversation if they need to refer to it.

End it

Some conversations go back and forth with *thank you* and *you're welcome* several times. You can avoid this by writing after the subject line: "No Action Required," "No Reply Necessary," "NFM" (no further message), or "<EOM>" (end of message). For example,

- Agenda for June 12 No Reply Necessary
- Meeting time tomorrow changed to 2 P.M. <EOM>

Use the Out of Office automatic reply when you are away

This lets the sender know that you are away from the office and will reply when you return.

How to write a business memo

Writing a business memo is a simple way of communicating information within an organization. It should convey information efficiently and effectively, and cut down on time-consuming meetings.

Memo is short for *memorandum*. You can use either term, depending on how formal a tone you want to convey. Most memos are similar in format. Some companies have memo templates (on a paper form or in a word processing template) that already have headers in place.

Use memos for communication inside your company. Use letters to communicate with people outside of your company. Emails are used for both of these purposes as well.

Memos are best used for …

- introducing information such as policy changes
- persuading people to take some type of action such as attending a meeting
- explaining a change to a current work procedure
- confirming a conversation or agreement
- requesting information
- transmitting data
- presenting goals or expectations

Guidelines for writing a memo

- Keep it short. Use only one page of up to 500 words.

- State your most important point right away. Your main point tells your readers exactly what you are writing about, and why they should keep reading. If your idea is useful to them, they will read the rest of the memo with attention.

Here's how to do it. Before you write a single word, ask yourself, "What's my most important idea?" If, for example, you are changing your company dress code for the summer, the idea might be expressed by the following:

New Summer-Casual Guidelines Effective June 5, 2015

If you can't express your idea in a simple statement like this, you will need to keep thinking until you can.

Use that statement as your first sentence. Then explain it, but don't over-explain it. Provide as much information as you need to prove your point.

Finally, close with a call to action, in which you ask the reader to do something.

Sample memo

Memorandum

To: Sales Staff
Cc: Mike Doe
From: Lisa White LW
Date: June 2, 2015
Re: New Summer-Casual Guidelines Effective June 5, 2015

New guidelines are needed for business casual dress in summer. We have developed a new dress code for the summer months, in effect from June 5 to August 31. Please read the guidelines that you receive from your manager, and pay particular attention to these points:

- Jeans and shorts are not appropriate for the office.
- Tops should have sleeves—no tank tops.
- Have a jacket handy for unexpected client meetings.
- Do not wear beach sandals or jogging outfits to the office.
- Anything see-through, too short, or too tight is not appropriate.

We appreciate your assistance in presenting a polished, professional business image to our clients.

Action requested: Please read the new guidelines and make any necessary changes to your wardrobe.

Formatting tips for memos

- Use short paragraphs.
- Double space between paragraphs to create white space.
- If you have too much information to fit within a memo, send an attachment.
- Use bullet points and lists where possible.
- Keep line lengths between 65 and 80 characters.
- Use a readable font such as Verdana, which was designed to be read on a computer screen.
- Use a font size of 10 to 12 points.
- Avoid light-coloured type, such as yellow or orange.

How to write a fax

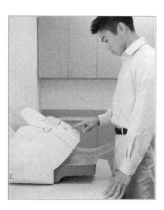

The fax machine is useful when you don't have access to email, or when you want to send longer documents or pictures. Faxes are usually used to send information that is not confidential. Sending a fax is quick and efficient, but the quality of a fax is sometimes poor, making it hard for the recipient to read.

As with business email and memos, keep your tone courteous and business-like. Write messages that are short and clear—don't waste words.

When you send a business fax, be as attentive as you are when writing other correspondence. Always include a cover sheet that includes your name, fax number, and phone number; the recipient's name, fax number, and phone number; the date; and the number of pages you are sending.

Here are some tips for writing and sending a fax:

- Include a subject line to let the recipient know the reason for the fax.
- Leave large enough margins so that your fax is easy to read.
- Use a large font—14 or 16 points—to improve visibility.
- Try to fax only black text or images. Other colours in your document, such as blue, may not appear at the other end, or may be too light to read.
- Some fax machines are only turned on at specific times, so check with the recipient before you send the fax.
- In large corporations, the fax machine may not be near the recipient, so you may need to call afterwards to see if they received the fax, and that no pages are missing.

Sample fax cover sheet

ABC Company

To: John Smith, Director of Marketing
Fax: (604) 457-8759

From: Jane Jones, Accountant
Fax: (514) 271-9384

Date: September 20, 2012

Pages: 4 pages including cover sheet. If all pages are not received, please call (514) 271-8657.

Subject: **Proposal for Marketing Budget for January**

Message: We will be discussing the marketing budget for next year at our meeting in Calgary. Your feedback will be welcome at that time.

How to write a business letter

A business letter is for external communication. It is more than just a message—it has substance. Business letters are permanent records that people keep. Individuals may file them for future reference or pass them on to other people.

Take time to write a concise, clear letter. Pay attention to the formatting, and check for spelling errors and typos. If English isn't your first language, ask someone to proofread important letters for you before you send them out.

Keep your letter brief. Try to ensure that each paragraph is no more than seven lines long. Don't put too much text on any one page. The body of the letter should be two to three paragraphs long. If your letter is longer, use a second page.

Your company will give you letterhead to use. The format will be either block style, with everything lined up on the left side of the page, or modified block style, with each paragraph indented, and the date and closing salutation on the right side of the page. Block style is more popular today.

 Canadian Business Concept: It is no longer necessary to include *st*, *nd*, or *rd* after the numbers in dates (for example, 1st, 2nd, 3rd). It is acceptable to write January 1, March 3, and so on.

Sample business letter in block style

Note: the words in italics, such as *mailing notation* and *reference line* are for your information only. Do not include them in letters that you send out.

HRL and Associates

August 19, 2015

REGISTERED *mailing notation*

Ms Bev Smith
Event Planner
ABC Hotel
1274 Prospect Street
Toronto, ON M3A 7K2

Ref. 94287 *reference line*

Dear Ms Smith:

Subject: **Change to September Sales Meeting** *subject line*

We reserved three conference rooms for our sales meeting on Sept. 21. We will require an extra room. Would it be possible to ensure that all four rooms are in the same area of the hotel?

We also require an LCD projector and screen for each room, and would like to order coffee and pastries for our mid-morning break.

Please confirm that the extra room is available, and that we can rent the equipment from you. Also please let us know the costs for the coffee and pastries.

Sincerely,

Patricia Oliver

(Ms) Patricia Oliver
Sales Assistant
HRL and Associates

PO: cs *reference initials*

Routine letters

If you are writing a letter that will go out to all your clients or suppliers, you can use a simplified version, called a routine business letter format.

Here are a few points to keep in mind:

- Include a subject line in capital letters
- Omit the salutation (*Dear ...*)
- Print the letter on company letterhead
- Keep everything aligned to the left
- Use bullet points if needed
- Omit the closing (*Sincerely*)
- Type the sender's name and business title in capital letters under the signature.

Sample routine letter

ABC Financial

May 18, 2015

Mr. Jim Smith
Financial Advisor
Ace Accounting Corp.
2284 Main Street
Vancouver, BC V3T 2M7

no salutation

MERGING OF ABC FINANCE AND XYZ INSURANCE
subject line in capitals

In order to serve you better, ABC Finances and XYZ Insurance have
merged their businesses to become ABC Financial Inc.
introductory sentence with reason for letter

We now bring you a complete package of services for all your financial
needs:

• Increased financial planning services for mutual funds, specialty funds,
  and RRSPs

• Health insurance, group insurance, and supplemental insurance

• New service offering—Fee-based financial planning to give you an
  objective picture of all your financial holdings.   *body in point form*

We look forward to working with you to increase your wealth.
goodwill statement

no complimentary close

Brad Smith   *handwritten signature*

BRAD and JIM SMITH
ABC FINANCIAL INC.

name and company name in capital letters under the signature

Tips for using the correct name and title

Sylvia, a human resources manager, frequently gets letters addressed "Ladies and Gentlemen," or "To Whom It May Concern." These letters generally end up in the wastebasket. Sylvia says, "I'm a busy person. When others can't be bothered to find out the name of the person they are writing to, I can't be bothered to read their letters."

This point is extremely important because some people won't read letters that address them incorrectly. Check people's business cards to make sure you have the correct spelling of their names. If you don't have their business cards, call their companies to verify the spelling. Here's how to start off your business letters:

- Use the honorific (*Mr., Mrs.,* or *Ms*) and family name for someone you don't know.

- Use people's first names if you have an established relationship with them, if they have asked you to use their first names, or if they have sent you letters signed with their first names.

- Some women want to be called *Ms* and some prefer *Mrs*. You can offend someone by calling them by the wrong title. If you have received correspondence from someone before, follow the format she used. If not, use her first and last names (*Dear Janet Smith*). Use the full name for a man as well, rather than *Gentleman* or *Sir*.

- If you don't know the recipient's name, use a generic title (*Dear Client*, *Customer*, or *Sales Representative*).

- When you don't know the person's gender, such as for someone named Pat Smith who could be male or female, use both the first and last names (*Dear Pat Smith*).

- Avoid writing *To Whom It May Concern*. No one likes to receive impersonal letters, and most people throw them away. Take the time to find out the name of the person you want to reach.

- You can use a comma or a colon after the name, but a comma (,) is friendlier. A colon (:) can seem cold or more formal. Here are some salutations you can use:

  Dear Mr. Smith,
  Dear Ms Smith,
  Dear Pat Smith,
  Dear Pat,
  Dear Sales Staff,
  Dear Client Services Representative:

- An appropriate close is *Sincerely,* for a formal letter, or *Regards,* for a less formal letter.

How to write a thank-you note

When your mail arrives every day, what do you open first—the bills and advertisements, or anything that looks personal? Chances are you'll reach for the handwritten envelope.

We all want to be appreciated and acknowledged, and sending a handwritten word of thanks or congratulations sets you above the crowd. This is because so few people take the time to write personal notes.

When should you write a thank-you note? Any time someone takes more than 15 minutes to do you a favour, write a note of thanks.

A thank-you note shows that you ...

- acknowledge and appreciate the gesture when someone does something for you

- are a professional who follows through

- are a person who goes the extra mile

A thank-you note doesn't have to be long. Three sentences can be sufficient. Here is the structure to follow:

1. Start with a salutation (*Dear Bob / Dear Mr. Smith*)

2. Express your appreciation and thanks in two to three sentences. Be specific about what the thanks are for. Explain briefly how the person helped you.

3. Close in a positive way, without repeating the thanks you gave before.

4. Sign your name clearly. You don't have to write *Sincerely*.

Sample thank-you note

Dear Bob,

Thank you for working overtime to complete the proposal for the ABC Company contract by the deadline. You made a big difference in getting it out on time. You will be the first to know if the proposal is accepted.

Pam

Use good quality writing paper or a card, and the formal *thank you* rather than the informal *thanks*.

Begin with *you* to make the person feel appreciated. Here are some ways to start your note:

- Thank you for the time you took to …
- You make it possible to …
- Your help was much appreciated in …
- Your advice / help / contribution / understanding was greatly appreciated.
- Please accept my thanks for your help with …
- I am grateful for your contribution / help …

How to write clearly and professionally

 Veena, who worked for a marketing company, was checking a new client's website to find out more about their services, and read: "As a proactive solution provider, we synergize world-class business-centric excellence, leveraging our breakthrough core competencies to enable a paradigm shift through the seamless but holistically diverse integration of our enterprise." After reading the words, she still had no idea what the company did.

If you don't understand this, don't worry—no one else does either!

This is just a small example of the business language we see every day. But just because you see it doesn't mean you should use it.

Use plain English instead of "business speak." Even if you use technical language to communicate with other professionals in your field, always aim for clarity. (See Chapter 6 for tips on using business language.)

Use words and phrases that sound natural, instead of business speak. This chart contains some suggestions of the natural language to use.

Business speak	Natural language
accordingly	so
in receipt of	received
awaiting your instructions	please let me know
commence	begin / start
expedite	speed up
facilitate	make easier
finalize	finish
quantify	measure / count
as per your request	as you requested
enumerate	list
fabricate	make
fluctuate	vary
in accordance with	as

Business speak	Natural language
paradigm shift	major change
parameter	limit
preliminary to	before
pre-plan	plan
procure	buy, get
ramification	result
remuneration	pay
subsequent	after / later
utilize	use

How to write concisely

Avoid saying the same thing twice, such as *advance forward*, where the first word means to move forward. Use concise words that deliver your message quickly and clearly. This chart contains a few examples.

Wordy	Concise
advance forward	advance
a majority of	most
at an early date	soon
combine together	combine
consensus of opinion	consensus
despite the fact that	although
final outcome	outcome
for the purpose of	for
for the reasons that	for
on a daily basis	daily
free gift	gift
free of charge	free
have the capacity to	can

Wordy	Concise
in light of the fact that	since / because
in order to	to
in the amount of	for
in the event that	if
it is often our opinion that	we believe
join together	join
personal in nature	personal
until such time that	until

Standard phrases

Here are some standard phrases that you can use in your correspondence:

- Thank you for your interest. Here is the information you asked for.
- We have received your information on …
- We believe
- I think
- I understand that …
- We would like to know more about your …
- We would appreciate the opportunity to …
- Although I would like to, unfortunately I cannot (help you / attend your meeting)
- Please reply by (date)
- Please send the information by (date)
- I recommend that …
- I suggest that …
- If you have questions, please call me at …
- Thank you for …

How to use respectful, fair language

The words you use have an impact on your readers. Use fair, respectful language—avoid negative references to gender, culture, disability, or age.

Gender-neutral language

Avoid   policeman / chairman / businessman
Use   police officer / chair or chairperson / business professional

Race, religion, and ethnicity

Avoid   references to religion or ethnicity, unless they are an integral part of the message
Use   specific terms, such as First Nations or Baptist, only when they are integral to the message

Disabilities

Be aware of the preferred forms or terms.

Avoid   cancer sufferer / handicapped
Use   person with cancer / challenged

Age

Don't use words with negative connotations, and avoid focusing on the age of the person unless this is integral to the message.

Avoid   the aged / kids or teens
Use   older adults / young people

Business Buzzwords

- business speak
- EOM
- FYI
- go the extra mile
- information overload
- netiquette

Chapter 8 Action Plan

1. Look at your company's existing written communication to understand the format, language, and tone. Notice the headings, signatures, and layout. Keep a selection of these items on file so that you can refer to them when you have to send out these types of correspondence.

   Write down anything you need to change from your usual writing style in order to conform to your company's style. _____

   _____

   _____

2. Look at your email inbox. Write down three or four subject lines from the messages you see. Are the subject lines clear and effective? If not, how could they be made more effective?

   _____

   _____

   _____

   _____

3. Create an email signature to make it easy for people to reach you. If your company has a preferred format, use it. If not, use the suggestions from page 160.

   _____

   _____

   _____

   _____

Section 3

Working Relationships

Getting Along with Co-workers

Working well with co-workers and teammates is vital to your success on the job.

In This Chapter

- How to get along with co-workers
- What not to do at the office
- Working well in a team
- Office courtesies—the everyday things that count
- The holiday season at work

How to get along with co-workers

At your new job, you'll be spending 40 hours or more each week with your co-workers, including people on your team and people working next to you. You may be wondering, "Who are these people?"

The most challenging part of any job is getting along with people. You probably already have the skills to do your job or you wouldn't have been hired in the first place. But working well with your manager and co-workers can make all the difference between enjoying your job and thriving, or having a miserable time and failing.

Some people go to work thinking, "My job is great. It's the people I can't stand." This is dangerous thinking. No one can succeed on his own, and people who make enemies soon find themselves isolated and unable to perform well in their jobs. You have to build allies. You and your co-workers are in the same boat, so it pays to row together.

Work relationships

 At Sorin Group, the majority of employees are immigrant women. They work together in close-knit groups for eight to ten hours a day. Judith Thompson, Senior Manager of Human Resources, says that team members always support each other. Instead of individual recognition, the company emphasizes team recognition for jobs done well. This results in increased group efficiency and teams meeting their deadlines.

Team members come from many different cultural backgrounds. They celebrate together frequently with potluck meals that feature dishes from around the world. They also celebrate everyone's holidays, from the Moon Festival to Chinese New Year. Canada Day is a big event in the workplace, with red and white decorations and many festivities.

Work relationships are a bit like family relationships. You can choose your friends, but you can't choose your family members. In the same way, you have to work with people who you might not have chosen on your own. You have to learn to get along with the various individuals you meet.

If you don't feel included at your new workplace right away, don't worry—it's not personal. People are busy and don't always make time to get to know their new co-workers. The following sections will give you some guidelines for building relationships with co-workers, so you'll fit in more quickly.

Build trust

As people get to know you, they will trust you more and become more relaxed around you. You will find the workplace more pleasant. There will be more give-and-take, with you and your co-workers helping each other out when one of you is in a bind. Building trust doesn't happen in an instant—it takes time and effort.

Be reliable

Do what you say you will do. If you say you'll call someone at 3:00, call him at 3:00—not 4:00, or even 3:15. Canadians are very punctual. If you have a phone call scheduled, call at exactly the agreed upon time. If you can't call for some reason, make sure you send a message by email, or make a brief call to reschedule your telephone time.

If you say you'll have a report on your manager's desk by 9:00 a.m. on Thursday, make sure it's there when he walks in. If you tell your co-workers that you'll buy a card for someone's birthday, make sure you get the card.

Under-promise and over-deliver

This means that if you think you'll have the report ready by Wednesday, say that you'll have it for Thursday. Then deliver it on Wednesday. You'll surprise everyone by your efficiency, and people will learn to count on you. You'll get better assignments and more promotions when you are known as a person who delivers more than you promised.

Be honest

Don't lie about your past jobs or mislead people in any way. Don't say you've done something before if you have no idea how to do it. Sooner or later, you will have to prove your skills anyway. However, if you have done something related, it's fine to mention this.

"If you don't know something, admit it and ask for help," says Srini Iyengar, Director of Multicultural Markets for the GTA Division of BMO Bank of Montreal.

"In my culture, people are sometimes too proud to admit they don't know something. They say, 'Yes, yes' because they worry about what people will think of them if they admit they don't know something. Be honest. No one will think you are less competent if you say, 'I don't know.'"

Be loyal

Show loyalty to your co-workers and manager. If someone says something negative about them, you can say something like the following:

"I'm surprised to hear that. Have you spoken to her about that? I'm sure she'd want to change things if she realized ..."

"Perhaps he didn't see things in that light. Would you mind if I spoke to him for you? He's very professional and I'm sure he'd like to know your views."

Share and care

Share your brownies at lunch. Even more important, share your expertise and time. If your co-worker is stressed because his manager gave him too much work, and you have a few extra moments, offer to help him. Most people will appreciate this gesture, and will offer to help you when you need it. If that person doesn't help you, someone else will. There's a saying that *What goes around, comes around*. This means that when you help others, they may not be in a position to help you, but someone else will—kind of like karma.

Be sure to share credit as well. Every project has a star—the person who gets the recognition for doing a great job. Generally, there are a few people who contributed along the way. If you are the star, acknowledge the people on your team. Use the word *we* instead of *I*. This will make you even more of a star. Your teammates will appreciate it, and will return the favour when the roles are reversed.

Be flexible about time off

One area that creates conflict among co-workers is scheduling time off. Everyone wants to take off the same days around the major holidays. Discuss the days you are requesting to take off, and try to work together so everyone gets to take off the days they want the most. For some people, religious holidays are very important, while for other they are not. Volunteer to work your share of holiday time or weekends.

Find creative solutions

"Early in my career, everyone in my office went out for drinks together on Friday nights," says Yasmin Meralli, Vice President of Diversity and Workplace Equity at BMO Bank of Montreal. "This was a problem for me, because I'm Muslim and I don't drink alcohol. However, I didn't want to be excluded from the group, so I thought about how I could make this work. I realized that there's nothing stopping me from ordering soft drinks. I went out with the group and became the designated driver. I had a good time, and built relationships because everyone looked to me to get them home safely.

"I realized that you can be true to your principles and values, yet still adapt to Canadian culture, as long as you are flexible and open-minded. When people do something that makes you feel uncomfortable, ask yourself, 'What are some alternatives?' Look for a creative solution."

Take responsibility

Everyone makes mistakes. Accept responsibility for your errors, apologize, fix them if you can, and move on.

Show respect

Be courteous to the people you work with. Don't leave your coffee cup or dishes in the sink. Keep your voice low when you are talking on the phone, so you don't disturb your co-workers. Be aware of how your actions affect the people around you.

Do your share

Everyone notices the people who don't get their work done on time, leave early, or put things off until the last minute, causing other people stress. Doing your job well helps others do their jobs well.

Participate in sports and activities

"The easiest way to gain entry quickly into your working group is through sports. At lunch, if people are talking about the game, make sure you watched it and know what's going on," says Baljit Chadha, founder of Balcorp.

If you don't understand a sport, ask your co-workers to explain it to you. Most people are glad to help. Also, join any company sports team that you can. This is a great way to build friendships within the company.

Expect respect, not necessarily friendships

In the business world, not everyone will like you, just as you won't like everyone you meet. It's important, however, to establish trust and have pleasant working relationships. It may take time to develop deeper friendships with any co-workers, but you can feel more comfortable right away if you make an effort to be helpful and friendly.

Take charge of your own emotions

No matter how good you are at your job, if you develop a reputation for being angry or difficult to work with, people won't want to work with you.

It can be difficult to deal with your feelings, especially negative ones. How do you behave when you feel stressed, anxious, or frustrated? Do you take out your anger on people around you? Do you hold a grudge?

If you find that you have negative feelings toward your co-workers, examine the issues that are bothering you, and learn how to handle them. Work on changing your own behaviour before you ask other people to change theirs. If you need help, find a life coach, mentor, or counsellor.

Perform acts of kindness and courtesy

"When I started a new job at a downtown corporation, everyone worked in their own cubicle. There was no common hall to gather together other than the corporate boardroom, so I decided to organize cubicle picnics to meet and greet my colleagues," says Judith C. Hart, Marketing Specialist at the Toronto District School Board, who came to Canada from Hungary three years ago.

"I brought in organic spreads, made with love, and arranged them creatively on top of my cubicle where many people passed by. I put up a small welcoming sign written with a touch of humour: 'Please help yourself to not only food for thought, but also for the stomach!'

"The ancient Greeks and Romans realized that the marketplace is where people can get together and experience the community. In Europe, many corporations provide spaces and even 'corporate playgrounds' for 'thinking minds' to nurture collaboration and creativity. The goal of my cubicle picnic was to contribute to that in a small way."

Just like mountain climbing, building relationships requires small steady steps.

Do nice things for the people you work with. This doesn't mean you have to buy them gifts—it just means you should be helpful. Ask co-workers if they want coffee when you're picking up some for yourself; lend a hand when someone is swamped with work; or throw out the food that is growing mould in the office fridge.

Treat the people around you with respect, and they will treat you with respect in return.

Show appreciation

Take a moment to say, "Thank you. I appreciate your help" to the IT person who gets your computer up and running.

Thank the person who shows you how the microwave works or helps you fill out your expense report. Also be sure to thank co-workers who go out of their way to help you when you're rushing to meet a deadline or when you don't know how to do something.

Pay compliments

In our hectic business world, many people complain when things go badly, but don't take the time to notice what goes well. Take an extra moment to say, "That was a delicious cake you brought to the office party last week," or "You're fantastic at formatting documents. You make them look so professional."

Make an effort to notice what people care about and compliment them on those things. People who are fashion conscious love to be complimented on their clothing and accessories. Women can talk about this to other women more easily than men can, but if you notice a woman who loves shoes or handbags, be sure you compliment her on them every so often. You'll make a best friend.

Listen and pay attention to the personal achievements that people talk about, such as their contributions to the community or being on a winning sports team, and compliment them on those subjects.

Find a small positive thing to say to everyone. Before you know it, you'll have many warm relationships, because everyone loves to be noticed and appreciated.

What not to do at the office

"We rely on others for our accomplishments," says Dessalen Wood, Senior Director of Human Resources for Airborne Mobile. "If people don't want you to win, you won't win. You need to have people trust you, support you and believe in you if you want to succeed at your job."

If you want to work well with your co-workers, **don't** do the following things:

✗ Gossip: Everyone talks about the people around them, but some people go out of their way to spread malicious rumours. By gossiping, you can cause a lot of damage to the people you talk about, and to yourself as well. Spend some time getting to know people. Be careful in your first few weeks on the job not to reveal everything about yourself. You may find out your new best friend is the office gossip. Wait a few months to see who you can trust.

✗ Get personal: It is fine to share your excitement or disappointment about big events in your life—an engagement or marriage, a new baby or puppy, a personal or professional award or triumph, or the breakup of a long relationship. But don't bring the details of your wedding plans or the sob story of your breakup to work, unless you have developed a close and trusting friendship with one of your co-workers.

✗ Discuss your religious beliefs during office hours: While you have every right to your religious beliefs and practices, many Canadians become very uncomfortable talking about religion in the workplace. They feel that this is a private topic that they do not necessarily want to discuss with co-workers.

✗ Boss people around: Do your work and help your co-workers when you can, but don't try to dominate or control the people around you, and don't report other people's behaviour to your manager (unless the situation is serious).

✗ Be negative: Don't be overly critical or put people down. No one likes to be around a person who makes them feel bad.

✗ Be a chatterbox: If you find that your co-workers are always making excuses to get away from you during conversations, you may be talking too much. You are probably chewing up their work time. Try to listen more and talk less.

✗ Cry, yell, or shout: Feeling stressed or angry? Go for a quick walk or call a friend. Don't yell at anyone in the office—you will be viewed in a negative way. If you are very upset, try not to cry at the office either. If you have to, take a few moments to go to the washroom and cry in a stall. Then wash your face and return to work. Adults don't act on every emotion, and people who cry at the office are seen as unprofessional. The only time it is acceptable to cry at work is in the event that something truly tragic happens. A manager saying something negative to you is not in this category.

✗ Argue for no reason: Playing the devil's advocate means that you jump into every argument, just for the sake of arguing. Why stir up trouble? If your co-workers feel they will be challenged on everything they say, after a while they'll stop talking to you.

✗ Call people at their homes: Don't call people in the evening or on weekends about work-related matters, unless it's an emergency. You'll look disorganized and unprofessional. Plan your work for normal business hours.

✗ Make enemies: If you really dislike a co-worker, or he loses his temper, don't let it develop into a personal war. Even if he has no real power over you now, anything could happen in the future: he could be promoted or move to another company where you might want to work in a few years from now. Try to be neighbourly and get along with him.

✗ Waste people's time: Everyone is in a rush these days, so don't be the person who wastes anyone's time. Be on time for meetings. Don't plop yourself down in someone's cubicle or corner them in the hall for a chat. Keep encounters friendly but brief during the day.

✗ Change or cancel appointments unless it's absolutely necessary: When you reschedule, the other person has to change her schedule as well, which can lead to stress and problems on her end.

Don't be a pain in the neck

We are often quite shocked to hear what other people think of us. You may consider yourself passionate, yet your co-workers think you are just loud. Maybe you see yourself as friendly: you ask people a lot of questions about themselves, and make suggestions about how they can solve their problems. Other people might find you nosy or bossy.

What people think of you really matters at work. Even if your manager doesn't notice your everyday behaviour, he'll eventually hear about your operating style from other people.

Maybe you've grumbled to your co-workers about how much work you have, or complained loudly about a client. If your behaviour has been a source of problems for others, your manager will notice your co-workers' frustration, anger, or disgust when they interact with you.

This can be a major problem because workplace success depends upon people working together. Most managers understand that people have to work together to be productive and effective. If you earn a reputation as a whiner, a nitpicker, or pain in the neck, it will be difficult to change people's opinions, and it will affect your ability to advance.

If your co-workers point out traits in you that are irritating other people, don't just dismiss them or become defensive. Listen carefully and consider whether they could be right. Perhaps you are talking too much or complaining too often. Or maybe you aren't talking enough or contributing to the group.

Look for help from a mentor or an understanding colleague. Read self-help books or, if necessary, get therapy. Your career depends on it.

Working well in a team

Terry, Jun, and Aimee are on the same team. Aimee and Jun communicate regularly and share information about their mutual customers. Terry says that he is taking care of the customers, and only needs to tell Aimee and Jun information that they specifically need. He feels that Jun and Aimee's meetings are a waste of time, and refuses to participate. The team's productivity is rapidly declining.

A team is a small group of people with complementary skills, committed to a common purpose. Teams can achieve far more than a group of individuals working alone. When you work together everyone benefits: the team members and the company.

One of the biggest challenges for teams is having members who come from both collective (group-oriented) and individual cultures. The unwritten rules for the two groups are very different, and being a good team player in one culture can make you a poor team player in the other.

In collective cultures, group loyalty is stronger than individual needs, and the group is the priority when decisions are made. The motto is *One for all, and all for one.* Tasks are considered the responsibility of the team, and the boundaries between tasks are not clearly defined. Team members share information freely, and there is strong commitment to the team.

Problems arise when team members from collective cultures work with Canadians, who are among the most individualistic people in the world. In individual cultures, roles are clearly defined and only one person is responsible for each task. Information is shared on a need-to-know basis. The idea is that when people take care of themselves and perform their jobs well, the team will succeed.

Teams often break down when their members have differing views on how information should be shared. Collective teammates share information, and feel excluded if they do not receive copies of memos and emails. Canadians feel that they are wasting time if they share information that is not needed by everyone. Misunderstandings about how and when to share information can lead to individuals within a team working in parallel, and possibly breaking into sub-teams.

Building a shared vision

Why does your team exist? You may be in a team that you wholeheartedly endorse, or your team may have been put together by management. Whatever the situation, if you are committed to your team you will reap the benefits of achieving your performance outcomes.

Teamwork isn't easy, and a multicultural team can easily become derailed. It's vital to have a kick-off meeting to discuss how the team will operate. The following are some items to talk about.

Cultural views of teams

For multicultural teams to work well, the group has to establish whether the members have collective or individual views of work, and decide how everyone will work together. All the team members have to feel that they are part of the same team, working toward the same goals. They have to establish how and when they will share information, and who is responsible for each task. They have to discuss and adapt their communication styles to work well together.

Goals and strategies

Teams have to establish their overall goals by outlining what the company wants from the team. Once they have clearly defined goals, they can decide on the steps to take to achieve them. Think of goals as the destination, and strategies as the route or steps to success.

Purpose

Next, define the purpose of your team. How will it benefit the members, both individually and as a group? What role will each person play?

Commitment

Each team member has to feel like a full partner in developing and implementing the project, and be committed to achieving its goals.

Group identity

All members should feel that they need the group, the group needs them, and that their tasks are worthwhile. Team members should talk in terms of *we* rather than *I*.

Trust

Members must care about and support each other. They should view each other as honest and committed to the team's purpose.

Resources

Teams need three key resources:
1. people who have the needed skills, knowledge, and experience
2. enough time
3. enough money

Without these resources, a team will have difficulty achieving its goals.

Decision making

Every team needs a clear decision-making process to move projects from concept to results. The team should discuss this at the kick-off meeting. Otherwise, the team might generate lots of ideas that don't achieve anything.

Communication channels

Teams have to develop ways to communicate regularly and effectively. From regular meetings to telephone calls or emails, team members have to know what they are expected to share, and how and when they should relay this information.

Belief

Team members have to believe that the team can achieve the desired results together, despite inevitable problems that will arise. Team members have to feel confident that there is a way around the obstacles they face.

Respect

Teams that get results are made up of members who have a high degree of respect for each other. This doesn't mean that team members agree with each other all the time. It means that they are open to exploring different ideas or perspectives and that they quickly resolve differences.

Seven tips for better team relations

1. Be sensitive to how people from different cultural backgrounds view teamwork, and discuss how much information you will share.

2. Respect your team members. It's difficult to get along with all of your co-workers all the time. This shouldn't be a problem as long as you give respect to, and receive the respect of, most of your teammates.

3. Make contributions to the team effort. Help your teammates when you can and when they need it.

4. Don't keep ideas or information to yourself. If you worry that a particular employee will steal or take credit for your ideas, explain your idea to the whole team at a meeting.

5. If your teammates have helped you, make sure to recognize their help in a public way. Team members will respect and admire you, and will be more likely to help you in the future. Never take credit for someone else's work.

6. Don't blame your teammates. If there is a problem, address the situation, not the person doing the work.

7. If a person on the team is having a negative effect on your progress, the team should address the problem first with the individual, and then with management if needed.

Office courtesies—the everyday things that count

Tina was helping her manager prepare for a meeting with clients from out of town. She got in extra early so she could have a quiet cup of coffee while she set things up. When she arrived at the office kitchen area, she found the coffee pot crusted with coffee from the day before. She scrubbed it out and made coffee. Then she rushed to make photocopies, only to find that the copy machine was jammed. The last person to use it had left it that way. By now her small window of extra time had evaporated, and she felt annoyed at her co-workers for not doing their parts in keeping the office running smoothly.

We live in a fast-paced world, and courtesies such as cleaning the coffee pot or fixing the photocopier often slip by the wayside. But without courtesy for the people we work with, the workplace is like machinery that's not maintained. After a while, things start to break down and the machine stops working.

Think of office courtesies as the oil that lubricates the machine. When you keep a machine in top shape by maintaining it, it will work well when you need it. You have to pay the same attention to the mechanics of working in your office.

Canadian Business Concept: In hierarchical cultures, people at certain levels do not perform tasks that are considered "beneath" them such as making photocopies. Canada has a more egalitarian culture and, while the CEO of a company may not make his own coffee, a manager who needs a quick photocopy might make one on her own instead of asking an administrative assistant to make it for her. Also, when clients need attention, employees are expected to go the extra mile and help them—even if it's not in the employees' job description.

Photocopier etiquette

The photocopier gets a lot of use and abuse. It's a delicate machine that provides hundreds of copies per day. But it's only as efficient as the people who take care of it. Here are some suggestions about how to respect your co-workers while using the photocopier.

- Pay attention to flashing lights. They usually indicate a paper jam or the need for a new toner cartridge. See if you can follow the instructions to solve the problem yourself. If you can't, call your office manager or service provider. Don't just walk away and leave the problem to the next person.

- Never leave the copier without paper. If you use up the paper that was in the machine, add more.

- If you use letterhead, legal sized paper, or coloured paper, remove it so the next person doesn't use it by mistake. This wastes paper and adds to environmental, as well as company, waste.

- Don't eat or drink while making copies, or touch the glass with greasy fingers.

- Remove paper clips, staples, and sticky notes from all pages before photocopying.

- Be considerate of fellow workers. If you have to photocopy a 200-page document, and someone else needs just one copy, let him go ahead of you.

- If you find a document that someone has accidentally left in the machine, don't read it. Look at the header to see who it belongs to, and take it to the owner. It may contain sensitive information, and you could be invading someone's privacy if you read it.

Kitchen etiquette

When you first enter the office kitchen, you may find one of two things: a neat, tidy environment with everything in its place, or a mess that smells of old cheese and a sink filled with crusty coffee mugs.

If your office kitchen is kept clean, simply follow your co-workers' cleaning routines. Be sure to wash your cups and dishes after you use them, and put them away where they belong. Here are some tips on being a good kitchen-mate:

- If you make a mess, clean it up. If you prepare food on the counter, clean the counter afterwards. If you drop food or spill coffee, wipe it up. If your food spills in the microwave, wipe this up as well.

- Don't leave cups, dishes, or lunch containers soaking in the sink— there is a good chance that you will forget them. Wash them and put them away. If your kitchen has a dishwasher, put your dishes in it.

- Don't leave food in the refrigerator longer than one week. If you don't have time to eat your lunch, take it home or throw it out.

- Don't take someone else's food from the fridge. If you take someone's lunch by mistake, apologize. If he is upset, offer to buy him lunch to replace what you took.

- If you take the last cup of coffee, turn off the coffee maker and rinse the pot. If people in your office regularly keep the coffee maker on, make a new pot when you take the last cupful.

- If you finish a box of doughnuts, throw the box away.

- Don't bring in food that is highly pungent, such as ripe cheeses, sardines, or foods with lots of garlic or curry. Your co-workers may not appreciate the smells that linger afterward. Choose food that won't offend anyone's sensitivities, such as salads, sandwiches, fruit, or yogourt. Also be aware of anyone who has food allergies, and keep your food separate from theirs.

Canadian Business Concept: Learn to make coffee, even if you don't drink it. Canadians are big coffee-drinkers, and keeping the coffee pot filled will really show your thoughtfulness.

Cubicle courtesy and privacy

If you come from a collective culture and now work in a cubicle, you may feel isolated if you can't see anyone over your cubicle walls.

One of your biggest challenges may be understanding how Canadians feel about privacy. In individual cultures, people value privacy because it allows them to work with few interruptions and be more productive.

Looking over a co-worker's shoulder at his computer screen, or reading a document that he forgot at the photocopier may not seem like a big deal to you, but may be considered invasions of privacy to your co-worker.

In fact, these things can be against the law. Under PIPEDA, Canada's Personal Information Protection and Electronic Documents Act, client information cannot be shared freely with co-workers. It must be kept private and confidential. This means that you should not leave files containing client information on your desk when you go to lunch or leave at the end of the day, because anyone could walk into your cubicle and read it. Also, don't leave confidential client information on your computer screen when you leave your desk. A person passing by can read it.

Here are some tips for cubicle courtesy in Canada:

- Be aware of how your voice carries. If you naturally talk or laugh loudly, make an extra effort to lower your voice, especially when you are on the phone.

- Keep personal and even business phone conversations brief and quiet. Make personal calls at lunchtime or after work.

- Don't discuss private matters with your co-workers while you are in a cubicle. Other people can hear you. Move to a private office or meeting room, if possible.

- Avoid anything that makes extra noise. Put your cellphone or pager on vibrate. Wear headphones if you like to listen to music while you work. When you go on vacation, turn off your phone's ringer.

- Keep eating and drinking at your desk to a minimum. It's annoying to hear someone rustling a bag of chips or crunching on candies. Be careful of slurping your hot tea or soup. Don't make your cubicle into a mini-cafeteria.

- Keep you cubicle neat and tidy. It's a reflection of you and it also affects people working close to you.

- Respect people's office space. They won't appreciate you walking in and interrupting their work. Knock, pause at the entrance, and ask whether it is a good time to talk. If your co-worker is on a deadline, or is absorbed in a project, ask when a better time to talk would be.

- Don't interrupt people who are on the phone by using sign language or passing them notes. Wait until they are off the phone to communicate with them.

- Never borrow anyone's supplies, such as scissors or a stapler, without asking first, even if the item is visible on the desk. Canadians value personal property and find it very annoying to return to their desk after a break and find that something is missing. Always ask permission to borrow anything, and be sure to return it promptly.

- If voices carry over from other cubicles and distract you, you can bring sound-blocking headphones to work.

- Keep your cubicle decor professional. It's true that you may spend more time in your cubicle than at home, and you want it to be comfortable. Just be aware of the message you send by putting up too many personal pictures, sexy photos, sports trophies, or holiday decor.

Canadian Business Concept: It's important to recognize that Canadians place tremendous value on personal property and privacy. Make a point of not interrupting others more often than is absolutely necessary, and always ask permission before you enter someone's workspace. Never borrow anything, including office supplies, without asking first.

Office Parties

In Sona's first month on the job, she was approached three times to contribute money and attend events. The first time someone asked her to contribute $3 for a group card and cake for a co-worker's birthday. The next time, a woman she didn't even know was having a baby, and a co-worker asked Sona to chip in $10 for a baby gift. Finally, someone in another department was retiring, and everyone was going to dinner at an expensive restaurant to wish him well.

Office parties are an important part of working in any company, and you may receive invitations and be asked to chip in frequently, either verbally or by email. Workplace parties (or after-hours dinners) are thrown to celebrate birthdays and new babies, and to say farewell to people who are leaving the company.

Generally, people gather to have cake and celebrate the event. For special occasions, such as retirements, the person being honoured may make a speech, and other people may say a few words about them as well

It is important to participate in office parties, even if you don't know the guest of honour well. An important side effect of these parties is that people bond and get to know each other better during the celebrations. If you don't attend the parties, you may find it much more difficult to fit in.

It is also important to take a small piece of cake if it's offered to you. If you don't feel like eating it, just take a small bite and leave the rest on your plate. (Be sure to clean your plate afterwards.) This shows that you are part of the office culture, and you respect the person being honoured.

At the office party, observe the rituals and do what other people do. Try to pay attention to the following things.

- How do people greet each other when they arrive?
- Where do people put their plates and glasses while they are eating and drinking—do they use coasters on the tables?
- Where do people put empty plates and glasses?
- How do people say goodbye to each other as they leave?

In the days before an office party, there will be a collection. You will be asked to chip in for co-workers' birthday presents, baby showers gifts, goodbye gifts, and so on. The expected amount may be $5, or it may be more. After a while, you may feel you are being nickel-and-dimed to the point that you can't afford to celebrate anymore.

A specific amount may be suggested, usually up to $10. You don't have to chip in for every gift, but if you work in the same department as the person who is receiving the gift, you should contribute. If there is no specific amount suggested, you can give an amount at the low end of the scale ($3 to $5).

You don't have to feel bad for not contributing to presents for people outside your department. Also, if you are an intern or on probation, you are not expected to contribute.

You should still attend the party, even if you don't chip in for the gift. If a card is passed around for everyone to sign, write a brief message of good wishes and sign your name.

The holiday season at work

The holiday season can be a tricky time in the workplace. In some companies, the holidays play a bigger role than in others. Every company has its own rituals for holiday parties and gift giving, and it's important to understand the way your co-workers do things, so you don't offend anyone.

Holiday tips

Here are some tips for enjoying the holiday season at your workplace.

Don't fall behind in your work

With all the holiday festivities, it's easy to get distracted and let your work fall behind. If too many company events disrupt your day, you may have to take work home in the evening, or come in early to complete assignments. Clients are still waiting for the work to be done!

Respect people's religions and cultures

Most Canadian companies today have individuals from a mix of cultures, and people may celebrate holidays in different ways. Try to be sensitive to different religious beliefs and ways of celebrating, and don't force others to celebrate in a way that makes them feel uncomfortable.

Behave properly at office holiday parties

Behave professionally at office parties and events. Dress appropriately, and don't drink too much. (See Chapter 16 for more tips on office parties.)

Don't push alcohol

Some people don't drink alcohol. If they say, "No thank you," don't push it. If you don't drink alcohol, you can just say, "No thanks," without further explanation, or "No thank you, I don't drink." You don't have to say why.

Gift giving tips

In some companies, everyone exchanges gifts. Other companies have a Secret Santa gift exchange, for which each employee randomly chooses one co-worker's name and buys a gift for that person.

What to buy

Usually, a price range is set in advance. If the range is from $10 to $20, for example, you can buy a bottle of wine if you are sure the person drinks wine. Other gift options for co-workers you know well are things like gloves or scarves.

If you don't know the person well, stick to neutral gifts such as chocolates, or business-like gifts such as good-quality pens or desk accessories.

If the price range is less than $10, many people choose gag gifts, or humorous items. You can look in a dollar store or drugstore for something useful or funny in that price range.

Gifts for co-workers

Speak to a co-worker you trust. Try to find out who usually gives gifts to whom, and the kind of gifts they give. If you have an idea of who will give you a gift, try to have something ready for them as well. These gifts don't have to be expensive—a $10 gift certificate to their favourite book store, music store, or coffee shop is often very much appreciated. It's the thought that counts.

Be careful about giving a gift to one colleague without giving to others in your office. Consider communal gifts, such as chocolates or a cheese platter for the lunchroom. Everyone will share it and appreciate it. If you want to give a gift to one special person who has helped you or mentored you, be discreet, and give it outside of office hours.

Never give anything too personal, unless you have become close friends with a co-worker. In that case, you should give the gift outside the office.

Gifts for your manager

Find out whether your co-workers give individual gifts to your manager or chip in to buy something together. If they don't give any gifts, give your manager a nice card or hand-written note of good wishes.

Don't give a gift above your rank. A gift to the company president is not necessary, and may be misinterpreted.

Don't feel obliged to reciprocate. If you receive an unexpected gift from your manager, you don't have to buy him something in return. If you choose to, it's not necessary to match the dollar value. Choose something that reflects your manager's taste, or give a box of good quality chocolates.

Gifts to clients

If you want to give a gift to a special client, find out your company's—and the client's company's—gift giving policy. Some clients expect gifts, while others don't. One sales representative caused embarrassment to herself and her company when she sent an elaborate gift to a customer who had to return it. The customer's company only allowed gifts valued up to $50. Before sending a gift to a client, call his company's human resources department to find out about any restrictions on receiving gifts.

If you are not allowed to give a gift because of company policy, send a hand-written note of good wishes. In fact, you can never go wrong sending a personal note or card.

Business Buzzwords

- chew up time
- go the extra mile
- in a bind
- in the same boat
- nickel-and-dimed
- play the devil's advocate

Chapter 9 Action Plan

1. Write down three things you can do to build positive work relationships and get along well with your co-workers.

   a) _____

   b) _____

   c) _____

2. List three office courtesies that you think your co-workers would appreciate.

   a) _____

   b) _____

   c) _____

3. How can you work well with your teammates? Write down one problem or challenge you have experienced in your team, and a possible solution.

Problem or Challenge	Solution

Good Boss / Bad Boss

Your relationship with your manager or boss is your most important working relationship. It may be similar to what you are used to in your country, or very different.

In This Chapter

- Understanding your boss
- How to develop a positive relationship with your manager
- Different "bad boss" types and how to work with them
- How to manage problems with your manager
- How to handle a performance review

Note: In this book, the term *manager* is used to describe someone whom you might refer to as your *manager*, *supervisor*, or *boss*. This is the person who assigns your work, and to whom you report. This person may also be the owner of the company.

The examples alternate between a male and female manager. The advice is the same for dealing with both, unless specified.

Understanding your boss

Your manager in the Canadian workplace

 Malaya, from the Philippines, was uncomfortable with her new manager. In her culture, managers and employees had a very structured, hierarchical relationship. Her Canadian manager, however, had a very relaxed, friendly manner. He often joked around with his employees, and everyone laughed at his jokes except for Malaya. Finally, he asked Malaya what was wrong, since she always looked so serious. Malaya replied, "I'm worried that if I laugh, you'll take it the wrong way."

Managers come in all shapes, sizes, and temperaments, and you will probably work with several variations throughout your career.

Some are open; they appreciate arguments and ideas that improve the department's efficiency and production. Other managers don't want to be challenged, especially not publicly. They would like you to follow their directions. Both kinds of managers can be competent or incompetent.

How Canadians view work

The first step in working well with your manager is to recognize how Canadians view work. Many Canadians define themselves by the job they do. You may notice this in the way people introduce themselves and others.

- When people first meet, they often ask, "What do you do?"
- When people introduce themselves, they often mention their profession: "I'm a financial planner."
- When introducing others, they do this as well: "This is Susan Lum, of ABC Company."

In countries such as France, work takes a back seat to pleasure. As an example, most Europeans take six weeks of vacation each year. Most Canadian companies give new employees only two weeks of vacation, and it's common for people to go without taking their vacations—sometimes for years—because they have too much work to do. Sometimes when Canadians do take vacations, they take their work along with them.

Many Canadians believe that this focus on hard work will lead to advancement, money, and happiness.

Taking responsibility for your career

To work well with your manager, you have to understand the concepts of power and authority in your new company, and understand how people make decisions. In traditional, hierarchical workplaces, people's roles and behaviours are clearly defined. The boss has the final word and employees follow the boss's orders.

Hierarchical companies place great value on job titles and protocols to maintain control within the organization. Managers are responsible for promoting the interests of employees, and employees are responsible for doing their jobs well and remaining loyal.

Canadian workplaces tend to be less hierarchal and more consultative. You can find out how hierarchical your company is by paying attention to job titles. Managers who are egalitarian will ask employees to address them by their first names and not use job titles, and employees will interact in an informal way with their managers.

In these workplaces, employees are expected to ask questions and work independently. People are encouraged to focus on the business objectives and take initiative. Canadians are taught that they are responsible for their own careers, and should work hard to move forward and be successful.

Problems can occur when managers and employees have differing ideas of their roles, with each assuming the other person sees things the same way they do. And although the workplace is changing, you will find both hierarchical and egalitarian managers in the same workplace. In fact, a manager can display varying degrees of hierarchical and egalitarian behaviours, depending on the circumstances.

The first step is figuring out which type of manager you have. Try to determine this in your first meeting by asking questions. You'll need to discover your manager's style, priorities, and how she communicates. This will help you determine exactly where you stand, and what she expects from you.

No matter which kind of manager you have, she is instrumental to you keeping your job and advancing your career. Managers may give you very explicit directives and details, or they may give you general directives and expect you to implement the decisions. In workplaces that are not very hierarchical, managers may coach or mentor you and help you develop your skills.

Watch and learn from your manager. You will develop strategies for working in your organization, including how to deal with corporate politics, how to communicate clearly, and how to network successfully.

The good manager in the Canadian workplace

In Canada, a good manager is a good leader who accepts responsibility and is ready to share the workload, as well as the glory that comes from it. Many managers love to work on the development of the people who report to them. They feel pride in shaping an employee who performs well.

Good managers delegate tasks and show appreciation for a job well done. They trust their employees to do a good job, and give them increasing responsibility. They deal with employees' shortcomings in a constructive way. This kind of manager can be a mentor, helping employees with their personal and professional development.

How to develop a positive relationship with your manager

If you want to succeed, you will have to develop an ongoing, supportive relationship with your manager. Some strategies are described here.

Find out what your manager wants from you

Grace, who came from a hierarchical culture, was eager to please her manager. Every time she finished a task, she checked to see if her manager's door was open. When she saw that her manager wasn't on the phone, Grace went in to show him the progress she'd made. One day her manager tactfully suggested that Grace make a list of all the things she wanted to ask or tell him, and save it for one meeting at the end of the day.

Grace was well-intentioned, but she did not understand that her manager wanted her to be more independent. She was consuming too much of her manager's time, and was considered a high maintenance employee. The term *high maintenance* refers to someone who requires a lot of attention.

If you come from a traditional culture, you may feel that you have to run to your manager to check for clarification on everything you do. In Canada, your manager may interpret this as showing lack of initiative. If you work in a company where your manager acts more like a coach, you'll have ask your manager what types of decisions you should make on your own, and when she wants you to check with her. Ask her how frequently she wants updates. When you need clarification between these updates, be sure to approach her with clear, well-formulated questions.

When dealing with a manager who is more egalitarian, take careful notes during your initial conversation to make sure you understand what is requested. Even if you have a great memory, it is virtually impossible to remember everything that is said during a conversation unless you write it down. Write down the details, and record them where you can refer to them later.

After that, do your homework before asking more questions. Take the initiative to research more information and come up with various options for proceeding with the project, supported with data. Avoid asking too many open questions such as "What do you think?" or "How do you want me to do this?" These kinds of questions will annoy a manager who expects you to be independent and get the job done.

If you are in a hierarchical workplace, be prepared to report to your manager more frequently, and to check in with her before taking new initiatives. When she makes a decision, do your best to implement it.

Make your manager your top priority

Your manager comes first

Answer or return her calls right away and never put her on hold. If she asks you to do something by the end of the day, make every effort to get it done—she probably needs it right away.

Find out her goals and priorities for the department

You can ask your manager the following questions:

- Are there written objectives or goals for this calendar year?
- What is the reason for our department's existence?
- What are our most important products or services?
- What are the top three things our department must accomplish this year?

Put your manager's needs at the centre of your work

Once you know her goals and priorities, identify her areas of weakness or her biggest challenges. What can you do to help? Does she hate doing research? Offer to check the statistics on her next presentation. Is she squeezed for time? Ask if she'd like you to help organize the handouts for the next departmental meeting.

Become indispensable to your manager

Find out the procedures in your company, how to order supplies, and how other routine tasks are done. Your manager will rely on you to get the job done, and when it's time for promotion, you'll be her logical choice.

Provide solutions

If your manager is not very focused on hierarchy, don't go to her with every problem you come across. Before you have a discussion with her, think of one or more solutions to suggest. You'll be seen as a problem solver who takes initiative.

Learn your manager's communication style

"Learn about your boss's leadership style and try to adapt," says Adrian Cheung, Director of Multicultural Marketing at BMO Bank of Montreal. "Some managers do not like too many questions, while others do. Some are very macro oriented while others have a micro perspective. Give a boss who is a macro manager a proposal that focuses on mission and strategies. For a micromanager, provide lots of details. After your manager gives you a task or project, get coaching and find out the approach so you will be able to do the task in your boss's style and taste. You can simply ask, 'Can you give me some coaching on this? Is there any approach I should use in executing the task?' When you complete the project, always ask your boss for feedback and how to do better so you can adapt to the Canadian ways of doing things."

Learn how your manager likes to communicate

If your manager likes casual conversations, study his schedule and strike up a conversation in the lunchroom. Does he prefer written communication? Send him an email to update him about your progress on a project or to pass along helpful information, and send him a card when he aces his presentation at the sales meeting. Before beginning a conversation about your work, always ask, "Is this a good time to speak to you?"

Know your manager's moods and quirks

If he isn't a morning person, steer clear of him until he's had his coffee. Some managers are easy to read. They'll let you know right away when they are angry. Others may just be quieter and act preoccupied. If your manager is frustrated and wants to vent, open up the lines of communication and listen sympathetically. This is not the time to tell him that you can't talk because you have a deadline.

Mirror your manager's style

Managers have their own styles that work for them. Watch how they operate, and do the same thing. When interacting with managers who are animated and energetic, pep up your style to match their pace. When dealing with managers who are more reserved, slow down so you don't overwhelm them. Does your boss work late every Wednesday? Do the same.

Take an interest

What business or industry magazines does your manager read? Subscribe to the same ones, so you'll be able to communicate intelligently about industry trends. Does your manager have a special interest or hobby? Ask the golfer about his game; ask the theatre buff about the latest shows in town.

Help your manager succeed

Victoria was working as the assistant manager of a private art gallery. Her job was to maintain the gallery, and deal with artists and visitors. She enjoyed working with people and appreciated the different types of art.

However, to the owner, the gallery was a business, and sales were a major concern. When sales were down, the owner always asked, "Why don't we have more people in? How can we sell more?"

Victoria's usual explanation was generalized and a bit philosophical. She talked about sales dynamics and cycles. "I don't think that my boss perceived the situation in the same way," Victoria said. "When I talked about the ups and downs of sales, my boss said, "I like your philosophy, but I want sales—as simple as that."

A major part of your job is to help your manager achieve his goals. When this happens, you'll benefit as well.

In a small company, this will ensure that your company stays in business and that you have a job. In a larger company, your manager will help you move up the ladder as he moves up—and he will generally be in a better position to know when promising opportunities open up. Additionally, other managers and executives will see how you support him, and may look for opportunities to help you advance within the company.

- Always support your manager in meetings. When your manager is presenting, keep your focus on her. Make eye contact and take notes. Laugh at her jokes (as long as they aren't offensive). Always arrive early, and never cause any distractions or embarrassments, such as letting your cellphone ring during a meeting.

- Go to your manager first. If you have big news or a great idea for the company, talk to your manager before talking to anyone else. Never make her the second person to find out about something. Never go behind her back to share information with someone else.

- Never correct or contradict your manager in public. Even if you are right in what you say, correcting your manager in public is a bad career move. You'll make both of you look bad. Even worse, other managers who witness your actions will never want to work with you. Never surprise your manager by asking a question in public unless you are sure she knows the answer.

- Never tell your manager, "I told you so," especially if she was wrong and you were right. If your manager is intelligent, she will know and remember that you warned her about potential problems, and she will be more likely to listen to your opinion the next time.

- Be part of her top initiatives. Find out what's on your manager's agenda, and ask how you can help. Is your manager being inaugurated as president of a professional organization? Offer to hand out information at the meeting, or listen to her speech ahead of time. If she's addressing the sales team, ask if you can attend for your professional development.

- Be loyal. If your manager makes a mistake, (as long as it's not illegal, immoral, or unsafe), protect her and cover for her, even if she deserves the consequences. Never do anything that puts your manager in jeopardy. If you find out something that will cause her problems, talk to her privately and give her a heads-up.

- If your manager treats you unfairly, through thoughtlessness or for reasons you don't understand, be prepared to deal with it. For example, if she gives an assignment that you wanted to your co-worker, you can say, "I had hoped to be assigned the ABC account, but I understand that you have your reasons for assigning it to Joe. Please let me know how I can help."

- Ask for more responsibility. This will help you grow, and take some of the burden off your manager. Offer to do the little things you will probably have to do anyway—even the unpleasant tasks. Your manager will love that, because it's so unusual and refreshing.

- Whatever you do, do it well. Never promise more than you can deliver. If the unexpected happens and you cannot meet a deadline or do the job that is expected of you, warn your manager as soon as you become aware of the problem.

- Remember that your work always reflects on your manager. If you try to hide problems and don't bring issues to your manager, you are really at fault.

Be a pleasure to work with

"Solve problems instead of spotting problems," says Adrian Cheung. "Be the one to make things happen, rather than watching things happen, by constantly offering constructive suggestions to help your department or company do a better job. Instead of coming to your boss with questions and problems, arrive with alternatives and solutions that help solve the problems. When you encounter challenges and problems, provide your boss with options and recommendations instead of excuses by saying, 'I think this is the root cause and I suggest the following ways to help fix the problem.' Remember to put your idea in writing so there is a formal record. Create value by providing recommendations to turn failure to success."

- Never argue with your manager. Although you may win in the short-run, you may cause damage to your career in the long-run. Keep your emotions even. Don't act overly disappointed if you don't get what you want, and never get angry. If you are able to handle your emotions, your manager will respect and admire your maturity. Keep a cheerful, positive demeanor. Be the employee your manager enjoys working with.

- Most managers don't want to hear about your personal problems. If you have a real problem, such as illness or a difficult family situation, tell your manager so he understands why you are upset or preoccupied. However, most managers don't want to hear about problems with co-workers or petty office issues. Solve the problems with your co-workers on your own. Present yourself as a person who is in control of your life and your relationships.

- Remember dates and anniversaries. Find out the names of your manager's spouse and children. Take an interest in special events in your manager's life—a wedding anniversary, a birthday, or the graduation or wedding of his child. Be aware of professional events as well—perhaps your manager will be receiving an award soon, or has been with the company for 15 years.

  Acknowledge birthdays with a card only, not with flowers or a gift. Only give a gift during gift exchanges at holiday time. However, a gift is appropriate if your female manager or the wife of your male manager has a baby. If your manager is sick in the hospital, flowers or chocolates are also appropriate.

  In most cases the employees in your department will get together to send a gift. Be sure to consult the company's policy about gifts, and your own department, before you do anything on your own.

- Make an ally of your manager's administrative assistant. The assistant knows everything that's going on, and can help you schedule time with your manager. She'll also give you valuable clues as to his moods and priorities, so you won't approach him with a request when he's reached his maximum stress level. What's more, if you treat your manager's admin with the utmost respect, she'll report great things to your manager about you.

- Be neat and organized. Get rid of clutter on your desk. Having a neat desk will reflect well on your manager. Even if your manager has a messy desk, he may still view your desk piled high with paper as a sign of your lack of organization. (See the note on privacy legislation in Chapter 9, page 201, for information about not leaving sensitive documents on your desk.)

- Make sure that your manager finds you useful. If possible, do the jobs that he doesn't like to do. Don't say, "That is not my job" to your manager, except in very extreme situations. If you would like a favour from your manager, such as time off to see your child's school play, be direct and honest with him.

- Don't be late to work or to meetings. If, despite your best efforts, you are late occasionally (perhaps once a month) call your manager and tell him that you are on your way. If he needs you and is waiting for you, he may become impatient and angry. If he knows he can expect you in a half-hour, however, he will put this out of his mind until you arrive.

Good boss, bad boss—different supervising styles

Managers come in all shapes, sizes, and temperaments. This section will discuss various negative behaviours that managers display, with strategies on how to deal with them. Keep in mind that no one person will fit any of these descriptions exactly, but many people display some of these characteristics.

Canadian Business Concept: The title of this chapter, Good Boss / Bad Boss, is a play on words, from the term "Good cop / bad cop." This usually refers to two partners or colleagues, one of whom is kind, the other mean or demanding.

Big ego manager

This person wants the spotlight to himself. If you excel in a project, he will take the credit because he thinks the big ideas came from him, and you are just a pair of hands.

Strategy: Make this manager look good by tying everything you do back to his goals. Never make him look bad.

At the same time, plant seeds about yourself. If you see your manager's boss in the elevator, and she asks how you are, in addition to saying, "Fine," you can say, "I'm really enjoying working on the ABC project. I'm happy that I'm almost finished. You'll see the results soon."

Competitive manager

The competitive manager may ask you to write a letter, and then show you her letter, which is better. She may ask for your ideas, but say that hers are better.

Strategy: Strange as it may seem, the best tactic is to praise this person. She usually feels insecure, so she has to show you she's best at everything. By stroking her ego, you'll make her feel more secure around you.

With this kind of manager, you may start to feel competitive yourself. Try to control your defensiveness, because she may not see her own competitive behaviour, and will think you are being too competitive. It's never easy being mistreated, but if you stay calm, eventually things will work out better for you.

Quick-change artist

This person constantly changes his mind or forgets what he told you. For example, on Monday he might say, "I'd like you to research everything about XYZ for a presentation I'm delivering next month." Three days later, when you mention that you're making good progress with your research, this manager may look puzzled and say, "Oh yeah. I may not need that. I hope you are still working on your main project."

Strategy: Verify everything in writing. As soon as you get a new assignment, send your manager an email saying, "I understand that you want me to work on XYZ this week, and that this is a priority before I finish ABC." Hopefully, he will confirm in writing that you should go ahead. Then, check in frequently for signs that he's changed his mind, so you don't waste days of work. If you bump into him during your coffee break, casually mention that you are working on XYZ that day, and ask a question about it. If he's changed his mind, this is his opportunity to tell you.

Regularly ask your manager to help you clarify projects. You could say, "We have several projects going on now. Can you help me rank them in importance?"

Inexperienced manager

This manager may be new to the company, or may just be young. She may lack skills in technology or operations for your department, or not have much experience with managing people. As more baby boomers retire, there will be more young and inexperienced managers.

Strategy: Find out what she *does* know. Ask about her previous experience and accomplishments. Then, ask for help in the areas where she excels. At the beginning, let her do the talking, and ask how you can support her in her transition.

As well, give your ideas and share your past experiences. Your manager may appreciate them very much.

Micromanager

This manager wants to check every detail of what you do. He constantly checks your progress and corrects all the details.

Strategy: Give him constant updates either verbally or in emails. Show him lots of reports. Give him more details than he wants, and he may stop asking you for more information.

Incompetent manager

At some point, you may realize that you have more talent and expertise than your manager, and wonder how she got promoted. You may feel upset or angry because she is creating problems that you have to solve, or messes up things that you've done well. You can't defend yourself easily because the manager holds your job future in her hands.

Strategy: There are two options for dealing with this manager. The first is to put up with the incompetence and hope that either you or your manager will be transferred to another department, or your manager will leave the company.

The second choice is to be proactive. Join networking associations and focus groups so other people can see how competent you are. Volunteer to work on projects with other people in the company.

You can even offer to help your manager in her areas of incompetence. For example, if you know she isn't a good public speaker, offer to do part of the presentation at your next meeting, to take the pressure off her. She may even hand over a larger part of the project to you. You'll learn new skills, and people will see you shine.

Let her rely on you. An employee who has a good relationship with an incompetent manager may be relied on for many things. This will provide the employee with beneficial experience.

Be sure to document everything, so that if the incompetent manager does something stupid, you don't get into trouble along with her. For example, when her manager was about to make an unwise decision, a smart employee advised against it and wrote an email: "I want to reinforce my point of view that this is the wrong decision for the following reasons ..., and that these could be the negative outcomes ..." She described her ideas in detail. When the manager left the company, her detailed email saved her.

You'll also have to connect the dots for this manager. This means that you'll have to talk to her privately, and explain clearly what you are doing. Tell her about the actions you are taking, and the results that you expect to see. Don't be surprised if she implements your actions and takes the credit. Make sure you have all your ideas in writing before discussing them with her.

Strangely enough, if your company doesn't realize that your skills are stronger than your manager's, a supplier or customer might. Many job offers come through these channels. A supplier or client who realizes that you are more knowledgeable and decisive than your manager may offer you a job at their company.

Unavailable manager

This manager is a poor communicator, or is unavailable when you need to speak to him. He may be shy or may just not work well with people. He makes brief appearances before going off to meetings or long lunches with clients, and always seem to be travelling. He keeps his door closed and has rules about when you can meet with him.

He may just be coasting until retirement, or may have outside activities such as community involvement, and he expects other people to pick up his slack.

Strategy: Figure out how your manager likes to communicate—face-to-face, or by email. Approach him only for important matters, and he'll see that you're not wasting his time. Observe his schedule and try to schedule meetings for times when he's most often in the office.

What if your manager is not available, or doesn't get back to you, and you have to move forward or you'll be in danger of not achieving your objectives? Send an email saying, "Unfortunately we haven't been able to meet. Here's where we are right now with this project, and these are the next steps. If you have any issues with us moving forward, please let me know right way because we're implementing the ideas on Friday."

If your manager does come back to you afterward, you can say that you sent a number of emails and gave him every opportunity to respond.

Impatient manager

This is the "Type A" manager, who is intense, demanding, impatient, and often aggressive. She is competitive, and tends to work long hours. She expects you to do the same.

Strategy: Don't bore her with the details. Some people give too much information, with long stories about why and how something happened.

Get right to the bottom line—give her the facts and figures. Say, "Here's the situation, here's my recommendation, here are the costs, and these are the outcomes. Do you agree?"

Screaming or moody manager

One day he's friendly and easygoing. The next day he's cold as ice. When he's under stress, frustrated, or angry, he yells.

Strategy: If the yelling is infrequent, try to be understanding. He will probably feel bad afterward. If it's his habit to yell, he may be surprised that you take this personally.

At some point, he probably had a manager who yelled in order to cope with stress, and now he thinks that's the way managers normally act. He may be a good manager in other ways—he may be knowledgeable and supportive—but he just doesn't express his frustrations appropriately.

Look for a time when your manager is calm, so you can talk with him. If possible, bring him some good news on a project to start off the conversation on a positive note. Take the approach that you want to work better together: "I would like to do a good job for you, and maybe it's just me, but I can't think well when you raise your voice. Can you work out a way to help me resolve this problem?"

A good way to do this is to say the following: "When you … I feel … because I … I want …" For example, "When you yell or scream, I feel paralyzed by the situation, because I don't deal with conflict well. I want us to discuss these types of issues calmly."

If he continues to yell, pick an appropriate time and say very calmly that you cannot accept this treatment. Never raise your voice. It is likely that no one has ever challenged him before, and he doesn't even realize what he's doing.

If the problem is severe, you can go to human resources or senior management for advice and guidance. Be aware that this can follow you when you apply for new jobs, because some people are reluctant to hire someone who "officially" had a problem with a manager. This should not, however, deter you from dealing with the situation.

In a small, owner-run company, a bullying boss is unlikely to change. You can learn to live with his behaviour or leave the company. If you find your manager's moods very stressful to live with, leaving the company may be your only recourse.

Slave-driver or workaholic manager

This manager is all work and no play. She works long hours and expects you to do the same. She doesn't have much of a sense of humour.

Strategy: Here's one way to deal with this manager. Send a few work-related emails from home at night. Even if you're not at the office, this shows your commitment because you are thinking about work in the evening. You can win some brownie points this way.

Additionally, talk to your manager about what is expected of you, and how often you might have to work overtime. Come to a clear understanding of what is acceptable for both of you. Send her an email outlining what you agreed upon. Keep the email. You may need to refer to it many times in the future.

Master / servant manager

This manager thinks you are his personal servant. He may ask you to pick up his dry cleaning, send flowers to his friend in the hospital, or take his car for a wash—none of which is in your job description.

Strategy: Ideally, you received a job description with a list of your duties when you began your job. Ask for a meeting with your manager and refer to this list. If you don't have a job description, choose a quiet time and request a meeting. Say, "I seem to be spending more and more time on your personal errands. I'd like to clarify what your expectations are."

How to manage problems with your manager
Have a positive attitude

Dennis and his team had been working on a training program for a new product. After weeks of work, their general manager announced that he was going in a different direction, and the project was being scrapped. Dennis was furious that weeks of work were going down the drain. He stopped by his manager's office and let out his frustration at the change of plans. His manager just frowned. Later on, his manager told him that he thought Dennis had acted very immaturely and needed to learn to control his emotions.

In the business world, there will be many times when you may feel like screaming, "This isn't fair!" However, if you develop a bad attitude, you will pay the consequences.

When you develop a negative attitude, you waste a lot of energy being unhappy. Worse, you become labelled difficult and immature. You poison the workplace atmosphere, and no one wants to work with you.

The things that happen at work may be beyond your control. The only choice you have is in how you react to them. It's not easy to change your attitude, but this is essential to your success and to your happiness.

You can change your attitude for the better by understanding that you create the thoughts that you focus on.

Here are some examples:

You've been working really hard and are surprised to hear that a co-worker received a promotion that you thought you should have received.

> **Negative attitude:** I'm really upset that I didn't get the promotion.
>
> **Positive attitude:** I'm going to find out what I need to do better, so next time I'll get a promotion.

Your manager asks you to work on a task that you feel you aren't qualified for.

> **Negative attitude:** I don't know how to do this. What if I do it wrong and get into trouble?
>
> **Positive attitude:** I'll try to find the resources I need and do the best job I can.

Before you tell your manager you can't do something, try to find a solution. This is your opportunity to ask a lot of questions and get clarification and direction. If you need more resources, you can ask whether you can get someone to help you.

If you are new to the organization, you can ask who else in the organization has information about the assignment, and whether anyone has worked on something similar in the past.

You'll be surprised how often you can figure out how to complete new tasks. However, if you start and then find you can't do the job competently, tell your manager right away.

How would you handle a disappointing raise?

You are disappointed to find out that your company is only giving employees small raises this year.

> **Negative attitude:** I worked hard and I deserve more than this.
>
> **Positive attitude:** I understand that our industry is having a difficult time now. At least I like my job. Perhaps things will turn around and I'll get a better raise soon.

As you see, it's normal to have a negative reaction or to feel frustrated about disappointing news. But when we hold on to negative feelings, they can turn into self-pity, panic, or depression. Over time, these feelings result in misery.

Make a conscious effort to find something positive to focus on. You'll be more productive, happier, and more likely to succeed.

If your job is so bad that you can't be positive, you may have to find a new job.

An important thing to remember is that everyone needs a friend to vent to—having one person at the office who you completely trust can make all the difference. People who have a best friend at work are more likely to succeed at their jobs.

You need to be able to go into your friend's office, close the door and say, "I can't believe that happened!" and then go on with your day.

Getting feedback from your manager

"Feedback is a gift," says Dessalen Wood, Senior Director of Human Resources at Airborne Mobile. "It means that your manager is interested in you and wants to support you. A good manager will give you clear direction, the tools you need to do your job, and encouragement. This shows that your manager is investing in you. If you don't get feedback, ask for it.

"Remember that it's not just what you do, but how your manager wants you to do it. People are hired for their education and skills, but they get fired because they lack interpersonal skills: the ability to work in a team, flexibility, communication skills, and creativity."

Canadian Business Concept: To succeed, you have to understand not just what your manager wants you to do, but how your manager wants you to do it.

No one ever said that feedback or constructive criticism is easy to handle, but getting feedback is essential if you want to succeed in your company. When your manager takes the time to let you know how you are doing, be grateful for his comments, even if you don't like what he says.

Take an active role in getting suggestions on how to improve. Ask your manager for time to discuss your performance. Don't be afraid to say, "What can I do better?" If someone else receives the promotion you wanted, ask what you need to do differently to secure the next big promotion.

Some issues are touchy to deal with. Your manager may hesitate to mention subjects like the way you dress, your grooming, or your networking skills, but these things can hold you back, so it's important to find out whether your image should be more professional.

You should also get input on how you perform within your team and how you relate to your co-workers. When your first language isn't English, understanding the nuances of the language can sometimes be difficult, and you may offend people without meaning to.

If you can't get feedback from your manager about these things, ask some valued co-workers and friends. You might not like what you hear, but at least you will know what to work on.

When people give you feedback, receive it respectfully and tell them that you are willing to change your behaviour. This lets everyone know that the process was not a waste of time and energy, and that you really want to improve your performance.

How to handle a performance review

 During Gordon's probation period, he had his first performance review with his manager. Although his manager was generally pleased with Gordon's performance, there was one specific area that needed improvement. Gordon's manager began the review by mentioning some positive things about Gordon's work. He then addressed the specific area that Gordon needed to work on, and finished on an encouraging, upbeat note.

Gordon left the meeting feeling very happy and told his co-workers, "My manager said so many nice things about me!" He didn't realize the importance of working on the area that needed improvement, and didn't make any efforts to improve on it. At the end of his probation period, Gordon was stunned to find that he was being let go. His manager felt that he didn't take his work seriously, and wasn't willing to work to improve on his weak points.

In Canada, employee performance reviews, evaluations, or appraisals can determine raises, promotions, and sometimes whether people get to keep their jobs. No wonder they make employees nervous.

The performance review should be a review of everything you and your manager have talked about all year—there should be no surprises. If there are, come up with some strategies to improve communication and expectations for the next year. Use your job description as a guide to what you will be evaluated on during your review.

Performance reviews are often delivered in a "sandwich." The manager says something positive about your performance, then explains what needs to be improved, and ends on a positive note. This practice may leave you confused—in your country, you may have received either positive or negative feedback, but not both at the same time. Employers use this sandwich method to encourage people to feel empowered and confident about making necessary changes without feeling upset or stressed.

It is important to consider the areas that need improvement very seriously. You may have to dig out what your manager is saying indirectly. If a manager mentions a problem more than once and you don't make an effort to correct it, he may lose patience. If he speaks to you in a stern tone of voice, you have to make quick changes to your behaviour or you may risk losing your job.

If you have a coach, mentor, or close friend at your company, ask her to help you interpret the feedback, then decide which actions to take to address the issues your manager brought up.

Canadian Business Concept: Your manager may give you sandwiched feedback by making positive comments, followed by negative comments, and ending with more positive comments. Never ignore areas of improvement that your manager brings up in a performance review. You have to change your behaviour in the areas on which you receive negative feedback.

Here are some ways to make the most out of performance reviews:

Learn about the review process. Find out how your company uses performance reviews to evaluate employees. The goals of an appraisal should be to establish expectations, increase communication, support good performance, and improve unsatisfactory performance.

Prepare for your review. Write down your achievements and list anything you want to discuss at the review. If you haven't documented your achievements, you should take some time to write down what you have accomplished. The most important thing to document is the way in which your employer has benefited from your work. Did you bring in new clients, build relationships with older clients, streamline systems, or increase profits?

You may be asked to complete a self-assessment. Provide specific examples to back up your assessment of your performance.

What should you learn from your performance review?

Think of your review as a learning opportunity. Listen carefully to what the reviewer says, both positive and negative. Think about how you can improve based on the negative feedback. Does your manager give you suggestions on how to do something differently? Do your **utmost** to follow these suggestions, or ask for help if you don't know how to do this on your own.

"Lots of decisions are made around performance appraisals," says Shelley Brown, President of Bromelin People Practices. Your salary and promotion will depend on how you are rated. You may have a short appraisal at 6 months, and a full one at 12 months. Take the time to prepare and do it properly." Brown suggests the following:

- Find out when you will be assessed. Will it be after 6 months? 12 months? Every January? This may depend upon when you were hired in the performance cycle.

- Ask for a blank copy of the review. Know what questions you will be asked, and how you will be assessed.

- Keep a file of your accomplishments so you'll be ready at the time of appraisal. Be specific about your results and achievements, using your job description as a guide for your priorities. Use clear descriptions of your accomplishments, such as, "I have regular client contact with X, Y, and Z." and "My sales increased by 10 percent this quarter."

- Resist the urge to be humble. You need to make sure your manager knows about your accomplishments.

- Attend any training sessions that are available. Many big companies give training on how to handle performance appraisals. If yours does not, read a book, do an online training program, or ask your HR representative for a coaching session.

How to ask for a raise

 Li, a technical professional from China, was an outstanding employee, but he had difficulty communicating in English. Li was unhappy with his salary. He was too shy to speak to his manager about it because in China, people don't ask for raises. One day he came to his manager and said, "I quit."

This story comes from Haakon Saake, Information Technology Manager at Toromont Industries. Saake says, "Li (not his real name) was one of the best programmers I had, so it's really unfortunate that he quit because of lack of communication. I expect people to tell me when something is bothering them, but Li was too shy to talk to me. If he had asked for a raise, I could have helped him. In Canada, you have to recognize that it is important to communicate with your manager when something is bothering you."

When should you ask for a raise? If you feel you deserve a higher salary, but your manager hasn't offered one, speak to your manager.

There are two deciding factors in whether you will get a raise: your performance and the job market. The job market is based on two factors: typical salaries for people with your job title, and the demand for people who perform your job. If there are few people who can do your job well, you are more likely to get the raise than if there are many people with your qualifications.

Also keep in mind that your personal circumstances have nothing to do with your request for a raise. Don't present your case from a personal perspective. The company is not concerned about your mortgage payments or the family you have to support. Always present from a professional point of view. Show them the value you bring to the company.

Here are some tips on how to ask for a salary increase:

Find out what to ask for

Do some research to learn about typical salaries in your field. If you belong to a professional association, ask whether they have salary information available, or check their website. Then consider where you fit in. This will depend on how long you've worked in your field, and the length of time you've worked for your current employer.

Evaluate your employer's financial health, and your industry's strength

What is happening in the economy? How is this affecting your industry and your company? An economic downturn may not be the best time to ask for a raise. Do your research: check your company's financial reports and the business news to choose the best time to ask for a raise.

Prepare your case

When you ask for a raise, you're really trying to sell yourself, just as you did to get your job. Make a list of your accomplishments, starting with the most recent, and working your way back. Be specific, especially if you can quantify your successes, such as increasing sales by 20 percent.

Make an appointment

Don't discuss your raise with your manager by email or by telephone, unless you work at different locations. Set up a face-to-face meeting. You'll come across as a serious professional.

Present your case

Wouldn't it be nice if your manager agreed immediately to give you a raise just because you asked for one? This could happen. If it doesn't work that way, you'll have to convince your manager to give you a raise by presenting the materials you prepared, including information about typical salaries in your field and your list of accomplishments.

Think ahead

Before your meeting, think about what you will do if your manager says "no" or offers you a raise that is much smaller than what you ask for. Will you quit your job? Try again later?

Ask your manager when you can discuss your raise again in the future. Get as much external data as possible. For example, if a similar job to yours is advertised online or in a salary survey, show your manager.

Your plan for what to do if your request is rejected may depend on what your manager says. Did she turn you down because of performance? If so, ask yourself whether her criticisms are valid. If they are, think about the changes you can make. If you feel she's being unfair, you may want to think about moving to a job where your skills are appreciated.

If you were turned down for other reasons, such as the economy, ask your manager when she expects the situation to change, and when you can discuss your raise again.

Business Buzzwords

- ace a presentation
- admin
- baby boomer
- cover for someone
- go to bat for someone
- heads-up
- high maintenance employee
- pick up the slack
- scrap a project
- stroke someone's ego

Chapter 10 Action Plan

1. Find out what your manager wants from you, and what his supervising style is. Does he want you to ask many questions upfront, or does he prefer that you work independently as much as possible? Write down three ways you can work more effectively with your manager.

   a) _____

   b) _____

   c) _____

2. Find out your manager's communication style. Ask her if she prefers to be contacted by phone, by email, or in person. How often does she want you to update her on details of your work? Write three ways you can communicate more effectively with your manager.

   a) _____

   b) _____

   c) _____

3. Ask for feedback. Schedule a meeting with your manager and ask for feedback on what you need to improve. Ask for suggestions on how to do this, including asking about which tools, resources, or training can help you. Write the information below.

   _____

   _____

   _____

Client Relations and Business Etiquette

If you work in sales, or for any professional service firm, you'll be meeting and working with clients at their offices or at business meals.

In This Chapter

- Working well with clients
- Making a good impression at a client's office
- Business etiquette for the 21st century
- Business dining etiquette in Canada
- Hosting a business meal

Working well with clients

A patient came into a pharmacy to renew a prescription. Mi Hi, the pharmacy intern, was from Korea. She told the patient, in a very negative tone, "You are late!" The senior pharmacist jumped in to explain that the pharmacy intern was only concerned with the patient's health, and wanted to make sure the patient didn't miss his medication. He later explained to Mi Hi that she had to speak respectfully to clients. She had difficulty understanding why she could not tell the patient that he was late in renewing his prescription, since he obviously was!

If you work in professional services such as accounting, IT, engineering, or health care, working with clients in Canada may be very different than in your native country.

Different cultures have different structures to represent which roles are considered most important within the business world. In hierarchical cultures, the manager is on top (he holds the most power or influence), the professional service provider is in the middle, and the client is at the bottom (he holds the least power or influence). In North America, the client is at the top, the manager is in the middle, and the professional service provider is at the bottom. This means that the relationships between professional service providers and their clients vary from culture to culture.

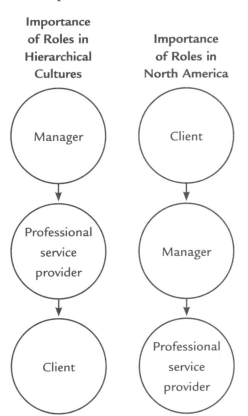

In hierarchical societies such as India, professionals have a much higher position. Professional service providers are expected to analyze their clients' situations in detail and then tell their clients what to do. Clients are thankful that their providers are helping them.

In Canada, companies and professional service providers are thankful to their clients for buying their products and services. They are expected to offer choices and let the clients decide on the best option.

In North America there is a saying that *The customer is always right*. While it's not true that every customer is right, the philosophy is that companies and service providers will do everything they can to make sure the customer is satisfied and will come back in the future.

A quick Internet search shows 350 million websites devoted to customer service, and hundreds of books on the subject. Clearly, customer service is an important concept in North America!

Canadians believe that if you don't acquire and retain customers, your business won't be profitable for long. The philosophy is that you have to keep your customers happy so they will return, and so they will also pass positive feedback about your business on to other people who may want your services.

The essence of good customer service is forming relationships with customers. Whether you like the customers or not, remember that customers pay the bills—they are the lifeblood of your company.

Canadian Business Concept: There's a North American saying, "The customer is always right." Canadian businesses spend a great deal of time and money to get and retain customers. While not every company succeeds at doing this well, most companies will tell you that customer service is a very high priority. When you meet clients, you are expected to treat them with respect and do an excellent job of providing customer service.

Good client service

"Give service to others," says Thomas Manuel from India, who works as an account manager with Royal Bank of Canada. "Many companies offer the same services—you differentiate yourself by your customer service.

"No one wants to be treated as a number. Everyone appreciates personal attention to their needs and problems."

Thomas offers these tips for great customer service:

- When a client has a problem, see it as an opportunity to help him.

- Never ignore a request from a client. Do your best to resolve the issue.

- If you don't have an answer for someone right away, get back to him in a timely manner. Clients will feel you are in control of the situation, and will appreciate that you're working on the problem.

- Stay organized and on top of issues, and see each issue through to its resolution.

If you deal with clients directly, here are a few basic rules to follow:

- Listen to your customers to find out what they need, and work to build long-term relationships.

- Respect your clients at all times, and take their complaints seriously. Some clients can be unreasonable or demanding, and you may not agree with what they say. If you can't meet their demands, be patient and explain why not, and offer another solution. Don't become angry or impatient. It's okay to be firm as long as you remain polite.

- Be helpful and take the extra step. If a client asks you for something that is not in your job description, most companies are happy if you take the initiative to solve the customer's problem. Ask your manager how much responsibility you should take in meeting a customer's needs on your own. When you become known for attracting and keeping customers, it will help your career enormously.

How to summarize a conversation

Learn how to recap or summarize a conversation. This has four benefits:

1. It demonstrates to your clients that you actually heard what they said and processed the information.

2. It forces you to listen carefully to what the other person says.

3. It helps clarify in your mind the customer's biggest issues and concerns.

4. It gives your customers the opportunity to hear exactly what they said to you.

Here's how to recap a conversation. Say to your customer, "Ms Bhatti, let me quickly recap what you told me." Then briefly restate the key points she mentioned. For example,

- "You typically have to hire three new employees per month."
- "You are seeing increased competition for product X."
- "Your new product launch will take place in October."

This simple technique will help you understand your customers' needs, so you can increase your sales and improve your relationships with them.

Making a good impression at a client's office

The first 12 seconds

When you meet with clients, you are representing your company. In the first 12 seconds of meeting someone, you make a first impression that can have a big impact on your business relationship. Here are three ways to make those first 12 seconds count:

1. The first 12 words you speak should include a compliment or a word of thanks. When you meet someone for the first time, thank them for meeting with you. Include their name in your opening words whenever possible.

    - "It's a pleasure to meet you, Ms Chan."
    - "Thanks for suggesting we meet today, Mr. Smith."
    - "It's great to see you again, Ravi."

When you meet people in their offices, you can also make a positive comment about the decor or the location. For example, "You have a great view of the city from your window, Judy," or "What a great location. It's right in the heart of downtown."

Be careful not to say anything too personal. Avoid commenting on people's looks or mannerisms, or other people in the office.

2. The first 12 steps you take should show confidence. When you are walking into a client's office, or into the boardroom for a meeting, walk with purpose, energy, and vitality.

3. The first 12 inches around your face should include impeccable grooming. Your hair, collar, and tie or jewellery should be clean, fresh, and classy.

In the client's office

Benoit had an appointment with Mr. Smith, a new client. After being greeted by his client in the reception area, Benoit followed Mr. Smith to his office and sat down in the nearest chair. Then he put his briefcase on Mr. Smith's desk, and spread his papers out. Mr. Smith looked annoyed, and the meeting did not go well.

When you meet a client or supplier at his office, ask, "Where would you like me to sit?" Don't sit down in the first chair you see, and don't invade the client's personal space by putting your papers, briefcase, or purse on his desk. Keep these things on the floor or in your lap.

Your client will most likely ask whether you want coffee or a glass of water. If you are meeting in a boardroom and everyone is drinking coffee, it's fine to have some as well, to show your appreciation for the offer. If you don't drink coffee, you can ask for water.

When meeting one-on-one in other people's offices, they will often ask whether you want anything to drink. In general, it's better to decline with thanks. Usually, they are just being polite, and don't want to run around getting you coffee. However, if a client comes to your office, you should ask your manager about the protocol for offering refreshments to visitors.

Timing for meeting clients

Mitch had a meeting with a client at 10:00. To make sure he wasn't late, he arrived at his appointment at 9:35. As he waited in the reception area, the client who was to meet with him looked up from her office across the hall and noticed Mitch waiting. Mitch saw her look at her watch in irritation.

By now you have heard that you should always be on time. Arriving late for an appointment is considered rude in Canada. It implies that your time is more valuable than the other person's.

Not everyone is aware, however, that arriving too early isn't courteous either. Business people are often pressed for time. They may be trying to meet deadlines or return phone calls between appointments. When you arrive too early, the person you are meeting may feel pressured to see you right away. The best time to arrive is five to ten minutes before your meeting is scheduled.

This takes a bit of planning. Always give yourself extra time when you are travelling to a meeting. There may be more traffic than you expect, or you may have to search for a parking spot. Also consider that if your meeting is on the 30th floor of an office tower, it can take an extra five minutes to wait for an elevator and get up to the floor.

If you allow yourself plenty of time and arrive earlier than expected, you have some breathing space. You can review your materials for the meeting at a coffee shop, or take a few minutes to wash your hands and comb your hair. When you enter your meeting, you'll feel calm and collected, instead of frazzled and frantic.

Knowing when to leave is important, too. When the meeting is scheduled, you can ask approximately how long it will be. When the person you are meeting with checks his watch, thanks you for your time, or starts to stand, conclude the meeting graciously and leave.

Looking organized and confident

Before a business appointment, take time to prepare. Focus on your goals for the meeting. What do you want to accomplish? Then plan ahead, both physically and mentally.

Organize any papers or other materials you have to bring. Review the meeting agenda, if you have one. Make sure you are prepared to discuss each topic.

Put your business card holder, with plenty of cards, in the pocket of your jacket, or another place where you can access it easily. Keep a pen and notebook within easy reach. Have everything at your fingertips. This will save you time, and you'll avoid fumbling or searching for things while under pressure.

Business etiquette for the 21st century

Marie, an administrative assistant, is headed toward the door with Robert, her manager. Who opens the door?

In some social situations, the man is expected to open the door for a woman. But the business world today is gender-neutral. This means that we treat men and women similarly, and we expect them to act similarly.

If you aren't sure what to do, use common sense:

- Whoever gets to the door first should open it as a courtesy.

- Never let a door slam in someone's face.

- If a man falls back on tradition and holds the door open for a woman, the woman should accept the gesture graciously, but should not expect it.

- When waiting for an elevator, train, subway, or bus, stand to the side to allow people to get off easily.

- If you are near the front of a crowded elevator, offer to push the buttons for people at the back.

- Whoever is closest to a revolving door or an elevator door enters or exits first.

- Never crowd into a revolving door—go through it one person at a time.

- A man or woman can help someone struggling with his or her coat, or open a door for someone carrying a package.

- Remember to say, "Excuse me" or "Thank you" when people move to accommodate you.

- If someone holds a door open for you, always thank the person graciously.

Business dining etiquette in Canada

Business dining is a big part of business today. It's also the area where most people are concerned about making mistakes. You may be worried because of cultural differences, or because you are new on the job. Business dining is different from dining with friends or family, and it's important to know the rules so you can make a good impression.

At the beginning of your career, you may be attending company dinners, or having casual lunches with co-workers. As you advance in your career, you'll be attending meetings and conferences away from your office, and dining with clients. At some point, you may be inviting clients out to lunch or dinner.

Whether the meal is formal or casual, remember that dining is about building relationships. Dining with customers gives you a chance to connect with them, away from the hectic atmosphere of an office. Dining with your manager or colleagues is also about building relationships so you get to know each other better and bond as a team.

At the dining table our manners are on display. Like it or not, we are judged by how we act. Mangers and clients notice when someone grabs the breadbasket without offering anyone a roll, or shovels food into his mouth. They may conclude that this person is aggressive, insensitive, or immature, and question his potential for advancement.

What if you are invited to a restaurant that serves a type of food that you don't eat? Perhaps you are vegetarian, or don't eat certain foods because of your faith. In general, if you are invited by your manager or client, it's best to go along without making an issue out of it. Most restaurants have at least one vegetarian dish that you can order, and you can usually order a salad without any meat or seafood on top.

Don't get confused about why you are at the table. At a business meal you are really at a business meeting that includes tableware. Use the time to focus on your dining companions, not on the food.

When you are invited to a restaurant

Here's how to make a great impression as a guest at a business meal:

- Always arrive on time.

- Place your napkin on your lap and use it frequently to wipe your fingers and dab your lips. If you leave the table during the meal, put your napkin on your chair. Never put a soiled napkin on the table until the end of the meal, when you place it, gently crumpled, to the left of your plate.

- Order the basics, such as soup, main course, and beverage. Only order an appetizer or dessert if the host suggests it.

- When you order, don't ask the server too many questions about how a dish is prepared. It's fine to ask if the fish is fried or grilled, but don't go into personal details about your special diet.

- Begin eating when everyone at your table is served. If your dining partner's food arrives before yours, encourage him to start eating before it gets cold. If three or more people at a large table are served, they can start eating so their food won't get cold.

- Keep briefcases, papers, keys, and cellphones off the table. Put your personal belongings in your briefcase or purse, under the table. Tuck the straps of your purse underneath, so they don't trip the servers.

Turn off your cellphone prior to a business meal.

- Turn off your cellphone before entering the restaurant. Taking phone calls during a meal sends the signal that other business is more important than the person you're with.

- Keep pace with others at the table. If someone is a slow eater, pick up the conversation to allow him time to eat. If you are a slow eater, ask questions to get others to talk, and to allow you to catch up with them.

- Make as little noise as possible while eating. Don't slurp or chew noisily.

- Don't put too much food into your mouth at once. Take small bites so you can avoid talking with your mouth full. However, although you shouldn't talk with your mouth full, learn to answer with a small bit of food in your mouth. It's exasperating to converse with someone who only speaks when his mouth is completely empty.

- You don't have to finish everything. If something is difficult to eat or you don't like it, you can leave it on your plate.

- Always thank the host in person at the end of the meal. Then send a note after the meal.

Canadian Business Concept: The purpose of a business meal is to build relationships with your customers—not with your food.

What to order

Pina, a new sales representative, was excited that her job offered the opportunity to dine with clients. When hosting a client at a chic French restaurant, she decided to order quail hearts, an exotic dish she had heard about. Her enthusiasm evaporated when her plate arrived, filled with small black balls that she found inedible.

A business dinner is not the time to experiment with unknown exotic dishes. And it's not the time to order your favourite finger foods. Choose foods that are easy to eat with a knife and fork, such as grilled chicken, meat, fish, or certain types of pasta, such as penne.

However, if your manager or client suggests a sushi or lobster restaurant, or a place that specializes in spareribs, go ahead and enjoy the food. Watch how other people eat these items and imitate their strategy, trying your best to be neat.

The following are some foods to avoid at business dinners.

Spaghetti: It's difficult to wind the long strands on your fork and avoid dripping sauce onto your shirt. Order pasta that is already in small pieces, such as penne or farfalle.

Lobster: It's hard to pull out the lobster meat from the claws without creating a mess. You don't want to spend your time wrestling with a lobster claw instead of talking with a client.

Cherry tomatoes: Eat them only if they are cut in half. Otherwise leave them on your plate, because it's almost impossible to bite into a cherry tomato without squirting someone, and cutting it can send it flying across the table.

French onion soup: This soup takes a long time to prepare, so other people will be waiting for you. Although it's delicious, it's messy to eat, and no one looks good with cheese dripping onto their chin.

Fried chicken: You'll have greasy fingers and lips no matter how careful you are.

Spareribs: These are finger foods that are fun to eat, but the barbecue sauce can get on your hands and clothes.

Canadian Business Concept: Remove a pit or seed from your mouth in the same way it went in. For example, if you eat an olive from a plate of finger foods, remove the pit with your fingers. But if the olive is in your salad, remove the pit by putting it back on your fork, and then placing it on your plate. For chicken or fish bones, use your fork as well. If you must use your fingers, do it discreetly by cupping your other hand over your mouth. Place bones or pits on your dinner plate, not your bread plate where they will be more visible.

Company dinners

At a gala company dinner there are round tables with place settings arranged very closely together. Which bread plate is yours? And which fork do you use?

Here are some tips for navigating the banquet table:

Locate your own place setting. It will be in the form of a square in front of you.

Your bread plate is always on the left. Glasses are always on the right. It's easy to remember: *Food* and *left* each have four letters. *Drink* and *right* each have five letters.

The utensils indicate the number of courses. Also, there will be a maximum of three of any type of utensil at a time.

Always pick up the utensils on the outside first. Then work your way inward with each course.

The fork and spoon above your plate are for dessert. Use the fork to eat your cake, and the spoon for ice cream or custard, or to stir your coffee.

Canadian Business Concept: A small cup of sorbet is often served to cleanse the palate between courses.

How to handle your knife and fork

There are two basic styles of business dining, the American style and the Continental (also called European) style.

American style: You hold your fork in your left hand and your knife in your right hand to cut your food. You switch your fork to your right hand to eat, and switch back and forth between cutting and eating.

Continental style: Your fork remains in your left hand, both while you cut your food, and when you bring it to your mouth. The tines always remain down. Extend your index fingers onto the handles for strength and control.

Although both American and Continental styles are correct, some people consider Continental style more sophisticated, because it implies that the diner is well-travelled. If you want to try Continental style, practise at home until you feel confident.

Here are some things to remember while dining out:

- Don't wrap your hands into fists around the knife and fork handles.

- Don't stab or saw your food.

- Cut one bite at a time and eat it. Don't cut all the food in your plate into little pieces.

How to use cutlery to signal the waiter

"I'm pausing"

"I'm finished."

The host signals the beginning of the meal by picking up his napkin.

The way you place your cutlery sends a signal to the waiter: "I'm pausing," or "I'm finished." When you pause between bites, separate your knife and fork on your plate in an inverted V-shape, with the knife and fork tips crossed at the top and the handles toward the outside of your plate.

When you have finished eating, place your knife and fork parallel to each other with the tips of the cutlery pointing towards 10:00, and the handles towards 4:00. The tines can face up or down.

To avoid soiling the tablecloth, never place used cutlery back on a clean tablecloth or hang it off the plate. Put your cutlery completely on the plate.

If you finish before everyone else does, engage some people in conversation to allow the slower eaters to finish. If you are a slow eater, it's okay to leave some food on your plate if everyone else has finished.

How to eat the basics

At a company dinner, John reached across the table for the breadbasket, put a roll on his plate, and then put the breadbasket down. Next, he cut the roll in half, buttered it, and took a big bite. In one minute, he showed everyone his lack of table manners.

Bread and soup are often the first food items at a business meal. To avoid making a bad impression at the table, observe the following etiquette:

Don't reach across the table. The person closest to the basket begins by picking it up and offering it to the person on his left, then puts a roll on his own bread plate, and passes the basket to the right.

When you receive the basket, don't put it down. Keep passing it. It goes from left to right, just like reading a book.

Pass the butter dish in the same way. Put a dab of butter on your plate and pass it from left to right.

Don't cut your roll in half, butter it, and bite into it. Instead, break off one bite-sized piece at a time, butter it, and put it into your mouth.

Sip your soup from the side of the spoon—silently. Don't blow on the soup to cool it. Dip your spoon into the soup at the edge close to you, and move it away from you. This makes it less likely to splash on your clothes. Rest your spoon in the soup plate, or on the saucer, wherever there is more room.

Buffet behaviour

Have you ever noticed what happens at a buffet? People attack the food as if it's the last meal they'll ever eat.

Avoid this "animal behaviour" by taking a moment to observe the set-up. Are there two lines, with utensils and plates at either end? Join the smaller line. The food is the same no matter where you're standing.

Don't heap your plate with food. It's okay to start with soup or salad, and return for the main course. If you notice that a particular dish is in short supply, take a small serving. Be sure to use the serving spoon or fork that is intended for each dish.

Don't double-dip. After you've dipped your carrot stick or potato chip into the sauce and bitten into it, don't return it to the bowl for more. Put some sauce or dip onto your plate, and dip from there.

When to talk about business

Business dining isn't only about the food. In fact, the conversation is the most important part. Most business meals are a mixture of small-talk, to allow the diners to get to know each other, and business talk.

The longer the meal, the more time there is for business discussion. However, some evening meals are not about business at all, and may be mainly for building relationships.

Breakfast

A breakfast meeting is an energizing way to start the day with customers. It takes less time and is less expensive than a business dinner. At a breakfast meeting, you can begin discussing business as soon as the coffee arrives.

Lunch

At lunch, make small-talk to get the meal started. (See Chapter 14 for tips on small-talk). Don't bring up business until after everyone has ordered, because you will be constantly interrupted until then.

You can discuss business while you eat, but time your questions so you don't catch your dining partners with food in their mouths.

Dinner

Business dinners are often more social occasions. Generally, at dinner meetings you don't talk business until after the main course. At a business event when spouses or companions are present you may not talk business at all.

Be sure to talk to everyone at your table, especially if spouses and guests are invited—this is common courtesy. Don't forget that your manager or clients will go home with their companions, so you don't want to make a poor impression on these important guests.

Hosting a business meal

Hosting a business meal is similar to organizing a business meeting, except that there is a restaurant and food involved. Just as you would plan your agenda before meeting with a customer, you have to plan your business meal carefully. Choose the restaurant and the time according to your objectives and your customer's availability and preferences.

Remember that whoever extends the invitation is responsible for paying for the meal. If you are invited by others within your company, the most senior person pays the bill. If you are inviting a client, you are responsible for paying. Never leave a guest wondering who is going to pay.

Here are some things to keep in mind as the host:

• Find out your guest's preferences, and offer one or two restaurant choices. For example, say, "I know a great seafood restaurant, and I can suggest an Italian restaurant as well. Which do you prefer?"

• Ask your guests if they have food allergies or any other dietary considerations, such as being vegetarian, or not eating pork or shellfish.

• Select a restaurant that your guest can get to easily, and where parking isn't a problem.

• Consider the time and the day of the week. A busy restaurant at noon on Friday may be so noisy that it will be virtually impossible to have a conversation.

• Cultivate a list of restaurants where the food and service are of high quality. You can get restaurant ratings from a local newspaper or the Internet.

• When travelling, check out the restaurant beforehand by having dinner there the evening before or speaking with the owner. Explain that you will be hosting an important meal, and you want to be sure everything runs smoothly.

- If you are hosting a meal with a client, speak to the server ahead of time so that the bill is brought to you. If you are a woman inviting a male guest, it is especially important to tell your waiter ahead of time, so there is no embarrassment or confusion at the last minute about who will pay.

Canadian Business Concept: When you don't know the restaurants in the area, choose a formal restaurant in one of the better hotels. You will generally have very good service and a large selection of food choices.

Duties of the host

Laura was having dinner with her client, Bob. Bob ordered a salad as an appetizer, but Laura wasn't very hungry and didn't order anything. When the salad arrived, Bob hesitated because Laura wasn't eating.

As the host of the meal, your role is to plan ahead so that everything runs smoothly.

Everyone at the table should eat together and finish together. Ask your guests to order first. If your guests order appetizers, do the same. If you aren't hungry, nibble on something to keep them company.

Other expectations of the host include the following:

- Arrive at least ten minutes early to check on the table.

- Offer your guest the best seat—the one with the nicest view, or away from traffic.

- Plan the seating arrangements. If the group will include two people from your company and one guest, arrange the seating so your guest doesn't have to swivel back and forth between the two of you.

- Don't eat bread or anything else at the table until everyone has arrived. Maintain a pristine table until all the guests are seated.

- If your guests order alcoholic beverages, order a drink as well. It doesn't have to be alcoholic. You can order a soft drink or sparkling water.

- Point out more expensive items so you guests feel comfortable ordering anything on the menu. When you're the guest, order something medium-priced.

Business Buzzwords

- engage (in conversation)
- gender-neutral

Chapter 11 Action Plan

1. How can you give better service to your customers? Write three steps you can take.

   a) _____

   b) _____

   c) _____

2. List three business etiquette tips from this chapter that you will put into action.

   a) _____

   b) _____

   c) _____

3. List three business dining tips from this chapter that you will use at your next business meal.

   a) _____

   b) _____

   c) _____

Office Politics, Gossip, and Romance

When you have groups of people working together, you will encounter office politics, gossip, and romance. This chapter helps you do the right things and stay out of trouble.

In This Chapter

- Dealing with office politics
- Avoiding office gossip
- Office romance

Dealing with office politics

Office politics—wherever you work, sooner or later you'll have to contend with them. From small businesses to large corporations, when you have people working together, office politics appear. This is simply human nature in the workplace.

What exactly are office politics? In the *Oxford ESL Dictionary*, one of the definitions for *politics* is "actions within a group that are done in order to gain power or control."

Steve Applebaum, professor of Organizational Behaviour at the Molson School of Business, describes *office politics* as "the way people behave in an organization." He says that we often think of office politics as tricky, devious, or underhanded, which they can be. But they are really a way of getting resources—and the way someone executes this behaviour can be honest or underhanded.

Professor Applebaum says, "The more political people are, the more powerful they become. Powerful people get more access to the top, and more resources for their employees, so they may gain esteem in their employees' eyes. To become more powerful, they may 'suck up' to their managers, and in some cases they cross the line between doing what's honorable and what's not.

"In life, everyone manipulates other people to get what they want, to a greater or lesser extent. Parents manipulate their children, and managers manipulate their employees. The difference is that some people do something for the other person's good, such as parents manipulating their children to protect them. Managers may get employees to do something for the company's good, which is positive, or coerce people to do something for their personal gain, which can be negative and harmful."

Office politics are about building and using relationships to accomplish something. Most people participate in office politics because they want to gain some advantage. Some people have to take part to survive in their office culture.

This is essentially about competition. Who will get the promotion, the raise, or the best project to work on? The stakes can be high. Play the game of office politics well and you can gain access to the manager's ear, which can further your career. Play the game badly and you can end up losing your job.

However, office politics can also represent a positive force in harnessing people's power to make the business more successful. For example, people can use office politics to launch a new initiative or to create better working conditions.

The pull of office politics

You may decide to stay away from office politics, but sooner or later you will probably get pulled in. Even if you intend to stay uninvolved, your co-workers will try to get you to take a side in their arguments.

At work, just as at home—if you live with a spouse, children, your parents, or a roommate—there are always areas of contention. Issues arise and personalities clash. Whether you like it or not, you may become involved because others pull you into an argument, asking you to support them. You have to decide whether you want to escalate the argument or try to find a solution.

The difference between conflicts at home and conflicts at the office is that, hopefully, the people you live with care about you and have your best interests at heart. In the office, some people may be looking for opportunities to cause trouble, and may not care about you personally.

People working in the same space have different personalities and values that can conflict, and this can lead to internal power struggles. The people in your workplace all have different goals and motivations, and do things that they believe will work out in their best interest. They don't always understand why others want different things than they do.

You may be fortunate to work in a company where everyone gets along most of the time. But there will still be times when you have different people in the mix. For example, your favourite co-worker might go on maternity leave, or your manager might be transferred to another department—suddenly the workplace dynamics will change. It only takes one negative person or one small gripe to change a positive atmosphere to a stressful one.

How to manage office politics

When you see office politics in action, try to figure out the dangers and opportunities of getting involved. For example, if two departments are fighting, the problem probably has nothing to do with you, yet you can still be affected by the outcome. Ask yourself, "Do I stay out of this? Can I keep a low profile?" If you don't know what to do, it's best to keep silent. However, keep in mind that silence isn't really neutral; it implies that you approve of, or agree with, what is taking place.

Office politics can have positive aspects as well. For example, if someone is trying to achieve something a bit risky or dramatic that will benefit the company, getting someone in power to be an enabler or sponsor can help to achieve this goal. Using the grapevine (gossip) can also be positive if you want to plant a good idea in people's minds. Co-workers who may not support you when you present an idea at a meeting may be more receptive when they hear others discussing your idea at lunch.

In almost every work environment, there are people who are negative and like to stir up problems. They may shoot down other people's ideas to make their own ideas look better. They may withhold important information so you look like you aren't doing your job efficiently. They may be ambitious people who are willing to step on others to get to the top.

Here are some thing to watch out for, and strategies to counter the problems:

Problem	What co-workers might say or do	Strategies
Co-workers put down your ideas	"We tried that before. It didn't work." "Has this been proven?"	In a positive tone of voice, ask, "What happened when you tried it before?" or "What do you suggest as an alternative solution?"
Co-workers do not give you information	Someone forgets to give you information or material you need for a meeting.	If you think you are missing information, call the sender right away to ask for it. At the meeting, tell your manager, "I want to do the best job possible. I only had a few minutes to look through this, and I'd like to study it more."

Problem	What co-workers might say or do	Strategies
Co-workers try to fix things for you	Someone criticizes you about little things by trying to "fix" your PowerPoint slides, or filling in missing details in your report.	Limit your access to these people. Thank them in front of your manager for contributing to that section. Find out whether they can actually help you improve.
Co-workers try to negate what they've done to you	Someone does something negative that impacts you, and says, "Don't make a big thing out of it. It's no big deal."	Don't argue—try to find a solution. Say, "I want to make this project a success. How can we work together?" Say, "I understand that you forgot to send me this email. For future emails, please make sure my name is on the distribution list."

Tips for managing office politics

Office politics are impossible to avoid, so you need to find strategies to minimize the effects. Aim to manage the effects of any office politics that relate to you directly.

Be careful with your words and actions, and use common sense. You'll begin to see where you fit into the environment, and how to ally yourself with the right people so you stay out of trouble.

Pay attention

If you're new to the company, you can learn a lot by studying your surroundings. Is the general climate in the office friendly and open, or do people hide out in their offices? Which people gossip? Which people offer a helping hand? In your first three months, watch and listen to those around you. This will help you figure out who you can trust, and who to avoid so they don't spread gossip about you.

Find the movers and shakers

Find out who makes things happen. Get to know them. Learn the techniques that make them successful, because they have already learned how to survive and thrive in your workplace.

Deal with the power-hungry

Most office politics originate with people who hold a lot of power, and blame other people for their mistakes. They often undermine their co-workers to make themselves feel better. The best strategy is to get to know them, and calmly stand up for yourself when necessary. These types are usually impressed by people who stand their ground—never get into a heated argument with them, however.

Become recognized as a serious worker

This doesn't mean working around the clock, but always offer to help. If people see you pitching in after-hours on an important project, they'll appreciate your dedication.

Be like Switzerland: remain neutral

If you hear people taking sides on a politically-charged issue, you don't need to jump in. Be cautious before you speak, as taking sides can create enemies. Be professional, not antagonistic—say as little as possible, and try not to agree or disagree. As soon as there's a pause in the conversation, change the subject.

This becomes especially important when your manager is deciding on an issue that affects everyone, and people are upset about the possible consequences. Don't take sides until you know the facts, which may be different from what people are saying. Remember that there are always two sides to any issue.

Even once you know the facts, let the manager handle the problem unless the consequences affect you and your work directly. If you side with the complainers, in your manager's eyes, you may get stuck in that category of people who are never satisfied. Think carefully and decide whether the issue is worth defending or not.

Don't bash anyone, especially your manager

Sure, there are things you may not like about your manager, and you may be unhappy about a particular run-in. Remember that you have to work as a team with your manager. Complaining to your officemates can escalate into a cycle of whining and feeling sorry for yourselves. You'll also be labelled as a negative person.

When you have an issue with your manager, speak to her directly. (See Chapter 10 for more tips on working with your manager.)

Build alliances

If you have a good idea, get an advocate: someone higher up in the organization who has more influence. Speak to your mentor or an experienced colleague about how to bring up your idea in a positive way. Network internally at parties and company events to build collaborative, long-term relationships. However, be careful not to go above your manager's head. Go to your manager first with your ideas.

Choose your friends wisely

Associate yourself with people who don't cause controversy. Avoid co-workers who start feuds over petty annoyances. Befriend the people who get along with others and do their jobs well.

Don't recruit allies for your grievance

If you have a problem at work, it feels good to have other people support you. However, most people will say they agree with you even when they don't, because they want to avoid conflict. If you have a legitimate grievance, speak with your manager or the person you are in conflict with. Don't pull other people into the fight.

Let things pass

Did someone do something that upset you? Either discuss it with her, or let it go. Don't get mad or try to get even. Of course this is easier said than done, but if you don't want to spend your working days at war with your co-workers, you have to learn to let some things go. Learn to pick your battles, and don't hold a grudge over small things. Chances are the other person has no idea she upset you. Try to shrug your shoulders and get on with your work.

Be prepared to defend yourself

If someone tries to undermine you, don't look the other way and pretend it isn't happening—the problem will just get worse. (See pages 276 to 278 for advice on how to deal with conflict.) Always be calm and polite. Use facts to back up your argument, and keep the discussion job-related. Remain professional, and don't take anything personally.

Stand up against them

When something is clearly wrong, you have to stand up against it. Sometimes a line is crossed, and you can't remain silent. For example, if you witness a co-worker being verbally abused by her manager, you can say,

"No one should speak to you that way. If you want me to, I'll go with you to HR because I was a witness to this behaviour." Most companies have policies to deal with these issues. Refer to them, and stay professional—don't let the situation get personal. (See the Appendix for ways to deal with serious problems.)

Avoiding office gossip

"Did you hear what Amir said about Ted? Did you know that Frank asked Dawn out on a date? Guess who is leaving the company? Can you believe that Raphael got the promotion? It should have been Tami's! And did you hear the latest about our raises?"

Gossip is called by many names: *the grapevine*, *the dirt*, and *the buzz*. Whatever you call it, it's everywhere. When people spend about 40 hours together each week, they're going to talk about who's getting promoted or let go, who's dating whom, what management is going to say next, who got into an argument, and what Person A said to Person B. Some people just love a good story: they are likely to be the source of most office rumours.

People have always gossiped at work. Chatting around the water cooler can be helpful or harmful. On the positive side, staying involved in the office grapevine can help you form bonds with co-workers and find out what's going on behind the scenes. You may hear news about a possible merger, or a new manager in your department. There's nothing wrong with listening, as long as you don't start spreading rumours before you know whether they are true.

How gossip is harmful

Talking about your officemate may seem innocent enough, but most gossip becomes harmful, even when it's not intended to be. People who say negative things about a co-worker are usually attempting to make themselves look good when compared to the co-worker. Or they may be retaliating for a real or perceived slight.

People will always talk about their co-workers, but it's important to ask yourself whether the things you say reflect badly on someone else. Gossip seems to take on a life of its own, with damaging stories spreading like wildfire. Contributing to a conversation that damages someone's reputation can lead people back to you, and if they think you are the source of gossip, your career may be harmed.

If you help spread gossip, you'll hurt your own credibility, especially if the rumour turns out to be false. You'll make enemies and people will think you have nothing better to do than sit around and gossip. Worse, you could hurt your co-workers deeply.

Managers hate gossip because they see it as a waste of time. Employees who gossip are wasting valuable work time and are less productive than those employees who avoid gossiping. Worse, the manager has to spend time putting out fires caused by stories that are untrue or half-true.

You may be wondering, "What's the difference between networking and gossip?" After all, doesn't everyone want to know who's doing what in the company? Isn't this critical to your career success?

The difference is that through networking, you build positive relationships and communicate to improve your performance. Gossiping is a form of networking that can help you develop strategic bonds that help your career. The problem is that gossip often turns malicious. When its main purpose is to say something destructive about someone, it is harmful, negative, and unnecessary.

For example, talking about last night's episode of your favourite sit-com is fun, and helps you connect. Saying something nasty about a co-worker's behaviour, faults, or appearance is harmful gossip.

Canadian Business Concept: The difference between networking and gossip is that networking is positive communication that builds relationships, while gossip is mainly negative communication about people that has the power to hurt them.

How can you protect yourself from becoming part of the gossip grapevine? Here are some strategies:

Get the truth

If you hear something that sounds unlikely, try to track down the person who said it, and see if it is actually true. There's a good chance the story got spun into something bigger, and took on a life of its own. Ask, "Can you please clarify something for me?"

Tell the truth

Don't embellish stories or fabricate them. Before you say something about someone, make sure it's true. Stick to the facts. And if it's negative, don't repeat it, whether it's true or not.

Don't participate

If you are always listening to gossip, people will think you are participating, and see you as a gossiper. If you meet the company gossiper in the kitchen, don't let yourself be cornered for a gossip session. Say, "Sorry, I can't talk now. I have a deadline to meet."

Don't pass it on

If you happen to hear something negative, simply let it stop with you. The fewer people who pass it on, the more quickly it will die. Repeating negative gossip can turn a positive working environment into an unbearable one.

Never discuss someone's religious beliefs or sexual orientation

These can be explosive issues. Check your company guidelines about discrimination, and be careful not to say anything that can get you into trouble.

Remain silent

You don't have to jump in when people are gossiping. You've probably heard the saying, *If you don't have something nice to say, don't say anything at all.*

Think about how you would feel

Imagine that people were gossiping about you. If you'd be upset if a rumour were about you, don't spread it about anyone else.

How to deal with gossip

Most gossip starts with people who don't really know us, and judge us by what they see or hear from others. When these people meet us, they may see that the rumours are not true.

If you feel that someone has the wrong impression of you, try to bump into her at the water cooler or kitchen. Start a friendly conversation. Offer to pour her coffee or get the sugar. As a friendly gesture, bring a bag of cookies for the kitchen, or keep some candies on your desk.

Be friendly and helpful. Offer to help with a small matter. Kill people with kindness. This is one of many ways to change people's opinions of you—it's hard to be mean to someone who is gracious and friendly.

Office romance

What if you find yourself attracted to a co-worker? Shelley Brown, President of Bromelin People Practices, says, "It's natural to be attracted to other people you work with. People often spend long hours together at sales meetings away from the office, and there's an adrenalin high in creating something together. However, you have to go into a relationship with your eyes wide open, and understand that you need an even higher level of professionalism.

"Be aware that if things go badly, you'll have to see the person every day, and everyone in your department will have insight into your personal life. It can leave a black mark on your reputations. Often, one person ends up leaving the company."

The reality is that co-workers spend most of the day—and often part of the evening—together. Because today many people get married later in life, there are more singles working together.

It's inevitable that some flirting will take place, and relationships will develop. People form social networks and get together after work, which sets up the ideal situation for dating. In fact, roughly half of married couples met at work.

Office romances can be the stuff of dreams, or the start of a nightmare. So what should you do if you find yourself attracted to a co-worker, subordinate, or manager, or if someone in one of these positions is attracted to you?

An office romance can be great if things work out well. If two people meet, fall in love, and get married, the story has a happy ending. But what if your judgment goes awry and you find yourself attracted to someone who is married? What if you fall for your manager, or someone you supervise? What if one of you wants to break up, and the other doesn't? You'll have to face the painful consequences of your past relationship, day after day.

Company policies about dating

Find out whether your company has any regulations about colleagues dating. These policies are intended to protect all the parties against legal liability.

Company policies vary. Management at a casual high-tech company full of young employees may be much more liberal about dating than management at an older, established law firm or financial services company.

Jean-Rene Paquette, counsel, deals with employment law. He says, "Directing staff not to date colleagues would be in contradiction with the private life of the employee. Dating a co-worker does not constitute a breach of law, but it may be considered so if this relationship creates problems within the company. It may eventually lead to dismissal, or one employee may have to transfer to another branch, section, or plant."

So, while dating someone at work is not a legal problem, it can create problems, mainly if the relationship does not work out.

According to Shelley Brown, some companies ask their employees to sign a code of conduct as part of their employee contract. It states that employees will behave with the highest ethical standards, in compliance with the values and behaviours of the company.

Understanding the dating signals

Let's say someone new comes to your department. This person is attractive and single, and so are you. Before you start flirting, wait and get to know the person better. In most cases it's acceptable, after you've become acquainted, to invite the person out for a drink or to a movie. If the invitation is declined, stop and leave it at that. Let the other person make the next move.

Repeatedly asking out a co-worker will put you at risk. You'll be seen as a pest or, worse, a harasser. Remember, you are at work, not a singles bar, and there are laws against sexual harassment in the workplace.

If you come from a culture where men and women don't work together on an equal basis, it may be difficult to interpret someone's actions. In Canada, women and men often have casual friendships. They may meet for lunch or coffee, or give each other a quick hug or pat on the back. This doesn't mean they are dating. Be very careful about how you interpret body language and social conversation. Friendly gestures are not necessarily signals of romantic interest.

Canadian Business Concept: Single co-workers often have casual friendships, but they are still professional. People working in the same department may have meals together, or even get together after-hours. Be careful not to interpret a casual gesture such as an invitation to lunch as a romantic overture.

If you aren't sure whether someone wants to date you or just be friends, think about your relationship so far. Is this a person you see regularly? How does this person act toward other people in the office? If she acts the same way toward everyone, she may just have a casual, easy way of relating to people.

Shelley Brown says, "According to many company policies, you can ask someone out once. If the person says 'no,' you are never allowed to ask again, or it can be considered sexual harassment."

What if someone flirts with you and you're not interested? Try to be honest without causing offence. Be careful about saying you want to keep your personal life separate from your office life: if you later start dating someone else, the person who asked you will feel hurt. You can say, "I'm sorry, but I'm not interested in taking our friendship further."

Romance between people of different job levels

A relationship between two people at different job levels, such as a manager and an employee, will raise suspicions, no matter how professional they act in the office. People will immediately begin to talk about unfair practices. The partner who is in the more junior position will have difficulty being promoted without people suspecting preferential treatment. And if the relationship ends on a bad note, the person with the lower-ranking position could raise issues of sexual harassment or abuse of power, which can be traumatizing for everyone involved.

Another concern is that the person with lesser power can be coerced into a relationship, or into staying in a relationship, because of fear of rejecting the person in the senior position, who may remain oblivious to the problem.

Problems can also develop if you work closely with a client or vendor who your company does business with. You may spend a great deal of time together; if a relationship develops and becomes serious, people will gossip. You'll create tension that may cause your company to lose an important account. In this case, you may have to remove yourself from this contract to avoid a conflict of interest.

According to Shelley Brown, in many companies you cannot date someone whom you report to, or who reports to you. If you wish to date the person, you have to transfer to another department, often at a lower level. If there is no opening for you, you may have to leave the company.

This is especially sensitive if one person works in human resources, payroll, or the legal department, where employees are privy to highly confidential information. The assumption is that people share information with the people they are romantically involved with. Brown says, "I've never seen this go well, and unfortunately this often works against the woman, who is frequently in the lower-ranking position."

Other relationships that are a definite *no* include a teacher dating a student, a health care professional dating a patient, and a manager dating an intern.

On the other hand, married couples who work in the same office, or people who were already dating and get married during their employment, are accepted more readily. Perhaps this is because they have a relationship that's already established.

Offices that ban romances

What can you do if your company policy bans office romances? You have several options:

- You can date in secret, and risk being discovered.
- One of you can ask to be transferred to another department without revealing the reason.
- You can end the relationship.
- One of you can find another job.

Even if your company allows relationships, it's usually a good idea to keep your romance under wraps for as long as possible. But don't think you can keep a relationship private for long. Sooner or later, people will find out and the rumours will start. People can spread gossip that will harm your relationship long before you even know whether the relationship will work out. Once you know your relationship is serious, you can speak to your manager and discuss your options.

You may also prefer to keep your relationship private for other reasons. Even though it's against the law to discriminate, in some work environments, same-sex or interracial couples may still be the target of unwelcome remarks from other people. If you don't want to discuss your relationship at the office, simply say, "I'm sorry, but I like to keep my personal life private."

Before you jump into a relationship

Here are some things to consider seriously before you embark on an office romance. The positive aspects are that you already know each other (so you're not going out with a stranger), you probably share some interests, and you know many of the same people.

Don't overlook the negatives, however.

Love can be distracting. If the object of your affection works in the next cubicle, you may find yourselves looking for ways to take coffee breaks or longer lunch breaks together, sending each other personal emails, and generally spending more time trying to get together than concentrating on your work.

Love can compromise your job. When you fall in love with your manager or co-worker, it can be difficult to give or receive constructive criticism about work-related matters without taking it personally.

In the workplace, fair and impartial judgment about issues of pay and performance is needed. If you are personally involved with the person who is supposed to complete your evaluation, that person can be accused of playing favourites. Or, your evaluator may try to compensate by judging you less than fairly. Remember that the person with the lower status job usually takes the brunt of any fall, and can lose her job if things get sticky. And keep in mind that in some offices, the person in the lower position will be immediately transferred to another department, if there's an opening.

Personal stuff spills over. If you have a fight outside of the office, you'll still be working together all day. The conflicting roles of your personal life and professional life can put a strain on both areas. You may find yourself discussing work outside the office, or personal issues at work.

What if one of you gets laid off, or has a problem with a manager at work? This can have an impact on the other person, who may begin to have negative feelings about the company.

Gossip follows you. You may be the centre of office talk when people find out about your relationship. It's difficult to keep a relationship secret, because if you confide in the wrong person, the cat will be out of the bag. Or some astute co-worker will notice you spending a little more time than usual with your partner and put two and two together.

Too much togetherness. Not every couple thrives on spending all their time together. If you see each other all day and then go home together, you may begin to feel smothered. And if you're trying to hide your relationship, having to pretend that there are no feelings between you all day can be a strain.

It's hard to break up. The real problem begins when one person wants to break up. All breakups are hard, but seeing your ex every day at meetings can be particularly gruelling.

You may want to end the romantic relationship, but worry that this will damage your work relationship. After a breakup, people are usually distracted and upset, and your distress can be magnified when you see your former partner every day—there's no way to get the space you need after the split. If things get really messy, one person may take revenge on, or even harass, the other person.

This all spills over to the workplace, which is why so many companies discourage relationships at work.

When you're in love

Sometimes love is so strong that you can't deny your feelings. If this happens, think about how it will affect you and your partner, as well as your co-workers who will have to witness the ups and downs of your relationship.

According to Shelley Brown, if you do start dating, tell your manager. Don't let her find out from someone else. Then, be careful not to mix your personal life with your office life. Don't go out for lunch together or travel to company events in the same car.

Here are more tips for managing your relationship:

Be discreet. With reality shows revealing people's most private moments to the world, it's hard to see the importance of being discreet. But when it comes to office romances, co-workers may feel uncomfortable seeing your displays of affection. Do your best to keep your relationship after-hours. You don't have to lie about it, just don't bring it up during business hours.

Set rules. Discuss with your partner how you will deal with your relationship at the office. Set up some rules for how often you'll meet for lunch, email each other, or try to find ways to work together.

Have an exit plan. Discuss what you'll do if your relationship doesn't succeed. Be honest about how you'll handle a failed relationship. You don't want to be on bad terms with someone you have to see regularly.

Don't compromise your job. This will be particularly difficult, but if your feelings or your partner's feelings make one of you compromise your job, you or your partner may have to look for new employment. If you are serious about the relationship, one of you should ask for a transfer or start looking for another job. Keep your work life professional and separate from your private life.

Stay within the law. Be aware of what is considered sexual harassment, and avoid anything that could invite accusations or lead to a lawsuit. (See Chapter 13 for what constitutes inappropriate behaviour in the workplace.)

Business Buzzwords

- movers and shakers
- put out fires
- take the brunt of the fall

Chapter 12 Action Plan

1. Think about the people in your workplace who spread gossip. What can you do to avoid helping to spread gossip?

    _____

    _____

2. What can you do if you hear gossip about someone you know? _____

    _____

    _____

3. What are some strategies for dealing with co-workers who use office politics to create problems for you? List any problems you have experienced, and some solutions.

Problem	Solution

Avoiding and Solving Problems

No matter how hard you try to prevent them, conflicts and misunderstandings will arise when people work together. This chapter helps you avoid problems, and solve them when they occur.

In This Chapter

- How to deal with difficult co-workers
- Unacceptable workplace behaviour
- Discrimination and harassment in the workplace

How to deal with difficult co-workers

"Learn to stop and reflect, but also develop a thick skin," says Yasmin Meralli, Vice President of Diversity and Workplace Equity at BMO Bank of Montreal, who came to Canada when she was ten years old. "I was a senior manager at a large company at the time, and I'm a conservative dresser. I was working with an executive who was very fashionable, and occasionally I would compliment this woman on her attire.

"One day she arrived at work with a huge garbage bag stuffed with clothes, and said to me, 'You and I are about the same size, and I thought you might like these clothes.' I was astonished. We weren't close enough friends that we would share clothing, and I thought it was quite presumptuous that she would think that I needed clothes because I'm an immigrant.

"Instead of being offended, I decided to make this a learning opportunity. I took the clothes to an immigrant family that was struggling financially. They were very grateful to receive the clothing. I wrote this woman a note, thanking her for the clothes. I also let her know that I had passed the clothing on to a family in need, and suggested to her that there was an opportunity for a larger effort in the company to donate clothing to worthwhile charities.

"I looked at this as a way of educating this woman and getting some good out of a situation, without humiliating her. When something happens from a place of ignorance, I always try to look at it as an opportunity, and ask, 'What can I or others learn from this?'"

Any workplace is filled with different types of people. Some are wonderful to work with. Others are not.

Some people criticize or bully their co-workers. Others talk constantly, never listen, and always try to get the last word in. Some co-workers compete for power and undermine other people's efforts. Some people form cliques and exclude certain co-workers. They gossip behind their co-workers' backs, forget to tell them important information, and try to curry favour with the boss.

All people bring their unique styles and personalities to the workplace, and it's impossible to click with everyone. It's easier to deal with a person who is obnoxious to everyone than an individual who is rude just to you. But whatever the reason, and however it comes across, you have to deal with the situation.

How to deal with criticism

It may not be pleasant, but it's normal for people to criticize each other. In the workplace, sooner or later, someone will criticize you. Acting angry and defensive will hold you back professionally. Remember that the most successful people accept constructive criticism and use it to grow. Here are five steps to receiving criticism:

1. Don't take it personally. Tell yourself, "It's my behaviour that's being criticized, not me."
2. Restate what you've been told: "I hear you saying that you don't like when I …"
3. Ask for suggestions: "What changes do you suggest?"
4. Ask yourself, "Is this valid? Should I make this change because someone has asked me to?"
5. If you agree to make the change, tell the person who has criticized you that you're working hard to change your behaviour.

How to deal with negative behaviour

"If someone reacts negatively to you because you look or sound different, it's worth avoiding a scene," says Tej Singh Hazra, Senior Manager, Corporate Diversity & Inclusion, IBM Canada Ltd. Mr. Hazra was born and raised in the United Kingdom, and came to Canada in 1996.

"Don't put someone in an embarrassing situation. Try to take them aside afterwards, and say something like, "I'm looking for feedback to improve my communication style. What do you suggest?"

Many people are generally positive, but occasionally have something specific to complain about. They may have legitimate grievances. If such a person says something negative to you, try to listen carefully to their complaints.

Sometimes people just want a chance to vent. If you sense that this is the case with one of your co-workers, ask questions and express concern. Offer to help. That alone can turn an angry, frustrated person into someone reasonable and pleasant.

On the other hand, some people are just plain negative. They hate their jobs, they don't like their co-workers, and they don't like life in general. They have a victim mentality, and believe that everything bad happens to them. Sometimes, the only way to deal with these people is to avoid them when possible.

How to stop offensive comments

 At a sales meeting in the United States, a small group of Canadian co-workers were discussing Canada's culture with their American counterparts. A woman from Ontario remarked that "People in Ontario don't really care about French Canadians, and wish they would just leave Canada and start their own country." The French-Canadian woman in the group was deeply offended.

There are times when you can't just walk away from offensive comments, particularly when you or someone you know is being insulted or defamed.

In this case, the French-Canadian woman explained to her Ontarian colleague that the remark was very hurtful. The Ontarian woman was surprised to hear this. She said, "I'm sorry. I was just saying what I believe many people think. I never realized I was offending anyone." This cleared the air and gave the Ontarian woman a new understanding of the impact of her remarks.

If something like this happens to you, don't just stew about it. You have to deal with the situation, or it will poison your relationship with the colleague who made the offensive remark. Ask to speak to your colleague privately. Frame your comments around the remark, not the person. Be specific: "You probably don't realize that when you mentioned my cultural background, I felt offended and hurt. These kinds of remarks are very upsetting to me."

People who make these types of remarks usually don't realize that such things are offensive. Often, just pointing it out will end the problem, as it did in the case above. In fact, having a discussion about a sensitive topic may bring new understanding to the relationship.

Some people don't take hints easily. For people who often bring up sensitive subjects such as race or religion, respond to the remark but don't make personal comments about the speaker. For example, "I think we're talking about race too much here. After all, your manager got the promotion because of her outstanding work, didn't she? It had nothing to do with her race or with office politics."

If the problem continues, you may have to speak to a supervisor or manager. If you are worried about retaliation, make your complaint in confidence. It's unlikely you will change the attitude of the person who made the comment, but she may stop making these remarks in the office.

How to deal with rude behaviour

Paul had a habit of interrupting people during meetings and belittling their comments. One day he made a sarcastic comment after Arjun, the new person in the office, gave his opinion. Arjun was stunned, and didn't speak for the rest of the meeting.

Being treated badly for no apparent reason often comes as a shock. You may retreat or become angry. Once a situation arises, you need to address it—otherwise the problem will simmer below the surface and erupt in a way that is very counterproductive.

Most conflicts start over miscommunication. Someone might make a comment that hurts your feelings, but you might have misunderstood what this person said. Things can grow out of proportion because both of you think you're right, and neither person wants to back down.

If you decide to do nothing, yet you constantly complain to other co-workers, you'll come across as a whiner and complainer. Your manager will wonder why you can't handle the situation—even though he may be part of the problem!

Even worse, you'll be labelled a difficult person. Once you get this reputation, it's hard to get rid of. If the situation continues, your relationships with people in the company could deteriorate, and your manager may become tired of dealing with you. If your boss believes you are a high maintenance employee, you may find yourself replaced by a more cooperative person.

The following are some strategies for dealing with a co-worker's rude behaviour.

Examine your own behaviour

Is this co-worker difficult with everyone, or just with you? If it's just you, are you doing something that may be provoking a negative reaction? Have you been inconsiderate, or caused the person to lose face with his manager without realizing it? If you think this is possible, your first step should be to apologize. Perhaps the conflict is the result of a cultural difference—you may have a different approach to your work than your co-worker, and acted in a way that he didn't understand, or that he misinterpreted.

Talk to a trusted friend

Ask co-workers you trust whether they understand why this person is acting so negatively. It's very hard to be objective about our own actions, and we all have "hot buttons," or areas of sensitivity. Perhaps this person pushed your hot button, or you pushed his. For example, if he's shy about speaking in public, and you made a joke about his forgetting to mention something at the last meeting, he may feel offended.

Assume the best

Maybe you and your co-worker just got off on the wrong foot. Perhaps you got the job he wanted, or maybe he is having personal problems that are spilling over into the workplace. He may be upset about something, but not with you personally.

Seven steps to resolving conflicts with co-workers

If the conflict continues and disrupts your ability to work effectively, you will have to take steps to resolve it. Most of us take the easiest approach: we avoid the person who has been rude to us, or we confront him in a negative way. This often comes back to haunt us.

If you don't feel good about the way someone treats you, you should speak up, and discuss the situation and possible solutions. Be clear about your objective—if it is to stop an unacceptable behaviour, focus on that behaviour until it stops.

Try these seven steps:

1. Define the problem. Separate the problem from your feelings. For example, Arjun would like Paul to stop interrupting him in meetings. This is separate from the feeling Arjun has about the situation, which may be anger or humiliation.

2. Be clear about what you can expect. You can't expect that the person you are in conflict with will experience a miraculous personality transplant, but you can probably get the person to stop interrupting you.

3. Make the first move. First, practise what you will say in a calm voice. You can try this with a friend, or even by yourself in front of your mirror. It will help you state your thoughts calmly. Then, suggest having coffee or lunch together to try to resolve the misunderstanding.

4. Invite the other person to speak first. Try to understand why this co-worker feels wronged, or why he has been criticizing you. Listen attentively to what he says. Most people are more cooperative when they feel you understand them.

5. Speak in a calm voice. Explain your needs and feelings. Stick to the issues and don't criticize or judge the person.

In the situation described on page 275, Arjun could say, "Paul, I felt upset when you interrupted me this morning during the meeting and said that my idea wasn't useful. Perhaps you are not aware that you are doing this. I don't appreciate it and I ask that you please stop." (Beginning with *I*, not *You* makes it easier to encourage a dialogue because you won't put the other person on the defensive.)

6. Remain calm while the other person reacts. Following steps 1 through 5 is usually enough to elicit an apology. If the person argues, becomes defensive, or goes on the attack, simply repeat your message calmly and firmly. There's a good chance that he will have some respect for you for standing up to him.

Speak in a calm voice and remain calm while the other person reacts.

His behaviour is unlikely to change toward everyone, but he'll probably find someone else to pick on. When you stand up to him firmly but calmly, you'll also gain the respect of other people in your office.

7. Reinforce positive behaviour. If the person acts in a more pleasant way after you've had your discussion, compliment him on something.

What if nothing works? Unfortunately, the only thing you can do may be to try to limit the difficult co-worker's access to you. Avoid working with him when possible. Don't volunteer for committees he's on, and choose projects he doesn't work on. Just be careful not to hurt your own career in the process.

How to handle an angry outburst

"Experts tell us that the average explosion of anger is 45 seconds long. Try being on the receiving end of 45 seconds of anger, frustration, and undoubtedly unprofessional behaviour. Sadly, it does happen in the workplace as well as in our personal lives," says Rhonda Scharf, Certified Professional Speaker, trainer, author, and president of ON THE RIGHT TRACK—Training & Consulting.

Here are Rhonda's suggestions for how to remain calm and avoid saying something you will regret when someone yells at you.

- Rather than focusing on your anger, focus on hearing what the other person is saying. Don't just listen to what he is saying—hearing and listening are two totally different things. Hear past the person's words, and try to understand what he is trying to tell you.

- When his outburst is over, avoid the temptation to ask whether he has finished yet. Let two or three full seconds pass before you say anything. Maintain eye contact. Remember that you still have to work with this person in the future.

- When the two to three seconds have passed, and you are sure he is indeed finished, with as much calm as you can muster, say, "I'm sorry you feel this way." This is a beautiful statement. It does not mean that you agree with what the other person is upset about; it does not mean anything, really. You probably are sorry he feels this way, because if he wasn't so upset, you wouldn't be at the receiving end of this explosion, and undoubtedly your day would be better.

- Don't say anything after that. Stop talking. Let him get the final bits of anger and frustration out. Don't become a sponge, and don't absorb what he is saying. Don't defend yourself, or even comment on what was said, at this point.

- If the person who yelled at you is your manager, following these suggestions is your best strategy. But if the screamer is a co-worker, you can simply walk away. Walking away and remaining quiet are two of the most important things you will ever do. You can't say the wrong thing when you walk away. And this gives you time to ensure that you say the right thing when you do speak.

- Before you walk away, you do need to indicate that this person's behaviour is not acceptable and that you both need to do something about it. Say, "I think that we need to talk about what just happened." (Be sure to avoid the word *you*. Don't say, "We need to talk about what you just said." Although it is honest, it will make the other person defensive and he will not listen to what you say.) Instead, say, "Let's get together again in two hours in my office to discuss this." And then leave. If the suggested time or place is not okay with your opponent, leave it up to him to reschedule.

- You do need to deal with the issue. But during an angry confrontation is not the right time. You need to prepare yourself for what you have to say and how you want to say it, and ensure that you are focused on the real issue and not caught up in the emotions of the situation.

Standing up to a bully is very difficult.

Standing up to a bully is very difficult. It can be very hard to take the high road. And while saying exactly what you are thinking can be very easy, refraining from doing so is well worth the effort.

The next time someone at work starts yelling at you, imagine that you are being watched by an invisible camera and strive to look as professional, calm, and in control as you possibly can—on the outside, anyway.

Unacceptable workplace behaviour

 Adolpho was new in the office, and asked a co-worker out on a date. After a few dates, he asked out another co-worker. Within a few months, he had gone out with several women in the company. The women began to compare notes, and Adolpho developed a reputation as a womanizer. Women in the office were reluctant to work with him, because they felt he didn't treat them with respect. This caused a strain on their working relationships with him and with each other.

In some countries, it is common for men to make remarks about sex, or to compliment women on their bodies. One human resources manager described a man who offered his services as a stud, and was shocked to find out that his behaviour was taboo in the Canadian workplace.

There are many workplace behaviours that can cause problems. Sometimes people just don't know when they have crossed the line.

Here are some things you should **not do** in the Canadian workplace. If you do, you risk being accused of harassment.

✗ Make comments or jokes about someone's race, national or ethnic origin, colour, religion, age, sex, marital status, family status, disability, pardoned conviction, or sexual orientation.

✗ Ask someone to date you more than one time. If the person says no, don't ask again.

✗ Look at someone's body in a suggestive way, or stare at any part of a co-worker's body.

✗ Laugh as someone leaves the room, or stop your conversation abruptly when someone enters the room.

✗ Make personal remarks about the way someone is dressed, such as, "You look hot in that sweater" or "I love your legs in that dress."

✗ Say, "If I were single, I'd ask you out."

✗ Label someone with a demeaning name, such as *sweetie*, *honey*, or *babe*, or call someone a slang name related to race, religion, or sexual orientation.

✗ Rub up against someone while dancing at a company party.

✗ Make off-colour remarks or tell sexual jokes.

Offensive behaviour often escalates during company events, when liquor is flowing and inhibitions are down. Often the intent is not to hurt anyone, but people may misread a co-worker's friendly gestures and perceive them as flirtation.

If a co-worker hits on you, you can try a polite rebuff, such as, "I have a boyfriend / girlfriend" (if this is true) or "I'm not interested in taking our friendship farther." You may have to repeat this several times. If the co-worker continues, say, "There's no chance of us going out. Please stop asking me."

It's not necessarily harassment if a co-worker asks you out once and stops when you say no. However, if the person approaches you repeatedly despite your rejections, this can be considered harassment.

Discrimination and harassment in the workplace

Psychological harassment

The Canadian Human Rights Commission defines harassment this way:

> Harassment is any behaviour that demeans, humiliates, or embarrasses a person, and that a reasonable person should have known would be unwelcome. It includes actions (e.g. touching, pushing), comments (e.g. jokes, name-calling), or displays (e.g. posters, cartoons). The *Canadian Human Rights Act* prohibits harassment related to race, national or ethnic origin, colour, religion, age, sex, marital status, family status, disability, pardoned conviction, or sexual orientation.

According to Jean-Rene Paquette, counsel, a single serious incident of such behaviour may constitute psychological harassment if it has the same consequences and if it produces a lasting harmful effect on the employee.

A gesture doesn't have to be aggressive to be considered hostile. For example, an employee could be the victim of repeated comments, actions, or gestures which, on their own, may each seem harmless or insignificant. But the accumulation may be considered harassment.

Psychological harassment can occur at every level of an organization. It can exist between colleagues; people in positions of authority may harass subordinates; and employees may harass their superiors. The parties involved may be individuals or a group of people. The harasser can also be someone from outside the company, such as a client, supplier, or visitor.

Sexual harassment

The *Oxford ESL Dictionary* defines sexual harassment as, "Comments about sex, physical contact, etc. usually happening at work, which a person finds annoying and offensive."

The Canadian Human Rights Commission defines sexual harassment this way:

> Harassment includes offensive or humiliating behaviour that is related to a person's sex, as well as behaviour of a sexual nature that creates an intimidating, unwelcome, hostile, or offensive work environment, or that could reasonably be thought to put sexual conditions on a person's job or employment opportunities.

A few examples are: questions and discussions about a person's sexual life; touching a person in a sexual way; commenting on someone's sexual attractiveness or sexual unattractiveness; persisting in asking for a date after having been refused; telling a woman she belongs at home or is not suited for a particular job; eyeing someone in a suggestive way; displaying cartoons or posters of a sexual nature; writing sexually suggestive letters or notes.

Sexual harassment is frequently more about power than about sex. It occurs in situations where there is unequal power between the people involved, and is an attempt by one person to assert power over the other. Harassment can also occur when an individual is in a vulnerable position because he or she is in the minority—the only woman, member of a visible minority, aboriginal person, or person with a disability—and is, for example, ostracized by colleagues.

Sexual harassment is a serious problem. If you are a victim, go to your human resources department. Your company will want to put an end to the harassment, and will want to avoid a lawsuit that could result if nothing is done to correct the harassing behaviour.

If you are accused of sexual harassment, stop your behaviour immediately, even if you do not think it constitutes harassment.

What to do if you are the victim of harassment

The concept of human dignity means that a person feels respect and self-esteem. According to Shelley Brown, president of Bromelin People Practices, if you feel you have been the subject of discrimination, sexual harassment, or psychological harassment, you should promptly report the charge to your immediate manager, any member of management, or your human resources representative.

You should not have to worry about retaliation through intimidation, coercion, or any other form of adverse action for reporting discrimination, sexual harassment, or psychological harassment, or for participating in the investigation of a complaint.

Here is a resolution process that Brown describes:

1. If you are being harassed, the first step is to speak to the person who is causing the unwanted behaviour. Express very clearly your wish to have the person stop the behaviour immediately.

2. If the problem persists, contact your manager. If the manager is the person harassing you, talk to another member of management or a human resources representative. Whatever route you take, it is important to inform management. In fact, employees are required to report any instance of discrimination or harassment immediately. This enables your company to investigate and resolve any problem promptly and effectively. Information disclosed during the investigation is confidential.

3. You can make a formal written complaint. For assistance in writing this report, you may want to meet with your human resources representative.

The following is an outline of the investigation process:

1. Within 48 hours of receiving the complaint, your HR department should begin to investigate it.

2. The investigation procedure should include discussions with the person who is complaining and with the person who is being complained about, as well as any potential witnesses to the inappropriate behaviour.

3. Investigations should be conducted in an objective, impartial, and confidential manner. If possible, interviews of witnesses should take place in a part of the workplace away from the workstations of the person who is complaining, the accused harasser, and any witnesses.

4. To prevent future challenges to the company's decision, the investigators should document their work. They should create a file with a report that states who was interviewed, what questions were asked, what statements were made, the conclusions about the complaint, and the resolutions and appropriate actions to take.

If you are accused of discrimination or harassment

If someone informs you that your conduct is offensive, take it seriously. Stop the offending behaviour immediately, and attempt to resolve the problem with the person who you have offended.

Jean-Rene Paquette says, "When attempting to resolve the matter, you should always have a witness and someone from the human resources department present with you, and document everything.

"An employee found guilty of harassment would be reprimanded, and may lose his job. It usually takes more than one event for this to happen, but depending on the level of harassment, it might be construed as sufficient grounds for termination with cause.

"If the harassment stops after the first warning, the person could continue to work in the same department. In companies large enough, the harasser could be transferred to another location."

Always take steps to resolve any conflicts with your co-workers. Don't let problems fester. Also, become familiar with the labour laws of your province and your company's policies. Ask your supervisor or HR representative—not your co-workers, who may be ill-informed—about these policies.

Business Buzzwords

- hot button
- take the high road
- vent

Chapter 13 Action Plan

1. List one or more behaviours you have seen or experienced in the workplace, such as criticism, or rude or negative behaviour. Write down a new strategy that you could use when you witness this behaviour.

   _____

   _____

2. What are some new strategies you can use to deal with conflicts with your co-workers? Write down any new ideas you can try.

   _____

   _____

Chapter 14

Networking, Small-talk, and Relationship Building

In This Chapter

- How networking can help your career
- Networking within your organization
- Networking outside of your organization
- How to network in Canada
- How to make connections at networking events
- How to use small-talk to build relationships

How networking can help your career

Now that you're becoming comfortable in the Canadian workplace, you may be thinking that you're all set. You just have to continue to work hard, and you'll have a long and successful career, right?

Not so fast. Skills, talent, and job knowledge are very important for success. But these are only part of the picture. If you want to get ahead, you have to build a wide network inside and outside your company. There's a popular saying: *It's not what you know, but who you know.* Even more important, your success can be determined by *who knows you.*

In a business world that is becoming increasingly impersonal, networking helps you build rewarding business relationships that are crucial to success. You'll benefit both personally and professionally, and make enjoyable social connections. Many networks are also active in helping the community, so you'll feel good while helping yourself. If you want to make more friends in Canada, networking is a great way to do it.

If you work in sales, networking is vital to finding new clients and building a broad base of people to work with. And networking at your national sales conference can help you connect with people in other parts of your company, such as different regions and divisions.

Cory Garlough, Vice-President of Global Employment Strategies at Scotiabank, believes strongly in the power of networking, both inside and outside of your organization. Scotiabank has many different networking groups, including resource groups for women, for different ethnic groups, and for LGBT (lesbian, gay, bisexual, and transgender) employees.

"These groups give employees a chance to connect and uncover different skills and areas of the bank," says Mr. Garlough. "At our networking events, people wear name tags that say, 'I want to learn more about …' to encourage them to share information. Scotiabank is a big organization, but after learning about different sections of the bank, some people get jobs in new areas that they never knew about."

Scotiabank also sponsors many business events in the community, such as Cricket Canada, Scotiabank Caribana, Masala! Mehndi! Masti! and programs such as the Toronto Region Immigrant Employment Council and ACCES Employment Services.

"We encourage employees to give back to the community, and it's a great way for them to meet and make strong connections," adds Rania Llewellyn, Vice-President of Multicultural Banking at Scotiabank.

Through networking you can …

- build connections and relationships inside and outside your company

- hear about sales leads

- increase your job security because you will have a network of professionals to turn to if your company downsizes

- constantly upgrade and polish your skills by listening to speakers at your networking groups

- make contacts that may help you discover good job opportunities that aren't posted publicly

- impress prospective employers because you participate in professional organizations and community groups

As an added bonus, you'll make new friends, and find professionals and services that can help you and your family. For example, in casual conversation with people you meet, you can find out about the best schools in your neighbourhood, or a trustworthy place to get your car serviced.

How to network in Canada

"Networking is the number one Canadian sport and best way for a newcomer to build a community," says Judith C. Hart, Marketing Specialist at the Toronto District School Board. She came to Canada from Hungary three years ago. "I believe you have to network all your life—it's the recipe to success and that is how communities evolve. Join several organizations, such as a cultural association, a business association, and an online business association such as LinkedIn. You have to be resourceful. Relationship building is an art."

You may be used to networking in your culture, and find that networking in Canada is different. For example, in some cultures people have large families and network mainly with family and friends. When someone is looking for a job, they turn to their extended family for help.

Catalina Duque, a Graduate Leadership Program associate at RBC Royal Bank, suggests, "When you are born here, you have a natural network. Immigrants don't have that background, so we have to make an effort to meet people. It's okay to join associations in your own culture, but also be open to meeting new people, so you won't be isolated. Learn about the sports here and attend games. Invite people for coffee to build relationships."

In some cultures, people network mainly within their alumni associations. Canadians do this as well, but for people who want to succeed in the workplace, professional associations are important avenues for networking.

Almost every industry and profession has at least one networking association, and often there are several associations with large memberships. These associations generally have annual conferences, and may also have other events during the year. Joining a professional association gives you the opportunity to do the following:

- Talk shop and get the latest information about your industry.

- Get career leads for new job opportunities.

- Find out how to solve problems or do your job better.

- Showcase your skills and knowledge by giving workshops and presentations on your areas of expertise.

- Put your skills and accomplishments forward to people who can help you in your career.

- Observe the leaders in your profession. Watch them in action to see how they speak, act, and dress.

"Attending these meetings gives you an idea of how senior executives carry themselves, and how you stand in comparison. It's very good exposure to hear them talk and to interact with them," says Gautam Nath, Director of Cultural Markets at Environics Research Group.

Mr. Nath says, "It's tempting to network within your own community because you feel comfortable and speak the same language. But don't rely only on this network. People from your community will have the same perspectives as you have, and you won't learn the skills you need for the Canadian workplace. It's a little like the blind leading the blind.

"Reach out to new organizations and associations to get the real benefits of networking in Canada."

Networking within your organization

"Networking is corporate survival," says Sandra Bizier, Account Manager with TD Commercial Banking. "You should constantly network with everyone at your company, from filing clerks to managers. Learn their jobs. Treat receptionists with the same respect you treat vice-presidents. You never know who is talking to whom, and who can boost you up the ladder."

According to Bizier, you should always network at meetings and company events. At any meeting you attend, say hello to each person. Make eye contact and shake hands. At the end of every meeting, make eye contact and shake hands again as you say goodbye.

Treat receptionists with the same respect you give vice-presidents.

Tina Bakin, Senior Manager of Human Resources at TD Bank Financial Group agrees. "We hold networking events so that employees can mix and mingle with company leaders. This gives employees visibility and exposure to leaders in the organization and to each other, which they may not get otherwise. It's a great opportunity to focus on career development."

After-hours events are good opportunities to network with your team. Doing this will help you develop team cohesion and expand your personal network. Colleagues will become three-dimensional to you, and you'll discover their hidden talents, which you can use productively in business. You'll also develop friendships, and so your teammates will be more willing to help you out. Regular events such as holiday parties, sales meetings, and birthday parties in your department are all occasions to network and build relationships.

Jane Lewis sees networking as a key to working successfully in Canada. The Human Resources Country Manager for P&G (Procter & Gamble) says, "We have many networks at P&G, and we encourage their growth. For example, we have an Asian network, a Latin network, a French network, and a Black Professional network. These networks provide mentorship and help employees grow more quickly. The people involved are enthusiastic and highly skilled, and help their members think strategically about the company's goals and how they fit in. What's more, people are passionate about their networks."

Lewis's advice to immigrants is, "Take advantage of any networks that exist in your company. Join a network and get involved. The networks help you think strategically and improve your leadership skills. It's a win-win situation."

Extend yourself in your company by getting involved in the social committee that's planning the office party, or by volunteering at the food bank that your company supports. You'll meet people from different parts of your organization, and make new friends and allies.

Alan Kearns, author of *Career Joy*, says you should look for people who are successful in your organization, and try to connect with them. Kearns says, "Ask yourself: Who do I naturally align with in this company? Who do I admire? What skills do they have? Let people know if you need mentorship. But remember that mentorship in not just one way. See how you can help these people, so it's a give-and-take situation."

Networking outside of your organization

 When Valeria first came to Canada, she didn't know many people. She joined a networking group in her industry. Although she enjoyed meeting the members of the group, it took a while to make real connections. Then the president of the group asked for volunteers to join the executive board. Valeria volunteered to be on the board's membership committee. This meant that she had to reach out to other people in her industry, and also that she worked closely with other executive members. She began to forge strong business relationships that helped her increase her sales. Networking brought her many benefits, both professional and personal.

There are many types of networking groups, and each offers different benefits.

If you work in sales, or if you are a professional such as an accountant or engineer, networking can help you bring more clients to your firm. This will definitely boost your career, because you will be contributing to the bottom line. Look into joining your professional association, and at least one outside networking group, such as a chamber of commerce.

If you do not work with outside clients, you should still join at least one professional networking association in your industry, or a cultural or community organization. Also be sure to take advantage of networking opportunities within your organization. These could be at annual company events, or in ongoing social, sports, or special-interest groups.

Canadian Business Concept: Once you join a networking group, you'll hear about other similar organizations. Most people who network belong to more than one group, and most groups are interested in increasing their membership.

Finding a networking group

Ask your manager and co-workers about organizations in your industry. They will be happy that you are taking an interest and want to keep your skills and knowledge up-to-date. Also ask people outside your company to suggest groups, or search online for other groups to join. Here is an overview of the different types of networking associations.

Professional associations

Almost every industry and profession has at least one networking association, from the aerospace to the pharmaceutical industry.

Benefits: You'll meet like-minded professionals who can help you increase your knowledge of your industry and keep up-to-date about changes in legislation and practices in your field. You'll also be well-informed about job and sales opportunities.

Board of trade / Chamber of commerce

Most cities have a main board of trade, with many smaller chambers for the city's various boroughs. For example, the Toronto Board of Trade has local chapters in North York, Scarborough, and Etobicoke.

Benefits: You'll meet business people from a variety of industries who can help you bring new customers to your company, and you'll gain professional skills and knowledge through the high-calibre speakers. Additionally, if you want to change jobs or industries, you'll have a network of people to help you.

BNI (Business Network International)

This is the world's largest networking group, whose purpose is to help people build their businesses through referrals. It's valuable for sales representatives, business owners, and professionals such as lawyers and accountants.

Benefits: In each chapter, only one person per profession is allowed (for example, one financial planner, one graphic designer), so you won't be competing with other members for business. Groups meet once each week for serious networking. Members help each other generate new business, while at the same time forming long-lasting relationships.

Local networking groups

Every major city has a host of other networking groups of various sizes and types. They may meet every other week, once a month, or a few times a year.

Benefits: You can find a group that meets your needs, close to where you live and work. You'll make new contacts and friends.

Specialized groups

In addition to professional groups that cater to one profession, you can find a group with another particular focus. For example, there are many women's groups which are subdivided into groups for women entrepreneurs, working moms, women in corporate positions, and women in the health care industry, to name just a few. There are also groups for young professionals and entrepreneurs, young presidents … the list is endless. You'll also find immigrant groups, such as the Canadian Immigrant Network, which can provide support and resources.

Benefits: Your group will have its own special culture. For example, new moms have different business challenges than young entrepreneurs. Find a group that supports you, and where you have fun and find camaraderie.

Meetup groups

Whatever your interest, you'll find other people who share your passion. An online search of "Meetup groups Vancouver" reveals a wide variety of meetup groups, including a tea enthusiasts' group, the Vancouver Tall Club, environmental groups, and ESL groups. You can join an existing group or start your own. To find out more, search for "Meetup groups (your city)."

Benefits: You'll make connections and have fun as you learn new skills.

Community service clubs

Kiwanis, Rotary, and other community service clubs are dedicated to helping the community. They are often rich sources of business contacts as well.

Benefits: You'll make a meaningful contribution outside the workplace while you network and make new friends and business contacts. You'll improve your community and make life more fulfilling for others.

School, athletic, pet, hobby, and special interest groups

If you have children in school, chances are the school has a parent group you can join. Do you have a dog? Take your pet to a training class and meet other dog owners. Whatever your interest, there are informal groups you can join where you can network.

Benefits: You'll be surprised at how often you will make valuable business connections and find new friends by networking with people who have the same interests and passions that you do. You can also get introduced to the people who your connections know—many people find new jobs this way.

Cultural associations

From the Chinese Professionals Association of Canada to the Mexican Business Association of Canada, these groups provide opportunities for interaction and networking. Large cities also have specialized chambers of commerce for many cultures, such as the Greek Chamber of Commerce, the Mexican Chamber of Commerce, the Latin American Chamber of Commerce, and many more.

Benefits: You'll find that cultural associations will help you integrate into and contribute to Canadian society. They can aid your career and your professional development, as well as represent your ethnic community

Toastmasters International

This is a great organization if you want to improve your public speaking. Look for a branch close to you. It may be located in a surprising place, such as a university or your own company. For example, Scotiabank hosts Toastmasters meetings for its employees.

Benefits: If you are shy about speaking, or want to speak more professionally, you'll gain confidence and public-speaking skills that will be of enormous help to your career.

Alumni associations

Here you can connect with people you went to university with, and help each other make new connections.

Benefits: You already have a natural point of connection with the other members. These associations often do a great deal of community work as well.

Online networking

If you already network on MySpace and Facebook, you know the power of social networking online. Online networking can help you in business as well. A popular site is LinkedIn, which helps people connect and build professional relationships. Immigrant Networks is another website—specifically for immigrants to Canada—that can help you make business connections.

Benefits: You don't have to leave your house to network. You can access people across Canada and around the world, and ask people you know to refer you to their contacts.

How to network in Canada

 Angela was invited to a business women's breakfast by Melissa, a co-worker. At first Angela hesitated. The thought of meeting strangers was frightening. She didn't know what to say or do, but she decided to try it out. When they arrived, she stuck by Melissa's side. Melissa introduced her to several people who were very friendly. By the end of the morning, she felt more comfortable approaching people on her own.

If the thought of networking makes you break out into a sweat, you're not alone. It can be intimidating to enter a room filled with strangers and make small-talk.

Studies show that over 40 percent of adults feel nervous about meeting new people. One survey showed that about 75 percent of people feel uncomfortable at business and social events.

If you come from a different cultural background, you may be proficient at networking, but not sure about the rules of networking in Canada. This next section gives you the skills and techniques for meeting and greeting people, and making small-talk. These tips will help you feel confident when you network.

Setting networking goals

Just as you set goals for other areas of your business, you should think about your networking goals. If you take time to network, you should think about what you are trying to accomplish.

You may want to

- learn more about your industry
- gain professional skills
- meet new potential clients
- strengthen relationships with clients
- connect with colleagues you don't see often
- build relationships with people from other departments in your company
- meet people higher up in your company

Your goal at a networking event should be to make contacts and build relationships. If you are in sales, don't try to sell anything at the networking event—networking is for gathering information. When you connect with someone who has business potential for you, ask for a business card and arrange for a workplace meeting, or a lunch or dinner meeting.

Always follow up. Nothing happens until you follow up.

Set achievable goals for yourself. For example, you can decide that you want to meet three new people and converse with them for approximately five minutes each. When you reach your goal, reward yourself by spending a few minutes talking to a colleague or have something good to eat. After all, you've reached your goal!

If you know the meeting planner, you can sometimes get a list of the people who will be attending the event. This way you'll know in advance who you want to meet.

At the event, spend a few minutes chatting with each person you meet. Then move on and talk with someone else. People understand that you aren't there to spend the evening with them, and won't be offended when you disengage after a few minutes. If you want to continue your discussion with someone, set up a time to get together later. Make sure to follow up because the business relationship can't progress until you have made contact outside of the networking event.

Who to approach, and how

If approaching strangers makes you feel nervous, here are a few tips to make it easier:

- Position yourself near the door. This way, you get to talk to a lot of people for a short amount of time.

- The best person to approach is someone standing alone. He or she is probably feeling awkward, and will be grateful to be rescued when you approach.

- There's an old saying: *Two's company, three's a crowd.* Two people who are deep in conversation may not want to be interrupted. Look for groups of three or more people to approach.

- Look for a group of people who are enjoying themselves. Approach the group and make eye contact with someone. Once you make eye contact, people will usually part to let you in. Then you can smile and say, "Hi, I'm ..." If you can't make eye contact, wait a moment or look for another group.

- When you approach people, face them directly so you can maintain eye contact. Don't cover your chest with folded arms or papers, because people perceive this as closed body language. When you keep your arms down, the unconscious perception is that you are opening your heart to others.

- People always congregate at the bar or food table. Approach the table and make positive comments about the food, the decor, or the event.

- If you come to the event with a colleague, once you arrive, you should separate to make new contacts and join up later. If you're shy about approaching people on your own, remember that people go to networking events because they want to make new connections. Most people are very welcoming if you approach them.

- Keep moving around. If you sit down or stand in the corner of the room, no one will see you. Welcome and encourage contact by showing that you are open to meeting people. To invite interaction, make eye contact and smile warmly.

- Try to become comfortable introducing yourself to others. Most people have been in your shoes, or are having their own first taste of networking at that moment, and will sympathize. Ask general questions about the function, why other people are there, or whether they have been there before. Most likely, someone will ask you about yourself and what you do.

- Remember to be sincere, smile, make eye contact, and show interest by listening. Expect acceptance and you will be accepted

Develop a tagline to capture attention

At BNI (Business Network International) meetings, each person has 30 seconds to stand up and present a "commercial" about his business. Since everyone wants to make the most of their 30 seconds, members put a lot of thought into how to present themselves quickly, and often with a touch of humour. They develop tag lines to tell people what they do. For example, Ron, who sells office supplies, says, "You call, I haul." Perry, an accountant says, "I'm an accountant you can count on." Who doesn't want that? And Diana, a naturopath, says she helps her clients "connect with calm." What a way to remember what she does!

How to introduce people

 Marco Della Rocca is a master at introducing people. He always begins by saying something positive about each person, so they are happy to meet one another. For example, when introducing Rosa to Jeff, he'll say, "Rosa, this is Jeff. He helps companies improve their training programs. And Jeff, I'd like you to meet Rosa. She's an excellent translator who can help you translate your documents between English and French." Now Rosa and Jeff both have some questions they can ask each other, and Marco can gracefully excuse himself from the conversation if he wants to. And since they both know Marco, they can talk about him as well.

At a business event you will often have to bring people together by introducing them to each other. On the following page are some ways to make this easier.

Introduce by hierarchy

Say the name of the person with the most authority or highest rank first. For example, at a national meeting you may be introducing your manager to someone you met in another division of your company. You would say, "Steve Jones (product manager), this is Doug Wong (a new sales representative)." You show respect to people by saying their name first.

If you are not sure who has more importance, you can fall back on tradition. Say the name of the older person, or the woman, first. For example, "Steve (40 years old), this is Doug (30 years old)," or "Nina, this is Steve."

Remember to look at each person as you make the introduction. First, look at the person with higher rank and say his name. Then, look at the other person you are introducing.

The customer is most important

In Canada, the customer is the most important person in a business relationship—even more important than the president of a company. If someone from your company and one of your customers are meeting for the first time, introduce the customer first by saying, "Mr. White, (customer), this is Lina Dahl, our president."

Help them connect

Always give people a way to start the conversation. For example, you could say, "Mr. White, of ABC Corporation, is at this conference to find out about …" At a more social event, if you know something about the people you are introducing, you can say, "Kai, you're a sailor. You might want to give Stephanie some tips as she is planning a sailing trip for this summer."

How to make connections at networking events
Business card etiquette

 Ken was at a networking event. He walked up to someone he didn't know, handed her a business card, and said, "I'm in Internet marketing." He asked for people's cards, and immediately stuffed them into his back pocket without looking at them. Without knowing it, he had insulted everyone in the group.

Exchanging business cards is part of the protocol of many business interactions, but the way you present your business card varies from culture to culture.

Most Canadians treat business cards casually. They may glance at a business card, or not even look at it before putting it into a pocket.

In countries like Japan, this is considered impolite. The Japanese treat business cards with great respect. They take time to examine a card carefully and make comments while accepting it. They also use both hands to present their card face out so people can read it.

Although Canadians do not behave as formally as the Japanese do, handling a business card with respect is a great way to show people that you appreciate both the card and the person presenting it.

Business cards are an ideal way to find out more about other people. You'll verify their name and the spelling, find out where they are located, and define their job title. Business cards also provide up to five ways to reach your new contact, including office phone number, cellphone number, fax number, email address, and mailing address.

Before you attend a networking event, make sure that you have some of your cards handy, and that they are in good condition. Don't hand out a crumpled or stained business card with information crossed out—this makes a poor impression.

When you receive someone's card, look at it and comment on it. Mention the person's specialty or the location of his workplace. Put the card carefully into a business card holder or briefcase, not your back pocket where you will sit on it. Taking time to look at people's cards shows your interest in them and makes them feel special.

In many cultures it's considered rude to write on business cards. If you must write on a card, write on the back—never on the front—and ask the card owner for permission first.

Canadian Business Concept: To exchange cards, you don't need to ask, "Can I have your card?" A polite way to phrase the question is, "What's the best way to reach you?" People will most likely offer their cards and you can offer yours.

Getting the names and titles right

Have you ever been introduced to someone whose name you didn't catch? We frequently miss names and then feel embarrassed about asking for the information again.

This often happens because during the introductions, we are thinking about the impression we are making. We aren't focused on the other people, and we never even hear their names.

Here are some tips that will help you remember the names of the people you meet:

- When you introduce yourself, say your name slowly and clearly. Pause between your first and last names. People tend to model each other subconsciously, and the other person may say his name more clearly as well.

- Make sure you understand the names as people are introducing themselves. If you didn't hear someone's name, ask him to repeat it, then say it immediately afterward to make sure you have it right.

- Ask for help. If you meet people whose names are unusual or difficult to pronounce, ask them to help you pronounce the names correctly. They will feel flattered that you care.

- Look at people's business cards or name tags. When you see a name written down, it's easier to remember.

- Write down the names of the people you meet in a notebook. This will help them stick in your mind.

- Use the name three times in conversation: "Nice to meet you, Miguel." "What kind of architecture do you do, Miguel?" and "It's been a pleasure talking with you, Miguel." Now it should be fixed in your mind.

If you meet someone who you know slightly but whose name you can't remember, don't panic or feel bad. Simply say, "I know we've met before, but my mind has gone blank. Please remind me of your name."

Never embarrass anyone by asking, "Do you remember me?" When someone seems to be struggling to recall your name, quickly reintroduce yourself. The other person will be grateful and may give you his name in response.

Help people remember your name. Your name may be unusual or difficult for some people to pronounce. Help others by spelling it, writing it down, or handing them your business card. You can smile and say, "I know it's difficult," but don't make a big deal of it. If possible, associate your name with something, or mention something your name rhymes with. When you do this, others will feel more at ease with you, and you can start a conversation about their names as well.

Canadian Business Concept: Pin your name tag on your right shoulder. When you shake hands, people naturally turn slightly, and they will see your name tag easily.

How to eat at networking events

At an industry cocktail party, Ryan approached a person standing near the canapé table, intending to introduce himself. The business woman at the table had her mouth full, so she put up her hand to stop Ryan from approaching.

Don't try to network and eat at the same time. It's difficult to make conversation while you juggle food and drink, and people will be less likely to approach you. Networking isn't about eating, it's about meeting people. If you are hungry, try to eat something before the event. Or sit down and eat when you arrive, and then get up and network.

If you still plan to eat and talk, here's how to do it:

- Choose foods that are easy to eat, like cut up vegetables, or cheese and crackers.

- Avoid anything greasy or sticky, such as fried chicken wings. Be careful of very hot canapés that can burst open or fall apart in your fingers. Also be careful of cherry tomatoes. They are likely to squirt tomato juice on the person in front of you.

- Always keep your right hand ready to shake hands. Hold cold beverages or your wine glass in your left hand. Keep a napkin in your left hand as well, so you can wipe your fingers after you eat.

- To hold both a plate and a drink, use the layering technique: Hold a small plate in your left hand. Put your wine glass on the plate and anchor it with your thumb. Put a napkin under the plate and hold it there. Every time you eat, wipe your fingers on your napkin. Voila! Now you can add finger food to your plate, and still keep your right hand available for shaking.

 Canadian Business Concept: Whenever possible, eat before you arrive at the event, or sit down and eat, and then get up and network. Networking is about meeting people, not about the food.

How to use small-talk to build relationships

"I learned how to make small-talk by selling water!" says Marvi Yap. When she first came to Canada from the Philippines, she was very shy. "In my country, we don't really make small-talk, and we don't normally talk to strangers, but I knew that I needed to learn how to make small-talk here.

"I was working at the Royal Alexandra Theatre. One day my boss asked me to help her. I said, 'Sure!' She asked me to get up on stage at intermission and yell, 'Water for Sale!' I was scared, but I did it, and it helped me feel more confident talking to people.

"Years later, when I started my own advertising agency, AV Communications, I learned how important it is to make small-talk. Before we talk business, I ask clients, 'How is your health? How are your parents and children?' This puts people at ease because they know I care about them as people—not just as clients."

How to prepare for small-talk at business events

"I didn't know who Martha Stewart was," says Nazia Bundhoo, who immigrated to Canada from Mauritius about six years ago.

"Professionally, I didn't find it very different to work in Canada. But socially, I didn't understand the topics of conversation. I was really lost when people told jokes or talked about TV shows. I had never heard about late night shows, and didn't understand the concept."

Nazia offers this advice for making small-talk:

- Observe, listen, and try to understand the topic before you speak.
- Read newspapers and listen to radio and TV news so you have a "heads up" on any topic.
- Learn about things that are important to Canadians. It's good to know who the major hockey players are, and who scored in the latest game.

"Become informed. It's your civic duty to know what is happening in Canada, since you chose to live here," Nazia says.

Making small-talk is an important business and social skill. It is the way you connect with other people. Small-talk builds the bridge to big-talk, which can be a business conversation, or a way to make a new friend.

Before heading out to a business or social event, you probably think about what you will wear, how you will get to the event, and even where you will park. How often do you plan what you will say once you get there?

Before the event, plan three or four conversation topics. This will save you from a frantic search for a new topic when the conversation grinds to a halt.

- If you are going to a business event, be sure that you know what's happening in your industry. Read professional journals and newsletters in your field to keep up-to-date.

- If you are visiting a new city, find out about local events. Learn about the home teams, movie releases, and books and cultural events that are in the news.

- Learn about current events. Read the local and national newspapers. Skim the headlines and top stories for topics of interest.

- Watch the local and national news so you know about new developments in your vicinity and all over the world.

- Look at three main types of magazines: news magazines, business magazines, and general interest magazines. This will give you plenty of conversation starters.

- Use a funny story from the newspaper or a personal anecdote to start a conversation. Humour brings people together.

How to begin a conversation

"I couldn't believe how much people talk about the weather here," says Felix Quartey, a loans operations officer at CIBC. I've lived in Japan and Australia, and people talk about the sunshine. When I arrived in Canada, I was fascinated by how much people talk about the weather in winter. People are always checking the temperature and the wind chill factor, which I never heard of before. (Mentioning the weather is) an easy way to begin a conversation."

If you become tongue-tied while searching for the perfect opening line, here's a simple way to begin: talk about the weather. It's a standard opening in Canada because it works. Everyone has something to say about the latest snowstorm, rain, heat wave, or glorious spring day, and this is a way to make an instant connection.

Another easy way to start the conversation is to begin with your shared experience, which is the event you are attending. Start by asking about the person's relationship to the event or group.

Here are some simple questions to ask to start a conversation:

- Are you a member of this organization?
- Have you been to this event before?
- Have you been to this place (city / restaurant) before?
- What did you think of the speaker?
- How do you like the event so far?
- What's the most interesting thing you've learned so far?
- How do you know (name of host or hostess)?

Any of these questions give you an instant connection because you've had the same experience.

A compliment is another great opener. If you aren't sure what to say, and the other person wears glasses, you can say, "Great glasses!" Many people express their individuality through their choice of eyewear. You could also compliment another person's unusual tie or necklace, but be careful about commenting on anything too personal. A woman can compliment another woman on her shoes, purse, suit, or jewellery, but a man should be more careful not to comment on anything that can be taken the wrong way, such as saying, "That's a nice blouse." The woman wearing the blouse may think that the man is trying to date her.

You can always comment on the wonderful hors d'oeuvres at the event or the ambience of the venue. Be pleasant and positive. No one wants to start a conversation with someone who is complaining about the food, the music, or the atmosphere.

How to find points of connection

 Kathleen was at an industry event. She didn't know anyone and was feeling uncomfortable. Then she noticed that the guest speaker was standing by himself. She summoned up her courage, and walked over and introduced herself. The conversation was a bit stilted at first, until the speaker mentioned his children in an offhand way. Kathleen immediately picked up on that, and asked about his children: How many did he have? How old were they? What were their interests?

The guest speaker became very animated as he talked about his children. Clearly, they were very important to him. And during their discussion, he and Kathleen found out that they both had children who loved to swim, and were close in age. They discussed swim classes and the best local pools. Within a few minutes they were talking like old friends because they had found a point of connection.

When you begin talking to someone, listen carefully to the subjects that he brings up. This will give you important clues about his interests and open up new avenues for discussion.

If the people you are talking to mention a new topic that is unrelated to your conversation, this topic is probably important to them. By asking about it, you give them a chance to speak about something that concerns them.

When this happens, people generally talk easily and freely. As an added benefit, they think you are a brilliant conversationalist because you are a good listener.

You can make powerful connections when you show sincere warmth and interest in the topics that your conversation partner brings up.

Canadian Business Concept: Look for things you have in common by listening carefully. When someone brings something up, ask about it. The conversation will flow easily after that.

Conversation patterns that encourage communication

Chapter 6 explored conversation patterns in Canada, and mentioned how a conversation is like a Ping-Pong game. Each person takes a turn to speak, and then listens while the other person speaks. Without this give-and-take, one person may end up delivering a monologue.

Here are some ways to keep the conversation going:

- When someone asks you a question, add something more (an interesting anecdote or a question posed to the asker) to keep the conversation going. Don't just say *yes* or *no*—this makes the other person do all the work.

- If you don't know what to say, ask others about themselves. Most people love to talk about themselves. As they talk, encourage them by saying, "Please tell me more about …" or "How interesting." Lean toward the person slightly and nod your head. Use verbal prompts such as *uh huh*, *yes*, or *I see*.

- Make eye contact. If you find it too intense to look into the speaker's eyes, look at any part of their face, from hairline to chin. Break eye contact momentarily when you are speaking, then return your gaze to the speaker. Use open body language, and remember to smile.

- Don't make negative remarks about what people say. Instead of, "We already tried that. It didn't work," respond with, "How would that work?"

- Don't try to top every story with a better one. Even if you have a similar story to tell, it's okay to let the other person have the spotlight.

- Don't interrupt people. This is the number one irritant in western culture. Just because someone pauses doesn't mean he has finished. If people frequently say, "Please let me finish," you may be guilty of interrupting without being aware of it. If you come from a culture where people have to interrupt each other to speak, try to hold yourself back from speaking too much or interrupting too often. You'll have more enjoyable conversations.

- Respond to what people say with attention and energy. Your enthusiasm will make people appreciate you as a conversationalist because they will feel you are interested in them. You will always be a welcome conversation partner.

Conversation topics to avoid in Canada

 At a company meeting, Rita met a co-worker from another department whom she hadn't seen for a while. The woman greeted her by saying, "It looks like you put on a lot of weight!" Rita was appalled.

On another occasion, this co-worker from a different culture asked Rita, "How come you only have two children? Do you use birth control?"

Every culture has subjects that are acceptable to discuss, and other topics that are taboo. Canadians generally don't like to discuss personal topics like their health, their weight, or birth control when they first meet someone. Commenting on someone's weight—particularly weight gain, is considered highly offensive.

In countries such as France, discussing politics is a safe topic, but many Canadians avoid discussing such topics because they do not want to get into emotional discussions at work-related events. There are certainly people who do want to discuss controversial topics, but they may prefer to wait until they go out for drinks or dinner after work.

In a business exchange, be sensitive to how other people react to what you say. Canadians commonly avoid topics that are likely to upset other people.

Here are some tips about topics and questions that can cause negative reactions:

- Avoid asking questions or making remarks about religious beliefs.

- Avoid asking about political views.

- Avoid asking questions about sexual preferences.

- Do not make negative comments about women in the workplace.

- Avoid asking about other people's weight, why they weigh so much or so little, or whether they have gained or lost weight.

- Don't say, "What's wrong? You look so tired." Or "You look stressed. Are you ok?" It will only make people feel bad.

- Do not make jokes about how old or young someone is, or ask people how old they are.

- Do not make jokes about race, religion, other cultures, or women.

- Do not contribute to damaging gossip about anyone.

- Avoid revealing too much personal information about yourself, such as talking about a recent divorce or marital problems in great detail.

- Do not discuss your health problems or a recent operation.

- Do not ask why someone isn't married.

- Do not ask when someone intends to get married or have children.

- Do not ask why someone doesn't have children, or only has one or two children.

- Avoid discussing salaries. Never ask how much money someone makes or has.

- Avoid direct questions about how much someone paid for expensive items like a house or car, or even less expensive items such as a jacket or pair of shoes.

"Business talk should be at a high level," says Srini Iyengar, Director of Multicultural Markets, GTA Division, for the Bank of Montreal. "You can talk about the weather or items in the news, or keep it strictly business. Don't discuss your religion or personal biases in the workplace."

"Also, in business conversations don't go on and on. In some cultures people love to talk, and go on forever. In Canada, it's important to get to the point, and keep the length of your conversation down. Don't ramble. Keep your message concise."

How to use humour without causing offence

Laughing with people is a wonderful way to create friendships. It helps people bond and enjoy each other's company. You release tension and make connections when you share a laugh.

The problem is that most humour is very cultural. Jokes are usually based on a culture's most taboo subjects, such as bodily functions, sex, politics, and religion—so it's very easy to offend someone without realizing it. Even worse, people who come from cultures in which people commonly use sexual innuendo can go too far, and even be accused of sexual harassment. (See Chapter 13.)

You don't have to tell jokes to show others that you have a sense of humour. It's usually safe to laugh at yourself, but never at other people. You can also laugh about a situation that everyone experiences in common, such as travel plans that go wrong. Watch other people to see what they laugh about, and then join in if you feel comfortable.

How to exit a conversation with style and grace

At some point, every conversation begins to wind down. If you don't know how to end the conversation gracefully, it may limp along after everyone involved has lost interest.

Watch for body language and signals from your conversation partner. He may break eye contact, glance at his watch, step back slightly, or make non-committal remarks such as *uh huh*.

If possible, introduce your conversation partner to someone else, so you don't leave him hanging. Once you get them talking, you can gently excuse yourself and ease out of the conversation.

A good way to end the conversation is after you have spoken, rather than after the other person has spoken. This way you don't appear rude by interrupting, and you don't seem to be waiting eagerly for the other person to finish so you can break away. You can say, "That's a good point, Bev. I've really enjoyed our conversation."

You don't need an excuse to leave. Simply say, "It's been a pleasure talking to you," shake hands, and move on. There's no need for explanations.

Take on the role of host

 Allie attended an association networking dinner once a month. When she began attending these dinners, she found networking very difficult. One day an event organizer asked her to greet newcomers and provide information about the association. Allie discovered that when she took on the role of host, she no longer felt shy and was able to connect with people easily.

Many people arrive at events and expect to be treated as guests. They wait for someone to offer them food or approach them to start a conversation. This role forces them to wait passively until someone notices them.

Taking on the role of host puts you in a different dimension. Think about how you welcome guests into your home. You make them feel comfortable by taking their coats and offering them something to drink.

At a business event you can assume host behaviour in the same way. Instead of thinking about how **you** feel, look for ways to make other people feel comfortable. Take on the responsibility of making connections by greeting people warmly and introducing them to other guests. Thinking of yourself as a host—even if you aren't one—means that you won't have time to focus on your own discomfort.

How to keep networking after the event is over

Going to a networking meeting without following up is doing only half the job. If you don't follow up, nothing happens.

Right after you meet new people, write down important information about them. You can write personal information as well. This will give you a reason to connect later. For example, if a potential client mentions that she's looking for a piano teacher for her son and you know about a good teacher, call with the information. Always approach the person with an attitude that says, "How can I help you?"

Contact people you want to build relationships with by calling or sending an email. Even better, write a personal note. You'll stand out from the crowd because so few people do this anymore. Arrange to meet for coffee or lunch so you can get to know each other better.

Finally, deliver what you promised. Send the brochure, article, or information you discussed. You'll build trust and credibility, which is the beginning of a valuable relationship.

Business Buzzwords

- boost someone up the ladder
- corporate survival
- talk shop
- two's company, three's a crowd

Chapter 14 Action Plan

1. Look for three different networking groups, either in your company or from the groups described on pages 292 to 295 . Plan to visit at least one group within the next two months. Write down the names of the groups, and put a check mark (✓) beside the group you will visit.

   _____

   _____

   _____

2. Find out about any company events in the next six months where you can network. This could be anything from a colleague's birthday party to a sales meeting. Write down the events and the dates they will take place.

Event	Date	Place

3. Write down the following information that you can use at any networking event:

   a) A tagline, or another way to introduce yourself _____

   _____

   b) Three small-talk topics you can use

   _____

   _____

   _____

   c) Three questions you can ask to get to know the people you meet

   _____

   _____

   _____

Section 4

Achieving Success

Managing Your Time and Being Productive

Canadian businesses are always concerned about saving time, and being productive and efficient in the workplace.

In This Chapter

- Understanding how Canadians view time
- Planning your time and being productive
- How to create a work / life balance

Understanding how Canadians view time

During Vito's first week of work, he arrived at his orientation session at 9:10 instead of at 9:00. He was five minutes late for his first meeting with his manager and he arrived ten minutes late for his first team meeting. By the end of his first week, he had made a poor impression because people had noted that Vito was not usually on time.

While five minutes here and ten minutes there may not seem like a big deal, in the Canadian workplace this is a big deal.

People from different societies deal with organizing time and information in different ways. In western culture, people are very concerned about using time effectively. This means that we take time commitments seriously.

Canadians view time as something tangible. They value promptness and talk about *wasting time*, *losing time*, and *saving time*. Time is seen as a scarce resource that has to be guarded carefully and managed. This is done by setting up schedules, prioritizing activities, and always looking for ways to save time. This view of time as precious also leads to the use of many labour-saving devices, such as laptops, fax machines, and smartphones.

Canadians are highly task-oriented, and generally focus on work before pleasure. *Time is money* is a phrase coined by the famous American Benjamin Franklin in 1748. Canadians embrace Frankin's view, as it highlights two of North Americans' most fundamental workplace values: time-consciousness and productivity.

Individuals are encouraged to focus on getting the job done—you may hear your manager tell you to *Keep your eye on the ball*. Canadians try to minimize interruptions and distractions in the workplace, such as irrelevant discussions that can cause them to lose sight of their goals.

Many common sayings and proverbs reflect the cultural view of time:

Common Saying	Meaning
Ahead of time / Behind time	Early / Late
The early bird gets the worm	The first person gets the prize, or the greatest advantage
Have no time for	Dislike, disrespect someone or something
In no time	Sooner than expected
It's about time! / It's high time!	It's good that you finally …
Lose no time	Do not delay
Make up the time	Do something at a different time that you can't do now
Racing against time	Trying to do something although there is not enough time
Time flies	Time passes quickly
Time is money	Time is valuable and shouldn't be wasted
Time marches on / Time stands still for no man	Time keeps passing

Refer to the *Oxford Idioms* dictionary for more expressions about time.

Canadians consider it rude to make someone wait for you. This is like telling others, "I think my time is more valuable than yours." It is also considered impolite to do two things at once, such as answering the phone while someone is in your office, or reading a newspaper during a meeting.

"The employer is counting on you being there to start working at the same hour every day," says Karen Wallis-Musselman, an HR independent consultant. "If you have a problem (getting to work on time), call. If it is before the office opens, leave a message and make sure to call after, in case no one got the message."

Being on time

"Being on time shows that you are professional, and shows that you mean business," says Thomas Manuel from India, who works as an account manager with RBC Royal Bank. "Respond to email and voicemail in a timely manner. When you say you will get back to someone within 24 hours, make sure you do it. You will show that you have a good work ethic, and this will help you succeed in Canada."

Many Canadian companies focus on short-term goals and measure success on a quarter-by-quarter basis. People spend time and money to learn techniques to be organized and save more time. Setting goals and objectives is a key concept for working in Canada.

In other cultures, people do many things at once and are casual about time commitments—what doesn't get done today will get done tomorrow. People are more committed to relationships than to tasks, and aren't as concerned with punctuality and promptness.

How will this affect you?

If you come from a culture that is casual about time commitments, you will have to understand and adapt to the Canadian idea of time management if you want to succeed. Here are some key points to keep in mind:

- Punctuality is very important. Being on time shows that you respect other people's time.

- Being late is considered rude. It implies that you are not considerate of other people, or that you are not well organized.

- Being organized is an important skill for success in Canada.

It's vital to understand the implications of time in Canada. Without realizing it, you can easily offend someone by keeping her waiting.

Arriving for a meeting or keeping a visitor waiting for five minutes is generally tolerable. However, you should always strive to arrive a few minutes early for any meeting. Keeping anyone waiting longer than five minutes implies that you consider yourself more important than the person you are meeting, and shows great disrespect.

How long someone is made to wait is based on status as well. People in senior positions in a company, and some professionals such as doctors, have enough status to keep people waiting for them. When a sales representative visits a client for a meeting, the representative may have to wait for a few minutes. But if the president of a company visits someone in another company, she would most likely be brought into the office immediately. The underlying message is, "You are important. Your time is valued."

The most important rule you can learn is to be on time. This actually means that you should aim to be five to ten minutes early for all meetings with clients, co-workers, or your manager. When you aim to be early, you give yourself a cushion of time in case you get delayed by a phone call in your office, or traffic jams on

the way to an offsite meeting. Schedule your time so that you get to every appointment on time—as often as is humanly possible.

If you realize that you are going to be late for an appointment because of unforeseen delays, call the person you are meeting as soon as you know you will be late, and reschedule. Sometimes the other person will tell you that it's okay for you to go to the appointment late. Always ask whether you should reschedule. This demonstrates that you respect the other person's valuable time.

Canadians schedule meetings to begin and end at specific times. This works better in some companies than in others. However, even if meetings habitually start late or run overtime at your company, as a new employee you should still make sure to arrive a few minutes early. You never want to be the person everyone else is waiting for.

Be considerate of your co-workers' time as well. They will not appreciate you keeping them waiting. People who are consistently late gain a reputation for being inconsiderate and undisciplined. This is one area that can easily destroy a relationship.

Canadian Business Concept: Whatever else you do on the job in Canada, be on time! You'll earn a reputation of being organized and considerate, which will go a long way toward helping you succeed in your job.

Being organized

Learning how to organize your work is one of the most important things you can do. This may seem overwhelming if you have never done it before—perhaps your previous manager gave you specific, short-term tasks, or was not very concerned about time.

Now you are expected to organize tasks on your own to meet deadlines. If you don't find a way to organize your work, you'll end up struggling to get through each day, running from task to task, and falling behind. You'll become exhausted and you won't accomplish much.

You must learn to manage your time strategically if you want to survive in your job and advance in your career. Being organized will help you know which tasks are most important, so you get the right jobs done on time. This will help you become efficient and effective, so you can do your job well and within the assigned timeframe. As a result, you will gain a reputation for being reliable and trustworthy. You'll be highly valued because people will know that they can depend on you.

Ask whether your employer offers a time management class. This may be the most valuable course you will ever take. If your workplace doesn't have one, find a local college or university program that does. There are also many books about time management that offer great tips on being more efficient.

Time management is not just about meeting deadlines and showing up for work on time. When you manage your time effectively, you communicate that you are a winner: focused, reliable, consistent, and professional.

Planning your time and being productive

Productivity isn't only about working quickly. It's about working efficiently and effectively. Efficiency starts with good planning.

To plan properly, you have to break down your responsibilities into project goals and tasks, and allocate the proper time to each task.

How to write SMART goals

The first step toward accomplishing anything is setting goals. Chapter 3 discussed the importance of meeting with your manager to discuss your overall goals and priorities.

Now let's look at how to organize your work so that you can deliver what's expected of you, in the way and within the timeframe that your manager wants it.

Your project or work goals should be defined, and they should emphasize what you have to deliver and the date by which it has to be delivered. Most time management books and courses talk about writing goals that are SMART.

SMART goals are **S**pecific, **M**easurable, **A**ttainable, **R**ealistic, and **T**imely.

Specific

Goals must be defined and clear. They should outline what you are going to do. Use actions words such as *write, organize, coordinate, plan, build*, or *complete*.

For example, a general goal would be, "Write the report on XYZ company." A specific goal would be, "Complete the outline for the report on XYZ company by June 12."

Measurable

Creating a measurement helps you know whether you have achieved your goal. Most long-term goals have several specific, short-term measurements built in. Choose a goal that allows you to measure your progress, and be specific in setting your goal.

Ask yourself questions such as *How much ...? How many ...? How will I know when this goal has been accomplished?*

For example, "My goal is to read and learn the 150-page company manual by December 15. My first task is to read 50 pages by November 15."

Attainable

Once you identify a goal, start thinking about how to attain it. You can attain almost any goal when you plan your steps and establish a timeframe within which you will carry out those steps.

List the activities you need to complete in order to achieve your goal. If you work on a team, write the name of the person responsible for completing each task. For example, "Marketing materials for the product launch to be completed by October 10: Randy."

As you accomplish each step and put a check mark (✓) beside it, you will feel a surge of pride that gives you the confidence to keep moving forward.

Realistic

A goal must be realistic. It must be something you are willing and able to do. This doesn't mean it will be easy. In fact, it may be very challenging. You may need to develop new skills to accomplish your goals.

Set goals that you can realistically attain with some effort. Goals that are too easy are not motivating, but goals that are too hard will set the stage for failure.

For example, if you want to increase your sales, setting a goal of 50 percent more sales in the next quarter may not be realistic. But a goal of 15 percent more sales in the next quarter might be realistic.

Timely

Every goal should have a timeframe. If there is no timeframe, there is no sense of urgency.

For example, if you need to complete a customer survey before you can create marketing materials, you should set a timeframe for doing this. If you say, "I need the results of the customer survey by May 1st," then you can start outlining the steps needed to create the survey.

How to organize your work

When you are given an assignment, you need to understand it and think it through. For projects that span days, weeks, or months, you'll have to break your project into a series of tasks.

Begin by identifying the main tasks needed to get your job done. Then break them down into smaller tasks. A task can take anywhere from five minutes to six hours.

Ideally, each task should take as long as you can work comfortably before you need a break. Most people can concentrate fully on work for between half an hour and an hour at a time. Very few people can concentrate on a singe task for two hours or more.

To organize your tasks, assume that you have 18 to 20 working days per month, based on an average of 230 working days per year. This takes into account the 104 weekend days, 10 statutory holidays, 10 to 20 vacation days, and 5 to 10 sick days per year. Some months, such as December and the months when you take vacation, have fewer days, while others have one or two more days.

Use your long-term plan for mapping out your work each day. Part of managing your time well is accurately estimating how long it will take to get things done. Discussing a project with a colleague, attending a meeting, or writing a letter to a client may take longer than you think it will. Monitor how long it takes you to complete different tasks, and compare this time to your estimates so you can plan your time better in the future.

In planning your tasks, make sure there is enough time to meet your deadline:

- Plan for six hours of productive work in any eight-hour workday.

- If a task will take more than six hours (or one day), divide it into smaller tasks.

- Expect between 45 and 50 minutes of work per hour, on average. Plan for a short break of 10 minutes each hour. You can use these 10 minutes to answer emails or return phone calls.

- If someone will have to provide you with a resource in order for you to meet your deadline, give her as much advance notice as possible. Follow up to make sure that the resource will be available when you plan to use it.

- If you attend meetings that take three hours, you'll have to make up these three hours of missed project work somewhere in your schedule.

- Strive to remain ahead of schedule because, invariably, something will come up to put you behind schedule.

- Work overtime when you fall behind or when an emergency comes up. Never plan to do your scheduled work during overtime hours. However, in many professional fields such as accounting and engineering, people are expected to complete their work on time, which often means working evenings or weekends.

- Do a "post mortem", or a review, to monitor how long it actually took you to do each task. You'll develop a feeling for how long you will need to allow for these tasks in the future.

If you come from a hierarchical culture, when your manager first gives you a task you may be tempted to ask many questions right away. In Canada, your manager may prefer that you show initiative by doing some research first.

Take a few hours to gather information and plan your work. There may be different approaches you can take. Narrow down your options and present your plan to your manager. You can say, "This is the approach I suggest. I plan to do A, B, and C for the following reasons (which you will explain clearly). What do you think? Am I missing anything important?"

By preparing well for your meeting, you show that you are doing your homework and that you are a person who presents solution, not problems, to your manager.

What if you are given a "mission impossible"? You organize your work and then realize partway through that you can't possibly get it finished within the timeframe allotted? Or what if you realize, at any point in your plan, that you can't meet your deadline? Perhaps a lot of work was added, there were unexpected glitches, the work is taking longer than you anticipated, or you were sick for a few days.

Visit your manager, armed with your plan. Show her why it will be impossible to get the work done within the timeframe. Again, it's important to go to your manager with suggestions, not just with problems. For example, you can ask for extra resources or the help of a co-worker so you can meet your deadline.

Canadian Business Concept: Never surprise your manager at the last minute by saying that you can't meet a deadline. Your manager will assume you are on schedule unless you tell her otherwise. Always come to her with solutions, such as getting extra resources or help, rather than dumping a problem in her lap.

How to plan each day

Now that you have your work organized, you will need to manage your time each day.

Remember that just because you have a list of priorities doesn't mean your manager won't drop new work on your lap, or co-workers won't ask for your help.

As well, there are many things that use up time during the day: the co-worker who drops by to chat, phone calls and emails that have to be answered, meetings that gobble up chunks of time, and routine paperwork that needs to be completed. Before you know it, your time plan has gone out the window.

However, even if you lose track of time through no fault of your own, you will still be held accountable. When the deadline for your report arrives, your manager won't be sympathetic if you say, "Sorry, I just couldn't get to it."

Here are some steps to organizing your day:

- At the beginning of each day, review your goals to decide how to spend each day.

- Write a to-do list of all the things you have to do each day.

- Ask yourself, "What do I want to accomplish today?" Then assign a priority to each task: A, B, or C. Work on the A items first, then the B items, and finally the Cs.

If you don't prioritize, you may end up doing things just because someone asks. When you have a written plan and priorities for each day, you can answer a request from a co-worker by saying, "This is my plan for today. Let's see if I can reorganize something so I can help you with that." It's okay to say, "Yes, I can do this, but not now. Tomorrow morning would be better for me."

However, if your manager asks you to do something right away, ask, "Is this a priority, or would you prefer I keep working on the XYZ project, which has to be completed by Wednesday?" Your manager should help you prioritize your work.

Prioritize new tasks

When you add a new task, identify its priority relative to your other tasks and slot it into your schedule, allowing enough time to complete it properly.

Take time to do a quality job

Aim to do the work well the first time. This may take more time at the beginning, but doing a quick job filled with errors usually results in redoing the job, which takes more time overall.

Focus on your task

Work in blocks of 30 minutes to 1 hour at a time. Then take a 10 to 15 minute break. If you are working on a computer, stop every 20 minutes to rest your eyes, and stand up and stretch for about two minutes.

Schedule regular tasks

Schedule time to respond to phone calls and emails, and block off this time in your agenda. It's disruptive to respond to calls and emails as they come in, and you can become sidetracked and never finish what you were supposed to be working on. Turn off your email while you are working on important tasks. You may want to answer some calls or emails during the 10 to 15 minute breaks mentioned above.

Evaluate how you're spending your time

Keep a diary of everything you do for three days to find out how you're spending your time. Look for time that can be used more wisely.

Plan the next day

At the end of each business day, take ten minutes to plan what you will do the next day. Planning the night before gives you three benefits:

1. You save time because the day's events are still fresh in your mind.
2. Once your priorities for the next day are written down, you can forget about them and relax for the evening.
3. You start the next day by immediately diving into your most important tasks, without having to wonder, "Where do I start?"

Add any items you did not complete that day to the top of your to-do list, and assign a priority to each item.

How to get more done

We all have peaks of high energy and valleys of low energy during the day. Use high energy times for high priority tasks or work that you generally find difficult. Use low energy valleys for routine jobs such as filing and completing paperwork.

During peak working times, do whatever you can to eliminate interruptions. If a co-worker drops by your desk, ask whether you can talk later. One trick is to stand up and say "It's too bad I can't give you my full attention right now because I have a deadline to meet. Can we meet at 3:00 instead?"

Of course, if your manager stops by to discuss something, you'll have to be polite and make room in your schedule to talk.

Tell people who call you that you would like to talk to them and ask, "When can I call you back?" Be sure to call back when you say you will. You will be considered professional because you are in control of your time.

Throughout the day, ask yourself, "What's the best use of my time right now?" After lunch, focus on tasks that are most important to complete that day, even if it means altering your original schedule.

To maintain your productivity, take a break when you need one. You'll refresh your brain and revive your energy. Take a short walk or do some quick stretches at your workstation. Be sure to get enough sleep and exercise, and eat nourishing food. You'll improve your focus and concentration, so you will complete your work in less time and do a better job overall.

How to make the most of face-to-face meetings

Marius, a new product manager, had been waiting for several weeks to meet with his manager. To prepare for the meeting, Marius defined three objectives for the meeting, and wrote them down. Because he was well prepared, the meeting was productive and both Marius and his manager were pleased.

If you are requesting a meeting with your manager, your team members, or a client, be sure to have a clear objective. For example, "At the end of this meeting, I'll be satisfied if we have identified three topics for next month's sales meeting."

Discuss a time limit for the meeting before it begins. For example, "I'd like 15 minutes of your time to talk about XYZ." If you do this, you will be more likely to have the other participants' full attention, because they'll commit that time to the meeting, and won't be thinking of other work that is waiting.

For a longer meeting, list the topics to be covered and prioritize them. Suggest a timeframe for discussing each point. You might allot 15 minutes for the first topic, 10 minutes for the second topic, and 20 minutes for the third.

During meetings, be sure to shut off your cellphone to avoid disruptions. Give your meeting partners your full attention.

How to use time-planning tools

You'll need several tools to help you manage your time. It's important to find the combination that works best for you.

Develop a system and use it consistently. Make time planning part of your daily routine. Carry your planner with you at all times and remember to refer to it every morning and every night. Here are the three main choices to make in selecting a planner:

1. **Paper or electronic:** Although we live in a highly technical age, many people still prefer paper-based planners. Other people thrive on the latest digital devices. If you choose the wrong planner for your work style, you probably won't use it regularly or effectively, so the first choice is deciding between paper and electronic.

2. **One location or many:** Do you do all your planning from your office, or are you on the road frequently? If you mainly work at your desk, you can use your computer or a paper-based agenda that sits on your desk. If you are in sales or if you travel to see clients, you'll need a portable system. This can be paper-based or electronic, but you'll want the smallest system that does the job to avoid carrying extra weight when you travel.

3. **Brands and features:** Once you decide on your preferred type of system, look into the brands and features of the various paper-based and electronic systems. Even paper-based systems have a wide variety of sizes and designs that you can customize to your needs.

Paper-based planners: pros and cons

👍 Paper-based planners make entering information quick and easy. There is no installation, and you don't need batteries. Writing feels natural, and you can flip back and forth between pages for an overview. You can also store old planner pages or booklets in your office for future reference.

👎 If you lose your system you're in trouble—there's no backup. Plus, you will still need other devices in order to do searches or to email people while you're travelling. Some agendas are big and bulky to carry around, and none of them allow other people to access your schedule.

PDAs (Personal Digital Assistants): pros and cons

👍 Digital planners offer many conveniences. You can back up information, easily group and rearrange data, search for information by keyword and date, and network with other people so you can access each other's schedules.

👎 It's hard to get a visual overview of information, because you can only see one screen at a time. Archived information is not as accessible as information in a paper-based planner, nor is referencing and accessing information as quick or as easy as it would be on paper. People who are visual and tactile often find such systems more difficult to use.

Creating your own system

You may need to combine several elements, such as a wall calendar, a place to write your to-do lists, and an electronic device for recording people's contact information.

Paper calendar: Use a large calendar on your wall to mark important meetings, holidays, company events, and project due dates.

Computerized calendar: Many companies use electronic calendars to schedule meetings with office staff and appointments with clients and suppliers.

Electronic reminders: Get a digital watch, cellphone, or electronic calendar system with an alarm to remind you of important meetings.

Combined system: If you love your electronic planner, yet find it difficult to manage your to-do list on-screen, add a small notebook inside your PDA carrying case. Write the date and your to-do list each day. You'll have the convenience and power of a digital planner, with the speed of pen and paper for quickly jotting down notes.

Tips on using your planner

Put everything in your planner. This will keep you from forgetting small but important items such as a lunch date with a colleague or a ten-minute phone call scheduled with your manager.

Remind yourself. When you write a due date in your planner, make a note in your planner—a day or a week ahead of the due date—to give yourself a reminder that the due date is approaching.

Block time. Once you've allocated time for all of your projects, block the time in your agenda to keep you on track. When you finish a task, write down how long it took. Later, you can go back and check the timing for each task to help you plan future tasks. The actual time spent on each task is often different than the amount you originally budgeted. Tracking this can help you evaluate and manage your time better.

Include all the information related to an event. For example, if you are driving to meet a new client, write the name of the receptionist and all the information for that client, including phone numbers and cellphone numbers, on the appropriate page in your agenda.

Include personal information to jog your memory. For example, if you know your colleague is getting married in June, record this information in your calendar for May so you'll remember to congratulate her at your May meeting.

Allow extra time for the unexpected. If you need an hour to write a report, allow 20 percent more time (10 to 15 minutes) for interruptions and delays. Adding a cushion of time gives you breathing space for urgent phone calls or traffic jams on the way to appointments, and helps you to feel less stressed.

Eliminate pieces of paper. Record the information in your planner as soon as you receive it.

Use flags. If you use a paper-based planner, buy sticky-note flags and use them as tabs to alert you to project due dates or important meetings and phone calls. This is a great visual tool.

Keep old pages. You will always have important information in your planner that you'll need to see again at a later date. You may need to access old phone numbers and notes from meetings.

As a bonus, these old notes can also be a useful record of your accomplishments for performance reviews. You now have actual facts to support your good performance.

How to use your time wisely

Phone calls

Write down, in point form, your reasons for calling. If you reach a receptionist, find out when the person you want to reach will be available. Summarize every call when you conclude it, to ensure that communication is clear and nothing is forgotten. Return phone calls within 24 hours, and emails within 48 hours.

Voicemail

Update your outgoing message every day. People often skip generic voice messages, but will listen if they hear the current date. Updating your message shows that you care, and tells the caller when you will call back. If a response is needed sooner, the caller can contact someone else. You will come across as professional, and you can relax knowing your callers are aware of when you can call them back. (See more tips in Chapter 7.)

Drive time

Listen and learn on the road. Buy audio programs to learn new skills, or record information about new products, and listen to them while you drive.

Be prepared before you start driving, so you can avoid wasting time while you're on the road. Check your car carefully the night before a business trip. Do you have enough gas and windshield washer fluid? Have you packed all the papers you will need to present to your client?

Delays

Take advantage of delays—always carry extra reading material with you to use waiting time productively. Even short periods of time can be extremely useful if you focus on one small task and get it done.

Filing

File papers so you don't have to look for them. Create a system that helps you find documents easily by asking, "Where would I look for this?" rather than, "Where should I put this?" Learn your company's filing procedures, and review Canada's privacy legislation for keeping documents secure.

Timing

Always give yourself a cushion of time between appointments. Your client may be late for a meeting, and this will make you late for your next meeting.

If you have to travel across town in bad weather, you can be sure there will be traffic jams that will delay you.

Schedule an extra 15 minutes between meetings in the office, so if one meeting goes overtime, your whole day doesn't run off track. If it turns out that you don't have to use up your cushion of time, you'll have some extra time to catch up on paperwork or get ahead in your work.

How and when to say *No*

Rebecca was new at the company. One day Jim, a manager from another department, approached Rebecca and handed her a stack of expense reports to process. Rebecca didn't know what to say. She had work of her own to complete, and would have to work late to finish Jim's work.

Do you have managers from different departments who drop work on your desk? What about a supervisor who piles on the work? Or perhaps you have a co-worker who chronically asks you to help her out in a time crunch?

Time-management gurus always tell you to say *no* to requests that don't fit in with your priorities. But when you are new on the job, it isn't always easy to say *no* to your manager or colleagues. You want to be seen as cooperative—a "can-do" employee. However, if you take on more than you can accomplish, you'll be sabotaging your own goals.

What can you do?

Instead of just staying late to finish her work and Jim's, Rebecca could reply politely that she would be happy to help, but she would appreciate it if Jim could check with her manager first. Jim may not even bother, and just find another solution. If he does go to her manager, her manager might tell Rebecca to do Jim's work, or she might refuse to let Jim pass on his work. In either case, her manager would help her establish her priorities.

If you frequently run into similar situations, a good first step is to meet with your manager to formalize your daily responsibilities. Find out who is authorized to give you work, and the type of assignments you can expect from each person.

What happens if Mike, your colleague, leaves you an urgent message to help him with a task? If he's in a bind, or if he's out of the office and needs information, do everything you can to help him.

However, if he routinely asks for help because he doesn't plan well, sit down with him and explain that you would love to help him when you can, but that you have your own deadlines to meet. Don't feel that you have to come to his rescue. It's not your responsibility to do other people's work.

What if your manager is the one overloading you with work? Let's say your manager just assigned a large project to you and you can't imagine how you'll get it done.

Before you say *yes* or *no*, make sure you understand exactly what your manager wants you to do by asking questions. Perhaps the task is more time-consuming than you originally thought. On the other hand, it may not take much effort at all.

Here are some questions to ask yourself:

- Do I have time to do this work, or do I already have several important assignments to complete?

- Which of my assignments is the priority?

- Can anyone help me with this?

- If I take on this assignment, how will it affect the success of my other assignments?

- Do I have the skills and resources needed to complete this assignment?

- Is there anyone else who could complete this assignment?

Once you've answered these questions, you have to decide how to approach your manager. You should never say *no* to your manager lightly, because you might pay the consequences. If the project looks difficult, or does not fall within your job description, you should still consider doing it. And never use a personal reason, such as being busy planning your wedding, to shirk an assignment.

However, there may be legitimate reasons to refuse an assignment. It may simply require too much time, and will cause your other work to suffer. Or you may not have the skills required to do a good job, and not have an opportunity to learn the skills in time to complete the assignment.

Have a conversation with your manager. Ask her for help in deciding where the new task should fall on the list of priorities. Remind her that you are working on other projects that she has already identified as priorities. You can say, "I'd be happy to work on this, but last week you asked me to research statistics for your presentation. Which do you think I should do first?"

Perhaps your manager isn't aware of all the assignments you're working on. Explain that you think your other work will suffer if you take on a new assignment. She will appreciate your honesty and your dedication to your other projects, and may help you prioritize your work.

If you are lacking the skills to complete this assignment, admit this to your manager. Don't pretend you can do something you can't. Ask if these are skills you will need in the future. If they are, see if there is some training you can take to help you gain the skills you need.

Canadian Business Concept: Never use the actual word *No*, or the phrase *I don't have the time*. Always present yourself as a hardworking, disciplined employee who has the best interests of the company at heart.

How to stop procrastinating

Do you find yourself avoiding certain tasks? We all procrastinate from time to time. Just because something needs to be done, doesn't mean we will enjoy doing it.

When you procrastinate, you will turn in projects late or not at all. If you find yourself playing solitaire on the computer when you should be tackling an important project, you have to discipline yourself and start moving forward. Here's how:

- Identify the tasks you are avoiding, and why you are avoiding them. If you are missing information, find out what you need to know. If the task is boring, think about the big picture, and how good you'll feel when you've accomplished your mission.

- Organize your work area.

- Break down each task into small manageable parts. Work on each part for a set amount of time, such as 15 minutes.

- Begin with the part that is easiest for you to complete. Once you successfully finish one section, you'll gain momentum and feel good about your accomplishment.

- Reward yourself for completing a task by taking a short break. Then work on the next part.

How to create work / life balance

The *Oxford Business English Dictionary* defines a *workaholic* as a person who works very hard and finds it difficult to stop working and do other things. This fits in with many Canadians who report that they spend more than 50 hours per week working, and worry that they do not spend enough time with family and friends.

"One out of every three Canadians identifies themselves as a workaholic," according to a study by Statistics Canada. The study found that "almost one-third (31 percent) of working Canadians aged 19 to 64 identify themselves as workaholics. About 39 percent of self-identified workaholics reported that they usually worked 50 or more hours per week, and 65 percent of workaholics worried that they do not spend enough time with family and friends. They were also more likely to report that the general state of their health was fair or poor, and that they had trouble sleeping."

Today more than ever, life seems to move at an impossible pace. For many people, there's a one-hour commute to work and another hour of stop-and-go traffic to get home.

The day begins early, sometimes with 7:00 a.m. or 8:00 a.m. meetings, and often ends much later than 5:00 p.m. There are lunch meetings, hundreds of emails to answer, and the constant stress of juggling family obligations with demanding work. No wonder so many people feel overwhelmed.

What can you do to avoid overworking and still build a great career? Here are some suggestions:

Take care of your health. Get enough sleep, try to exercise several times each week, and eat nutritious foods. These suggestions sound obvious, but they are often difficult to act on. Remember that you'll be more efficient, productive, and happy when you take care of yourself.

Create time for balance in your life. Just as you plan time for your work, plan time for friends, family, hobbies, and fitness. Don't let work overwhelm you. You need recreation time to recharge your batteries.

Set boundaries. To keep balance in your work and personal life, set boundaries so that you can feel generous and available without feeling depleted and overwhelmed.

Yes, your work life is important, but that doesn't mean that you need to give up your personal time. It's okay to say *no* to volunteering for a committee when you are overloaded, or to helping a co-worker after-hours. Some experts recommend keeping your answer short. This way, you can say *no* without feeling the need for a lengthy justification. (For example, "I'm sorry, I'm not available that night.") On the other hand, others say that giving a longer answer with reasons reinforces your credibility. Let the situation help you decide.

Recognize that sometimes things get out of control. Peak times at work, a sick family member, or other life circumstances can force you to work overtime, or to abandon your exercise routine or favourite pastime. No one can keep everything in balance at all times. Go with the flow, and sooner or later you'll get the time you need for the things that are important to you.

Business Buzzwords

- go with the flow
- keep your eye on the ball
- mission impossible
- post-mortem
- pros and cons
- to-do list
- workaholic

Chapter 15 Action Plan

1. Get information about managing your time more effectively. Find out whether your company offers any time management courses. Look into programs in your community, or ask your manager to recommend any books on the subject. Write the information about programs or books here.

   _____

   _____

   _____

2. Write down your overall goals for the year, using the SMART goal format on pages 321 to 323. Revise or add any information to make your goals SMART.

   _____

   _____

   _____

3. Write down three changes you could make to save time and work more effectively. Aim to put one new idea into action every month for the next three months. You may want to show your ideas to your manager, and demonstrate your progress each month.

Changes to make	Date to complete

Business outside the Office

You may be travelling to meet clients or suppliers, or to attend trade shows, conferences, or business events outside the office.

In This Chapter

- The ins and outs of business travel
- Trade shows and conferences
- Parties, events, and dinners outside the office

The ins and outs of business travel

Your job may have many different components that take you out of the office. You may have to travel to meet clients and attend company sales meetings, trade shows, or conferences. You will also be meeting with colleagues and people from your company at events like the annual holiday party or barbecue. You may also be invited to the homes of your co-workers or boss.

This chapter walks you through everything you need to know to make a good impression outside of the office.

Road warriors—learning the art of business travel

When Juanita made her first trip to represent her company at a national meeting, her flight was scheduled to arrive at 10:00 p.m. The first meeting was at 8:30 the next morning.

The flight arrived on schedule, but Juanita's luggage didn't. Fortunately, Juanita's travel clothes were passable for the meeting, but she was missing several items she needed, and she felt uncomfortable. Instead of projecting a confident image and concentrating on business, she was focused on herself and the impression she was making. Now, as a seasoned traveller, Juanita always packs the essentials in her carry-on bag so she is never caught off guard if her luggage goes astray.

If your new position requires business travel, you may be delighted to get away from the office for a few days. You'll look forward to staying at fancy hotels, sleeping in king-sized beds, and tasting local cuisine at the company's expense.

While all of these perks exist, you'll also find that you will work very long hours, and return to a week's worth of emails and a suitcase full of dirty laundry.

Travelling to conferences and trade shows can be exciting. You'll build closer relationships with your company members as you spend more time together, and meet new people in your industry. You'll broaden your knowledge when you attend sessions , and you'll gain new insights into how to do your job better.

Canadian Business Concept: Travelling to conferences and trade shows gives you the opportunity to build closer relationships with your company members and to broaden your horizons as you meet other people in your industry.

Here are some tips for successful business travel:

Be professional

Just because you're out of the office doesn't mean you're off the job. It's just the opposite—you are representing your company, and people will judge your company by the way you act. This doesn't mean you can't have fun, but remember that you are still on company time, and people from your company will be watching your behaviour.

Know your travel itinerary

Find out exactly where you are going, where you are staying, what you need to bring with you, and where you are supposed to be at all times. If you are going to a large city, make sure you know which of several airports you'll be departing from when you return. It's a good idea to contact the tourist office before you visit a new city, to find out about transportation from the airport to your hotel. This way you won't broadcast that you are a tourist when you arrive.

Know the purpose of your trip

Find out who you will be meeting, and set up an agenda to make the most of your time. If you will be attending a conference, look over the program when you receive it—you may be asked to register for sessions ahead of time. This way you won't arrive and find that the sessions you wanted to attend are all filled up. Make sure you know when and where to register as well.

Keep important materials with you

If you will be presenting to a group, keep a hard copy of all your materials in your carry-on bag. It's a good idea to keep them on a USB flash drive or CD as well. You never know when your laptop will have a temper tantrum and refuse to work.

Make the most of your carry-on bag

Always carry a change of clothing and your personal necessities in your carry-on bag. If you will be presenting the morning after the flight, it's a good idea to take your suit, or a least a jacket, in case your luggage doesn't arrive when you do. Pack essential toiletries, any medications you take, and your contact lens case and solution.

Know how to handle expense reports

Find out your company's rules. How much are you allowed to spend on meals per day? Will you be reimbursed for taxis to and from the airport, or do you need to take the shuttle?

Keep your receipts together

Put an envelope in your briefcase or handbag, and put all your travel receipts directly into it. This will save you time when you're back at your workplace, because you won't have to search through scraps of crumpled paper looking for restaurant bills.

Carry some cash

In these days of credit and debit cards, it's easy to forget to carry cash. But you should be aware that not all taxis take credit cards. Be sure to have enough cash to cover your taxis and to buy snacks and small items when you arrive.

Keep some essentials packed

If you travel frequently, keep a bag packed with essential toiletries, medications, business cards, and extra power cords for your laptop. This will save you from frantically running around at the last minute, trying to get your things in order.

Dress to impress

This is the time to dress up, not down. You will be representing your company, and you may mix and mingle with managers and executives from your company. Wear your best business suit. Make sure it is cleaned and pressed. Use the hotel iron to freshen up any creased clothing.

Pay attention to your accessories. Make sure your shoes, briefcase, and jewellery are polished and business-appropriate. If you'll be standing for long hours at a booth, find shoes that are comfortable, yet appropriate for business (a challenge for women!).

Dress well for the flight too. You may end up sitting next to other people from your company or a potential client.

Conserve your energy

Fly during business hours when possible. You'll be working long hours, and if you take the red-eye and lose a night's sleep, you won't be productive. Flying is stressful enough that it pays to arrange your schedule to make it easier for you. During the flight, it's fine to rest or read. Don't try to cram in extra work. And try to get a good night's sleep before you leave on the trip.

Carry snacks

Flying isn't always easy. You often won't get a meal unless you are on an overseas flight, and the food available for purchase is limited. Keep your energy up by carrying a few high-protein snacks like health bars or trail mix. Buy a bottle of water or juice after you've cleared security, and keep yourself hydrated.

Stay in touch

Don't make your boss think you've dropped off the earth. Keep him updated by email or voicemail. Check your email and voicemail once a day, and respond to clients or important departmental issues. Most hotels have Internet access, so you can log on to your email server from your room. You can also use the Internet at the hotel's business centre.

Adjust your internal and external clocks

If you're travelling across time zones, be sure to reset your watch when you arrive. Since adjusting to a new time zone can be disorienting, make sure you wake up on time. Don't rely solely upon the alarm clock by your bed. Set it, and also call the reception desk for a wake-up call. This way you'll double your chances of waking up on time. Believe it or not, hotels do sometimes make mistakes with their wake-up calls, so do not forget to set your alarm.

Take advantage of the hotel's business centre

You may be presenting at a conference and need to make a few extra photocopies, or send an email, or check something online. The hotel business centre is there to help you. But be aware that making photocopies here can be much more expensive than a regular copy shop, so only use these services in an emergency.

Monitor your expenses

Small things, like taking a few snacks from the fridge in your room or using the hotel phone, can add up to a lot more than you realize. Hotels charge a lot for these conveniences, and you can use up a good part of your meal budget by paying $4 for a bottle of water or a chocolate bar. Use your cellphone or a calling card for phone calls, and buy bottled water or snacks at a convenience store if there's one near the hotel. Even the shops in the hotel lobby are usually less expensive than the food in your room.

Schedule relaxation time

We often try to pack in too many activities when we travel. Take a brisk walk or go to the hotel gym and work up a sweat. Plan some relaxing activities as well, such as going to a play or a museum, or taking a short break for a bit of local sightseeing or shopping. If you're attending meetings or standing at a conference booth all day, you are getting very little fresh air, and you will start to feel tired. Get out of the hotel at some point and you'll feel energized.

Use after-hours well

Conferences and meetings are ideal times to meet new people and make connections. If you're with people from your department, there will probably be some team-building activities and meals after-hours. If you're on your own representing your company, look for opportunities to meet with other people who are on their own. It's more fun to go to dinner with a group than to eat by yourself.

Have fun!

If your company is sending you to stay in New York from Tuesday to Friday, it's a shame to miss out on the sightseeing. Find out if you can pay for two nights at the hotel on your own, and take the weekend to explore the city.

Business etiquette on the road

You may have to wait in long security lines, board a crowded plane, and find yourself trapped like a sardine between two large individuals. Being in such close proximity to strangers can add to your stress. In tough times, humour and pleasantness will help you cope.

Be courteous

Whether you're dealing with an overworked flight attendant or the person next to you, a polite *hello*, *please*, and *thank you* help to smooth the way.

Keep your perspective

It's easy to lose your temper when your luggage goes to Calgary while you're headed to Vancouver. Keep in mind that when you yell at the customer service representative, you may be one in a string of people blaming her, and she may be on the verge of screaming herself. Act professionally and she will be more likely to help you.

Look for solutions

If the child in the next seat is crying or fidgeting, quietly ask the flight attendant if there is an empty seat somewhere on the plane. If so, calmly mention to the child's mother or father that you have a report to work on, then move to a new seat.

When travelling by car, have it cleaned

If you have to pick up a client before a meeting, you won't feel embarrassed at having candy wrappers on the seat or trash on the floor. Even if you don't pick anyone up, you'll feel organized and efficient.

Focus on your goal

What really counts is what you accomplish after you arrive. If you meet your objectives, the trip will be a success regardless of what it takes to get there.

How to deal with hotel staff

Your hotel will be your "home away from home." When you become familiar with the hotel and its staff, you'll be able to concentrate on business. Make sure to treat the staff well—it can be embarrassing to have the bellhop take your luggage, and then find you don't have the right change for a tip. Here's a rundown on who's who, and what to tip them.

Porter: Carries your luggage at the airport or on a train. Tip $1 per bag, $3 to $5 for several bags.

Doorman: Handles the arrivals and departures of guests and gets you a taxi when you step out. Tip $1 to $3, depending on the service provided.

Bellhop: Takes luggage from the car or taxi and delivers it to your room. Tip $1 per bag, $3 to $5 for several bags.

Concierge: Acts as a resource who responds to guests' needs. He can direct you to a restaurant, get you tickets to the latest play, or track down a battery for your cellphone. No tip for small services, $5 to $10 for making reservations or getting tickets.

Taxi driver: Tip 10 to 15 percent of the cost of your fare.

Room service: Tip 15 to 20 percent of the cost of items delivered. Be careful, because the service charge and gratuity (or tip) are often added automatically to the bill.

Valet parking attendant: Tip about $2 per day

How to travel safely

No matter where you travel, safety should always be a priority. Here are some important things to keep in mind when you're travelling.

- Stow your belongings in the overhead bin across the aisle from your seat. The bin above you is invisible to you, and you never know what someone is doing with your possessions when they fumble around up there.

- Before going through the metal detector, transfer everything from your pockets to your carry-on bag. You'll avoid emptying your pockets into a bowl that has carried the pocket contents of many passengers before you, some of whom have colds or other unwanted germs.

- If the front desk staff announces your room number out loud while there are people nearby, ask for another room. This is especially important for female travellers.

- Ask for a room that offers the most security without compromising convenience. Ground floor rooms are prime targets for thieves. And although elevators are noisy, you don't want to be at the end of a long, winding hall with no easy exit.

- Remember that fire safety is important. Check where the closest emergency exit is and count how many doorframes you would feel along the way if you were making your way to the exit in the dark. Keep your door key in your pocket or handbag so you can grab it if you have to leave quickly. You will need your key to reenter your room when you return.

- Have an emergency first aid kit in your briefcase. Over 50 percent of travellers suffer from some kind of ailment. It's hard to conduct business when you have a headache or indigestion.

- Photocopy all your contact information, flight details, and credit card numbers, and leave the information with a friend or family member. Call to let this person know when you arrive at your destination.

- Confirm flights, hotel reservations, and business appointments ahead of time. Plans can be forgotten or be changed unexpectedly. Never assume that an appointment made weeks or months ago is still on the agenda. Confirm by phone, fax, or email before you leave.

How to travel with your boss

Travelling with your boss gives you uninterrupted time together. You can uncover different dimensions of his personality. You may find out about a hobby or interest that you have in common, that you would never have known about otherwise.

Here are three important tips for travelling with your boss:

1. Be respectful and considerate. Let you boss have the better seat on the flight or at the restaurant. Let him initiate the conversation. Allow him to take the lead in deciding how and when things will be done.

2. Be helpful. Take charge of tasks such as getting cabs, checking out restaurant reservations, and tipping service people.

3. Be professional at all times. This is a chance for your boss to get to know you. By acting professionally, you will shine in your boss's eyes.

Trade shows and conferences

A business conference is a gathering of people who all work within a specific field. At such conferences, you will attend sessions or workshops to increase your knowledge and find out about the latest developments in your industry. Larger conventions may have one or more high-profile speakers, often people who have written books in your industry, invented or discovered something, or who are noted for their business wisdom.

Trade shows are usually run in conjunction with these conferences. There will be a specific area where suppliers have booths set up to sell the latest products for your industry. Although trade shows are often part of conferences, some trade shows stand alone or have just a few sessions that you can attend.

Most business conferences take place in hotels or conference centres. Smaller conferences take place at resorts or hotels and have up to a few hundred people. Industry-wide events may be held in cavernous conference centres, run for 2 to 5 days, and have thousands of visitors. These types of events can be overwhelming the first time you attend, but they are also exciting and stimulating. You'll find that you are pepped up and on-the-go from early morning until late at night.

Attending conferences usually means travelling to another city, or even country, and the social aspect is a big attraction. Most conference organizers plan group excursions in the evening, such as dinners, shows, or local cruises. If you attend a conference with your company or department, you will usually have some planned events with your co-workers as well. And if you meet with suppliers, they will often invite you to lavish dinners, tours of the city, or local entertainment.

While you may want to take advantage of all the fun activities, don't let your guard down completely. You should participate, but don't take advantage of all the free liquor. While one glass of wine or beer may help you feel more relaxed, more than that may make you a little too uninhibited. Dress professionally as well. You can wear business casual in the evening, but don't dress in a way that attracts the wrong attention. Remember, you are still on a business trip, and your boss or clients will notice your behaviour.

Be sure to pace yourself and get enough rest. It's easy to stay up late at night with your group, but remember that most conferences start very early. There is often a group breakfast beginning as early as 6:30 a.m., with workshops and booths opening around 8:30 or 9:00 a.m. If you habitually miss breakfast and stagger in to the morning events, your boss will be aware of your after-work activities.

How to make the most of conferences

If your boss sends you to a conference, he is telling you that you are a valuable employee. He is investing in your education so you can be more beneficial to the company. When you return, he will also expect you to share what you have learned at the sessions. Be sure to attend all the sessions you can, and bring back the handouts you receive and the notes you take. You may be asked to present what you learned at your next departmental meeting.

Before you attend the conference, go over the agenda carefully. See which sessions are most interesting to you. You may want to discuss with your boss which sessions you should attend. If you are going with one or more co-workers, you may want to split up the relevant sessions and then report back to each other.

Learn about the speakers. If the keynote speaker wrote a book, it's a good idea to read it before the conference. This will give you a depth of knowledge, and make the content come alive. You'll also be more exited to hear the speaker because you'll feel like you know him after reading his book.

If you know of people from other parts of your company or your industry who will be attending, contact them ahead of time and set up a time to meet so you don't have to arrive alone.

Be on time for all the workshops. Walking in late disrupts the session. Don't forget that you are representing your company, and your name will be on your name tag, so you aren't anonymous!

Conferences are ideal places to network. During the breaks and at lunch, try to sit with people from different companies. Although this may be unnerving at first, you'll find that people are generally very friendly and like to find out what's going on in different companies in their industry.

While it may feel more comfortable to stick with your co-workers, remember that you already have a starting point for conversation with everyone at the event. It's easy to begin a conversation by asking any of the following questions:

- Which sessions did you attend?
- Which sessions did you find most interesting?
- Where are you from?
- How do you like this city?
- What did you think of the keynote speaker / yesterday's event / etc …

At a conference, you'll want to look and feel your best, so plan your wardrobe carefully. Take clothing you feel confident and comfortable in. Find out the dress guidelines. This will depend on your industry and where the conference takes place. For example, in New York or Montreal, people tend to dress formally, in business suits. Conference organizers in some other cities may expect attendees to dress more casually.

For conferences at resorts or in hot climates, business casual wear is often suggested. However, the hotels are typically overly air-conditioned, and attendees may find they are freezing by mid-morning. It's always a good idea for both men and women to have a business jacket with them. There are always some people who wear suits, and you'll impress others if you dress well.

Finally, bring lots of business cards, and follow up with new contacts. You never know when a lunch meeting will blossom into a valuable business relationship.

Trade shows

Attending trade shows can be lots of fun. There are endless displays from exhibitors competing for your attention. The noise, crowds, and size of it all can be overwhelming, but the atmosphere can also be energizing.

If you are attending a conference with a trade show, take the time to visit the booths. You'll find resources and suppliers for many of your needs, and you will learn about the latest technology or products on the market. You can also get demonstrations or samples of products to bring home.

The people at the booths are eager to talk to anyone who ventures near, and can be a great source of information about your industry. If you are interested in being contacted, give them your business card. Take their pamphlets or brochures, and write a note to yourself so you'll remember what you discussed with them. Otherwise, by the end of the conference, it will all be a big blur to you.

Parties, events, and dinners outside the office

 Sandra started working at a small law firm in Montreal in late November. The annual office party was scheduled two weeks later, and Sandra received an invitation that said "Tropical Island Theme." She spent considerable time putting together an outfit with a grass skirt, a straw hat, and a seashell necklace. She arrived at the party and stared at her co-workers in horror. All the men were dressed in dark business suits, and the women were in chic black dresses.

Every office and company has its own culture, and its own rituals for celebrating holidays and events. If you are invited to a company event, find out how it will be organized, who will be there, and what the dress code will be.

These are occasions to get to know your co-workers better and chat with people you don't normally socialize with. Parties and events are also used by employers as a way to assess people's behaviours outside of the office.

Office holiday parties

Attending an office party is usually mandatory, which means you don't have much choice in the matter—you have to show up. There's an important concept you should keep in mind: office parties aren't social occasions, they are business situations. Have fun, but still be professional.

Attend

Don't pass up an invitation because you are shy, or because you would prefer not to go. Attendance is not really optional. This is a great opportunity to show off your manners and social savvy. Companies judge their employees by job performance, but also by how well they fit into the office culture. When you attend, it shows that you're a well-rounded person who cares about your job and the people you work with.

If you have other responsibilities on the day of the party, you don't have to stay for the whole evening. Arrive for an hour, say hello to everyone, and then leave discreetly. If anyone asks why you are leaving, explain that you have another obligation that evening, but you still came because you wanted to see everybody. You don't have to be the last to leave, but plan to stay for at least one hour.

Arrive on time

Whether the event is at your office or at a restaurant, the organizers have planned a sequence of events and a schedule for the food and entertainment. It's rude to walk in late and interrupt the plan.

Dress appropriately

This is not the time for women to wear their lowest-cut, shortest, or most revealing party dresses, or for men to go completely casual. You can wear something festive, with colour or sparkle, but remember that it's still an office party.

Be on your best behaviour

Your manners are on display for managers and people higher up in the company. You should look like you're having fun, but don't take advantage of the free liquor. Alcohol lowers your inhibitions and alters your judgment. It can make you do things you may regret. Even if alcohol has little effect on you, you don't want to look like you're drinking too much. Remember, perception is everything.

Network

Think of the office party as a networking occasion. It's your chance to meet people from different parts of your organization who you don't see regularly. Don't just chat with your buddies from the next cubicle. Take the extra step to meet someone new. Make sure to introduce yourself to upper management. You don't have to talk for long—just say hello and tell them how much you enjoy the event. After a few minutes, you can say, "It was great talking with you." Shake hands, smile, and move on.

Make small-talk

Don't talk shop all evening. Present yourself as an interesting, well-rounded person with a variety of interests. Be careful about telling jokes. You may think your jokes are entertaining, but they may be hurtful or offensive to other people.

You'll be judged on the company you keep

If you arrive with your spouse, date, or guest, brief them on appropriate behaviour beforehand. If they act badly, it will reflect on you. Be sure to introduce them to your boss and co-workers. Help them find common interests to discuss with these people so they don't feel awkward.

Include other guests in your conversation

They won't know anyone, and may be feeling awkward. If you go out of your way to make them feel welcome, you'll score big points with your co-worker or boss. And don't forget that your boss's spouse can have a big influence on your career. Besides, it's just common courtesy to make everyone feel included.

Don't pig-out at the buffet table

Eat something small before the event so you aren't ravenous when you arrive. Remember that office parties are not about eating, but about building relationships.

Don't gossip or talk about people behind their backs

Just because someone isn't at the party doesn't mean you can talk about him behind his back. You never know who's standing behind you, or who's dating or best friends with the person you're talking about.

Thank the host or sponsor before leaving

Someone has spent a lot of time organizing the party, and will appreciate your gratitude. After the event, write a thank-you note to the organizer of the party. It can be brief:

> Dear Amira,
>
> Your time and effort paid off. The office party was a huge success. Thank you for doing such a great job.
>
> Sincerely,
> Bob

Cocktail parties

Cocktail parties are part of mixing business with pleasure for many industries. If you are invited to a cocktail party, there are some things you should keep in mind:

- Make sure to RSVP (reply). Don't assume the hosts know whether or not you will be attending. They need to plan the appropriate amount of food and drinks.

- Dress as you would for the office. Cocktail parties are generally not casual. Check with your host to find out what the dress code is.

- Walk around the room and meet people. This is the time to make pleasant small-talk with people for five to ten minutes, then politely excuse yourself and meet someone else. Cocktail parties are often stand-up events, so everyone is mobile.

- Carry your drink in your left hand, so your right hand is always ready to shake someone else's hand.

- The food is usually finger food. Use a small plate or the napkin to hold your food, preferably with your left hand so your right hand is ready to shake someone else's hand. Wipe your fingers on your napkin frequently so your hands aren't greasy.

- Don't overeat or expect a full supper. If you are famished after work, have a protein-rich snack before the party, so you won't be eating everything in sight. It's difficult to talk and eat at the same time.

Company picnics

The company picnic is a family affair, where employees get together in an informal setting. People take along their spouses and children, and everyone gets to know each other better. However, it's still important to make a good impression with the people you work with.

- Volunteer to help with the organization and cleanup. Everyone will appreciate your help and graciousness. This is a good opportunity to get better acquainted with your co-workers.

- Participate in the games or activities. Don't be a wet blanket. Join in the fun, even if you aren't athletic. It's important to be considered a good sport.

- Introduce your family to your co-workers, and make the time to meet your co-workers' families.

- If you have children, supervise them to make sure they act properly. Try to find them playmates of their age, or help them join the activities that have been set up for them.

- Thank the hosts after the event, with a warm but brief thank-you note.

Dining at your co-workers' homes

How to eat unfamiliar foods at other people's homes

Frederic, from Belgium, was invited to his Canadian co-worker's house for a casual dinner. It was summer, and the co-worker barbecued on the back deck. Frederic was served a plate of food that included corn on the cob. He had never seen food served this way, and was unsure of how to eat it. He felt more comfortable as he watched his co-worker pick up the corncob with his fingers and bite into it.

When you eat at someone's home, you may be served food that is new to you. It's difficult to refuse food that is offered to you. When you accept someone's food, it's as if you are accepting the person who is serving the food. Here are some tips for eating unfamiliar food:

If you are served an unfamiliar dish, taste it.

- If you are not sure how to eat something, watch how your hosts and other guests eat it.

- If you are served an unfamiliar dish, taste it. If you don't like it, play with your food. Cut it up and move it around so it looks as if you are eating. If your host asks how you like it, say with a smile, "The flavour is very distinctive," or something similar.

- If you've tried something before and know that you don't like it, you can say, "I understand this is a delicacy, but I had trouble when I ate this before."

- Watch your alcohol consumption. Wine or beer may be part of the meal, but drinking too much is never a good idea.

Don't eat and run

Bill invited a group of new employees from another culture to his house for dinner. The evening began with drinks and canapés, and dinner was served at 8:00 p.m. As soon as the dinner was over, all the new employees got up and left at the same time. Bill was surprised about this, because in Canada people usually stay for a few hours after the meal to talk. However, this group of employees came from a culture where the meal was the last event of the evening.

There is a common saying that applies here: *Don't eat and run.* In Canada, a typical meal starts with some canapés, and drinks such as wine or beer. There may be three or four courses. This may include a salad or soup, the main course, which is often some kind of meat or fish accompanied by rice or potatoes, and vegetables. This is usually followed by dessert and coffee.

When the meal is over, guests are expected to stay and get to know each other better. If the meal ends around 9:00 p.m., people generally stay about two more hours, and start leaving around 11:00 p.m. Of course, this varies greatly depending on the relationship between the host and guests, and on how far people have to drive to get home. Some parties continue much later than 11:00 p.m. On weeknights, they may end earlier.

Dining at the boss's house

Having dinner at your boss's house can be intimidating. Your behaviour can have a big influence on your career. What's more, your boss will be observing your spouse as well. Try not to be nervous, and make this an opportunity to bond with your boss and co-workers.

These same rules apply for dinner at a co-worker's house, but without your boss, the atmosphere will be more relaxed and informal.

- Ask about the dress code, and dress tastefully. If it's a dinner party, men should wear a jacket unless you are told to dress casually. Women can wear a skirt and blouse or a dress. Pay extra attention to your grooming, and make sure your shoes are shined. For a more casual gathering, such as a summer barbecue, men should still dress in crisp pants and a shirt, and women can wear a linen or cotton summer dress with classy sandals.

- Arrive on time. The hosts will have a schedule for serving food, so it's important to arrive on time—not early, but not late either. If you don't know the area, check a map carefully, or even drive there the day before so you don't get lost. Allow for traffic and weather conditions that can slow you down.

- Bring a gift, or send one ahead of time. A good gift is a bottle of wine; a plant; fancy cookies, candies, or chocolates; or a nice box of unusual teas. Flowers are always appreciated, but send them ahead of time so the host doesn't have to run around looking for a vase when you arrive. If you bring wine or some kind of food, don't be offended if the hosts don't serve it at your meal. They planned everything carefully, but they will still appreciate your gift.

- Be sure to compliment the hosts on their house, and say something specific about the décor. People usually appreciate when you mention how spacious the house is.

If they have many paintings on the walls, you can also comment on their artwork. You may get a tour of the house, but don't wander off into rooms on your own.

- Don't discuss business unless the hosts bring it up, because spouses and guests won't be able to participate in the conversation. This is a good opportunity to discover your boss's hobbies and interests.

- Compliment the hosts on the dinner at least once. If the food is unfamiliar to you, watch how the other guests eat it. If you don't like something on your plate, don't make a fuss about it. You can decline it for medical or religious reasons. Otherwise, eat around it (for example, eat the vegetables but not the meat, or vice versa), and carefully move your food around on your plate so it looks like you ate part of it.

- If the atmosphere is informal, offer to help clean up. If you are eating outside in the summer, you can help bring the plates inside, but if the hosts say they don't need help, retreat graciously. They may not want guests in their kitchen.

- Don't wear out your welcome. When the evening seems to be slowing down and the first guests get up to leave, depart as well.

- Send a thank-you note the next day, to show your appreciation for the invitation. Here is an example:

Dear Susan and Robert,

Thank you so much for inviting us to your home on Saturday. We really appreciated your wonderful food and warm hospitality.

Warmest wishes,
Carmella and Luis

Potluck parties

A potluck, or BYO (bring your own), is an informal party, often at a co-worker's home. Everyone brings something to eat—a main dish, salad, or dessert. Often, the host will ask each person to bring something specific.

This is a popular type of party for people who have busy jobs and don't have much time to entertain. When everyone pitches in, it's more fun and makes it possible to have a party.

If you are asked to contribute something, you can make it yourself, or you can pick up something from the market or deli. It's nice to bring a family recipe, especially if you can make something that the other guests may not have tasted. Everyone likes to try something new.

Dining out with co-workers

When you eat out with colleagues, the big question is how to divide the bill. If you eat at a Chinese restaurant, you will generally order several dishes for the table and share with the group. In this case, it is easy to divide the bill equally at the end.

However, if everyone orders his own dish, some people may order more than others, and it may seem unfair to make a lighter eater pay the same amount.

It's important to iron out, ahead of time, how the bill will be divided. If everyone will pay for her own meal, tell the servers this when they take your order so they can create separate bills. Servers don't like to be told at the end of the meal that you are each paying separately.

If your co-workers dine out together regularly, and it's common practice to divide the bill at the end, you'll have to go along with their system. Be conscious of what you order, and try to order food that costs more or less the same amount as what everyone else orders. If you order less, you'll resent having to pay for someone else's meal. If you order a more expensive meal or more drinks, offer to pay the difference.

If one person offers to put the whole bill on his credit card with the idea that everyone will pay him back, be sure to pay promptly. People tend to forget about small amounts they owe to other people, but it's annoying for the person who paid to have to run around asking to be paid back.

Business Buzzwords

- red-eye
- road warrior
- talk shop
- wake-up call

Chapter 16 Action Plan

1. Find out about at least one conference or trade show in your industry. Research the subjects that will be covered, and ask your manager if you are eligible to attend. You may have to make a case for attending by stating some of the benefits from this chapter. Write down how this conference or trade show can help you and your company.

   _____

   _____

2. Prepare for a business trip, conference, or trade show you will be attending. Write down:

   Your goals for the trip: _____

   Who you plan to meet: _____

   How you plan to network: _____

3. List any upcoming company events or informal gatherings with your boss or co-workers. This can include lunch or dinner with co-workers. If you don't know of any events, could you arrange to have lunch or an informal dinner to get to know one or more co-workers better? List the events you know of, or any events you can organize.

   _____

   _____

Meetings and Presentations

Meetings are a way of life for many business people. When they are well-run, meetings can be very effective tools for getting things done.

In This Chapter

- How to make your meeting time count
- How to plan and organize a meeting
- How to give a presentation
- How to speak effectively

How to make your meeting time count

It's a typical 9:00 a.m. departmental meeting. At 9:10 people are straggling in with cups of coffee, chatting about a TV show. Some people are reading the agenda. During the meeting, one person brings up an irrelevant point, which several people debate for 15 minutes, while others silently doodle on their papers. The meeting goes overtime, and some people have to leave. Another meeting is scheduled for the next day because a key topic wasn't covered.

Does this sound familiar? Many people in offices spend up to 50 percent of the work week in meetings. In fact, about a year of the average worker's life is spent in meetings.

The purpose of a meeting is to make decisions. Meetings have a bad reputation because too many of them turn into an unproductive waste of time.

Despite the negatives associated with meetings, gathering together can be an excellent tool for getting things done. Meetings are a way to enable people to come together for a common purpose, discuss information, and work as a team toward a common goal. A good meeting can provide a creative spark to stimulate group thinking and help people make decisions.

For meetings to be effective, all the participants have to play their parts. The people organizing the meeting should have a clear reason for calling the meeting, and they should know and communicate what they want to accomplish. The attendees have to understand the meeting's purpose and be ready to participate in achieving the objectives.

Think about the role you play in a meeting. As a participant, you can demonstrate your skills and talents, and also learn more about your colleagues.

Types of meetings

Well-planned meetings can be productive, but many meetings tend to be boring, pointless, and last way too long. People call meetings for all kinds of reasons, including to delay making a decision or to form a new committee (which will involve more of its own meetings).

A productive meeting has a genuine business-related purpose. The person who is calling the meeting should know why she is organizing it, and the outcomes she wants. Then she should decide who to invite, and where and when to hold the meeting. In order to avoid wasting people's time, only individuals who need to be at the meeting should be invited.

Although the word *meeting* means a gathering of two or more people, there are many types of meetings. Here are a few:

Departmental meetings

These scheduled meetings, often called Monday Morning Departmental Meetings, develop their own structures, and can range from formal to informal. They deal with work in progress and weekly work reviews, including announcements about such things as new employees and new clients. Attendees should know the purpose of these meetings and should arrive prepared to report on their work in progress or on new issues.

Project meetings

A project meeting focuses on a specific project. This is not the time to bring up general issues or grievances, such as who forgot to clean the coffee pot.

In these meetings, you'll be doing an in-depth review of your project plan. This is the time to bring up issues specific to the project you're working on, such as lack of time, being pulled off a project unexpectedly, not getting the resources you were promised, or needing more resources than you anticipated.

Participants should arrive at the meeting prepared to move quickly through the items on the agenda. Attendees should know what topics they are expected to contribute to, and be ready to intelligently report or discuss their areas of concern.

Crisis meetings

These meetings are called when there is an industry or company crisis, such as a change in the economy that affects your sales, an explosion of sales for which you can't provide the product, or a lawsuit that's been brought up against your company. If you are invited, you should consider your attendance to be mandatory.

Problem or issue meetings

These meetings are called when you have specific issues to solve. They are frequently called at short notice. This is not an invitation to a complaining session, but a time to look for solutions to the problems.

Presentations

Presentations may involve a guest speaker, or someone from your company, presenting on a specific topic, such as a new sales initiative, new insurance policy, or new system being put into place. This type of meeting is very structured. A video conference may also be part of this meeting.

Conference call

Also called a teleconference, this is a meeting for people working from different locations. People listen and take part over the phone, either from their own offices or from a conference room with speakerphones.

Conference or seminar

This is usually a formal educational event, presented by an industry expert. The meeting may be conducted at your company, a hotel, or another meeting facility.

Getting the most out of regular meetings

Regularly scheduled meetings are the most common type of meeting, and take up the most time. To make the most of these meetings, the meeting leader should go over the agenda and explain the objectives to the other participants.

The leader should refer to the agenda regularly, mention any changes to the agenda at the beginning of the meeting, and stick to the time allotted for each item. Items that need more time should be assigned to small groups or individuals for resolution, or be listed on the agenda for the next meeting. Most important, the meeting leader should begin and end the meeting at the time stated on the agenda.

As a participant, you should respect the agenda and pay attention to each item under discussion. Avoid bringing up topics that are unrelated to the agenda, or bringing up something related to item number four on the agenda while item number two is being discussed.

Arrive at the meeting prepared to succinctly discuss, and contribute to, the areas where you are concerned. If you are reporting on something, know what you have to report and how much time you will have, so you can prepare properly.

How to be a productive participant

"A successful meeting, for me, is one in which everyone participates," says Tina Bakin, Senior Manager of HR at TD Bank Financial Group. "At our weekly departmental meetings, everyone provides updates on their week and their projects. We talk about what's working well and where we need to move in a different direction.

"We had two employees who were raised in cultures where it was not acceptable to actively participate in discussions and debate solutions. They felt that they should only speak when spoken to, and didn't feel it was their place to contradict their boss or to provide better ideas. I explained to them that even if they don't agree with me, I want to hear their ideas. Their experience and perspective is key to helping us find the best solution."

In Canada, everyone who attends a meeting is expected to participate and contribute in a positive way. If you feel shy or are not sure whether you should communicate your ideas, keep in mind that companies are looking for people with leadership skills. People who can articulate their ideas and bring something to the table are more likely to advance within the company.

"If you're invited to a meeting, you're not invited as a tourist. You're expected to participate," says Michele Caba, Senior Technology Career Manager at BMO Financial Group. "Canadians are less formal than some other cultures. If you attend a meeting, put yourself on the agenda by speaking up. People want to hear your opinions."

Here are some tips for being a good participant:

- Always respond promptly to a meeting invitation if a response is requested. If you have something work-related in your schedule that conflicts with the meeting, you can phone the person who invited you to say you can't make it. This lets the person planning the meeting know that you  have a legitimate reason for not attending. If many people can't attend for the same reason, the leader may reschedule the meeting.

- Review the agenda in advance. If one hasn't been sent to you, ask the organizer for it.

- If a topic that you feel is important has been omitted, ask the meeting leader to add it to the agenda. You may have to explain why it is important to include this item.

- Be prepared. Try to familiarize yourself with the purpose of the meeting and the topic. If you will be contributing, review your materials so you are able to present them professionally and efficiently.

- Arrive for the meeting five minutes early, and plan to be available for the entire scheduled time. Assume the meeting will run overtime by 15 minutes.

- Take along any materials you want to refer to, or discuss. Make sure you have enough copies for everyone who will need them.

- Listen and be open to new ideas. Respect other people's points of view.

- Wait for your turn, and don't interrupt. However, if everyone is talking and not giving you a chance to speak, you can put up your hand to signal that you want to say something.

- When talking to the group or answering a question, speak clearly and loudly enough to be heard.

- Try not to dominate the discussion.

- Don't have side discussions with your neighbour.

- Turn off your cellphone or use the vibrate mode.

- Take notes on areas of the meeting that affect you.

- Stay focused. Don't work on your computer while someone is speaking. People won't know if you're taking notes about the meeting or planning your child's birthday party.

> **Canadian Business Concept:** In some cultures, employees are not encouraged to debate problems or challenge their managers. In Canada, everyone who attends a meeting is expected to participate and contribute in a positive way. Employees are encouraged to bring up new ideas or suggest alternative ideas— as long as this is done respectfully.

Telephone meetings

For some teams, regular telephone meetings are the only way to get together. Telephone meetings are convenient in saving travel time, and are sometimes the only option for people who work across the country or around the world to connect with one another.

However, telephone meetings tend to be less personal than face-to-face meetings because you can't see the people you are talking to. Other possible difficulties include not being able to hear other speakers clearly due to poor reception; having trouble  staying focused while someone drones on; not being able to signal to others when you want to speak; and losing track of who is talking.

Here are some tips for staying focused in telephone meetings:

- Review the agenda before the meeting. If you don't receive a copy of the agenda, ask for one.

- Call in on time, and plan to be available for the scheduled time.

- Organize your thoughts and information so you can answer questions clearly and succinctly.

- Prepare your questions—in advance or as they arise throughout the meeting—and write them down. This way you won't forget them, and they will be formulated clearly so you won't feel shy about asking.

- Listen and be open to new ideas. Respect other people's points of view.

- Try not to dominate the discussion.

- Have a glass of water available in case your throat gets dry from speaking. Also have a pen and some paper for taking notes.

- If there are many people on the call, say your name before you speak.

- Minimize distractions by calling in from a quiet place. Let people around you know when you will be on the conference call, and when it will end. Close the door to your office, if possible, so you won't be interrupted.

- Take notes on items you need to act on.

- Stay focused. Don't work on your computer or check your email during the call, or you'll lose track of what is going on.

How to plan and organize a meeting

Meetings can be productive and useful, but only if they have been planned carefully. When the purpose of a meeting is not clearly defined in advance, it can waste everyone's time and cause frustration.

If you are in charge of organizing a meeting, start by clearly defining your goals. Why are you calling this meeting? What should you and the other participants gain from it? What topics will you review from the last meeting? What new topics will you discuss?

Here are seven steps to planning a productive meeting:

1. Define the objectives. Decide what you want to accomplish at the meeting, and decide whether it will be possible to accomplish those tasks within the allotted time.

2. Select the participants. Think about who should attend. Invite only key decision-makers and people who can make a valuable contribution to the meeting. Don't waste the time of people who don't really need to be there.

3. Book the facilities. Decide where you will hold the meeting, and how many people you will have to accommodate. Make sure you have enough tables and chairs, and that the room is large enough to seat everyone comfortably.

4. Check your equipment and supplies. Depending on the type of meeting, you may need audiovisual equipment, speakers, a microphone, or flip charts. You may have to take your laptop or a projector to an off-site meeting, or you may need to rent the necessary equipment. Check that you have everything you need, such as handouts, extension cords, and markers and erasers for flip charts and whiteboards. Test all the equipment—to make sure the projector works and the markers have ink—before the meeting begins.

5. Organize the food. Refreshments are served at most meetings. Smaller or departmental meetings may have coffee with pastries or doughnuts. Larger meetings or events with clients may have more elaborate food platters that could include cheese, fruit, or sandwiches. For longer meetings, there may be a buffet lunch, or sandwiches may be brought into the meeting room.

Think about how and when the food will be served—such as before sitting down, or during the break—and aim to avoid interruptions.

Make sure to accommodate people who have special needs, such as vegetarians and people with dietary restrictions because of religious beliefs or allergies. You may want to send an email a few days before the meeting, asking participants about any food restrictions.

6. Create the agenda. Create and distribute the agenda to participants. (See the next section for tips on creating an agenda.)

7. Establish the rules. Decide on the **ground rules** that will keep the meeting productive. For example, know ahead of time who will speak, for how long, and about which topics.

Think about how the meeting will meet the participants' needs. Meeting attendees will be more likely to take action after the meeting if they understand the value of what has been discussed.

How to create an agenda

A meeting without an agenda is a recipe for disaster: participants won't know what they are supposed to do, and everyone's time will be wasted. An agenda is like a road map. It tells everyone where you are going, and shows that you value their time.

To create your agenda, outline the topics to be covered and prioritize them. Assign a specific amount of time for each item. (Refer to the sample agenda on page 373.) If you have three hours worth of material to cover but only one hour for the meeting, you won't cover all of your topics. Your lack of planning will reflect badly on you as the meeting leader.

Use your agenda as a guideline, but be prepared to adjust the timing if some topics take more or less time than you had planned.

Here are some tips on creating an agenda:

- Make sure to read some of your company's previous agendas, and follow the same format. Don't try to reinvent the wheel.

- Write the purpose of your meeting in one clear sentence, such as, "The purpose of Tuesday's meeting is to review and agree on the details of the marketing plan."

- Use strong, powerful verbs that describe an objective you can measure. Some examples of strong verbs are *agree on*, *compile*, *complete*, *assign*, and *finalize*.

- Include the start time and end time.

- List the topics to be discussed, and allot a specific amount of time for each item. This will help presenters prepare their material.

- Include the location. For off-site meetings, this should include the street address, floor, room number, and a map if necessary.

- Distribute your agenda as early as possible—give it out at least one day in advance at the latest—to make sure attendees have sufficient time to prepare.

- When you distribute the agenda, ask attendees whether they have any topics to add. Ask them to respond at least one day prior to the meeting. Then decide which items should be added. You may not want to spend meeting time giving out specific information. A meeting should really be to discuss important topics and create plans. You can use email or regular mail to send out information.

- Prioritize the items in a logical sequence, according to what is most important. Create the final agenda, allotting time for each item.

- At the top of the agenda, include the names of everyone who will be attending the meeting.

- Distribute the agenda to all the participants. You can send it out as an email attachment.

Checklist for running a successful meeting

As the organizer of the meeting, your job is to stick to the agenda, maintain a positive atmosphere, and help people discuss the items and stay on track. It's a good idea to have a time-keeper and a note-taker to help you keep the meeting on target.

Here is a checklist for running a successful meeting:

✓ Remind participants about the meeting one day in advance, through a memo, email, or phone call.

✓ Greet people as they arrive. Start the meeting at the time stated on your agenda. Don't repeat information for latecomers—this is rude to the people who were on time.

✓ Clearly state the reason for the meeting. Although the objectives should be listed on your agenda, this will remind attendees of why they are there, and focus the meeting. Explain why the objectives are relevant, and re-emphasize them if people get off track.

✓ Quickly review the topics and time allotted for each, as well as the ending time of the meeting

✓ Appoint a secretary and a note-taker. Ask one person to keep the minutes of the meeting, and the other person to record ideas and discussion topics on a flip chart or whiteboard. You can ask either of these people (or appoint someone else) to watch the clock and help you manage the time.

✓ Follow the agenda. Cover the most important items first, in order of the priority you established. Don't try to cover all the small or easy items first, because you may get sidetracked and never get to the most important items.

✓ Manage your time. If an item needs more discussion than you have time for, assign this further development or discussion to an individual or group to take care of. Or add it to the notes on your flip chart to be discussed at a future meeting.

✓ Keep the discussion focused. As the leader, it's your job to make sure that discussions remain on the topic and participants don't get sidetracked by other issues. Listen carefully when people speak or ask questions, and make sure everyone has a chance to give an opinion.

✓ Clarify the actions that you expect people to take. Different individuals can leave a meeting with completely different ideas about what was said and what actions they should take. This is why it's important for the meeting leader to review the decisions, and state clearly who is responsible for which items. A good way to do this is to ask each person to state the action they are accountable for and write it down. Each item should have a deadline for completion, or for checkpoints along the way. This creates a follow-up action plan.

✓ Have a note-taker write down all the action items that are discussed at the meeting. After the meeting, you can type a clear action list and distribute it to all the participants. The action list should include information about who will do what, and when it will be done.

✓ Summarize the meeting. Review the decisions reached, and ask whether anyone has any questions or is confused about anything. State how the meeting was useful, the objectives you achieved, the steps to be taken, and who is responsible for each step.

✓ Thank the group for their participation and inform them of the date of the next meeting, if one is scheduled.

Handling difficult participants

What do you do when one participant rambles off topic, another participant tries to hijack the meeting with a different agenda, and a silent person refuses to contribute? Here are some tips for dealing with difficult participants:

Big talkers

If someone tries to take over the meeting or change the subject, decide whether the idea has merit. If it doesn't, try to get back on topic by saying "Did we want to wrap up issue X before we move on?" If the idea does have merit, you can thank the person for contributing and ask her to put together a report on her thoughts. If the topic warrants it, you might even suggest that the person form a committee to pursue the topic.

continued on page 374

Sample Meeting Agenda

Agenda

ABC Company
Departmental Meeting, May 10, 2015
10:00–12:00 a.m.
Conference Room

Purpose: To review and agree on the details of the marketing plan

Participants: Nadia Holt, Mindy White, Rich Smith, Deta Gan, Bob Ellert, Lu Wong, Dino Capellin, Sashi Vermani

1. Call to order; attendance
2. Approval of agenda
3. Approval of minutes from previous meeting
4. Committee reports

	Presenter	Time
a. Website update	Nadia	5 minutes
b. Sales meeting decisions	Mindy	5 minutes

5. Old business

	Presenter	Time
a. Review marketing initiatives	Rick	5 minutes
b. Internal newsletter	Deta	5 minutes

6. New Business

	Presenter	Time
a. Agree on new marketing strategy	Bob	15 minutes
b. Complete marketing campaign details	Lu	15 minutes
c. Assign tasks	Dino	10 minutes
d. Finalize details for product launch	Sashi	10 minutes

7. Announcements

8. Summary; establish date of next meeting

People who argue

There's often at least one argumentative person in the group. One way to defuse a heated statement is to acknowledge the value of the person's point of view and ask other people for their opinions. "Dawn, it's important to hear from someone as concerned about this issue as you are. I'm grateful that you brought this to our attention. Does anyone have any suggestions for how to handle this situation?"

People who have private conversations

If people are chatting about private matters while the meeting is in progress, stop talking. When the talkers hear their own voices instead of yours, glance at them quickly. Then continue talking while making eye contact with the other participants.

Shy people

Participants who are shy may not feel comfortable giving their opinions in meetings. Try to draw them in by increasing your eye contact with them, or ask, "Does accounting have anything to say about this matter?"

If these people are intimidated by large groups, give them time to discuss their ideas first with a partner or a small group. Give positive reinforcement when they participate.

How to host a meeting with a guest speaker

If you are in charge of bringing in a guest speaker to talk to your group, you'll want to make sure that things go smoothly. Here are some recommendations:

• Discuss the meeting objectives with the presenter ahead of time.

• Give the speaker information about the audience: who will attend, how much they know about the topic, and what you need the attendees to learn. Discuss how the speaker will cover the content, and encourage her to be as interactive as possible.

- Go over the logistics, including the meeting location, starting and ending time, and audiovisual needs. Make sure the speaker knows what time to arrive and where to sit before presenting.

- Ask for the presenter's biography so you can prepare an introduction.

How to give a presentation

The first time your boss asks you to formally present something to your department or a client, your reaction may be to panic. But remember that being asked to present is a compliment. Someone believes that you have valuable information to share with the group, and wants to listen to your ideas.

It's understandable to feel nervous, but developing presentation skills is one of the most valuable things you can do for your career. Most business professionals make presentations to their co-workers or clients on a regular basis. Also, if you belong to any networking groups, you will be asked to stand up and introduce yourself. The more you practise public speaking, the better you will become.

Planning your talk

Find your big idea

You may be asked to speak about a topic you are familiar with, but you still need to define exactly what you will say during the allotted time. Try to hone your idea down to one sentence. What do you want your audience to remember or learn as a result of listening to you? This is your "big idea."

Remember that people have short attention spans, and tend to have many things on their minds. If you try to tell them everything you know about a topic, you will confuse them. Instead, find one memorable idea about your topic that will stick in their minds.

Develop your topic

Think of three main points you want to make to support your big idea. Develop a story or anecdote to illustrate each main point. This could be something that happened to you or someone you know, or something you read in a newspaper or magazine.

Add some interaction

Even if you only have five minutes to speak, you can still involve the audience. For example, you can ask a question that begins, "How many of you …?" Raise your hand when you ask these questions, so audience members will do the same.

During longer presentations, you can use many interactive techniques. For example, you can survey the audience by asking them to raise their hands to show whether they prefer option A or B. You can ask participants to discuss a situation in small groups and report back, or use a training game to break the ice or energize the group.

When you engage the audience, they will have fun and remember what you say during your presentation. You'll be considered a better speaker than someone who just drones on.

Create excitement with visuals

We've all heard the saying, *A picture is worth a thousand words.* Think about how you can add visual excitement to your talk. Props are a wonderful way to make your presentation come alive. You could do something as simple as putting on a hat to signal a different part of your presentation, or holding up a toy telephone receiver when talking about customer service on the phone.

Use slides effectively

One of the classic mistakes of inexperienced presenters is to put large blocks of text on PowerPoint slides—and sometimes on handouts as well—and then read the text out loud. This is boring for the meeting participants for several reasons:

- Your audience may be squinting as they attempt to read the lines, and will not be listening to you at all.

- If they are able to read the text, they will read it more quickly than you can speak, so they'll be way ahead of you (and will not be listening to you).

- Most people will reason that if everything you say is written down, you should have just sent out a document to read and saved everyone the time spent attending the meeting.

Include only a few words per slide, in bullet-point form. The accepted rule is to use no more than six words per line, and no more than six lines of text per slide. Even better, use a picture, chart, or graph instead of words to convey your message instantly.

Be sure that each slide has a headline as well, to orient people to the topic.

Capture attention

Think of a dynamic and unusual way to start your presentation. This might involve holding up your prop or telling a story that relates to your topic. Never begin with, "Thank you for inviting me here to talk with you today." You'll put your audience to sleep right away. Start off strong so they will listen with curiosity and interest.

After your dynamic opening, introduce yourself briefly and thank the audience for taking the time to listen to you.

Plan your ending: Try to end in a memorable way as well. Remember that people remember best what they heard at the beginning and at the end of a presentation. Finish with a humorous story or by asking the audience to do something (giving them a call to action).

Practise, practise, practise

Don't try to memorize your talk or read it word-for-word. It will sound stilted and boring. Instead, practise your dynamic opening and closing until you can deliver them effortlessly. Rehearse your opening in front of the mirror or for a friend, until you feel confident. Once you are in front of your audience and the opening goes well, you'll feel a burst of confidence that will help you sail through the rest of the presentation.

Giving a polished performance

Once you have organized your presentation and know your opening and closing remarks, all you need are a few platform skills to make you look like a pro.

Make eye contact with your audience and smile

This is the most important thing you can do to create a positive rapport with your audience. You have to connect with listeners to keep them engaged and listening.

To gain their trust, look at one person in the audience for two to three seconds, as if you were having a one-on-one conversation. Then move to another audience member and do the same. Making eye contact will also give you a clue as to whether your audience is becoming bored. If you see people looking at their watches or getting restless, ask them a question or try to engage them in some way.

Stand and walk tall

Keep your shoulders back and your head up so you look self-assured. Use your arms to gesture.

Don't fidget

Many presenters jingle coins in their pockets or unconsciously play with a watch or ring. Nervous habits will distract your audience. Remove everything from your pockets, and keep your hands by your side when you're not using them to make a point. Use purposeful movements, such as counting off points with your fingers.

Speak with confidence

Don't drone on in a monotone voice, or you'll lull your audience to sleep. Vary your pitch, volume, and rate of speech. Pause occasionally to emphasize your points and let your message sink in.

Dress the part

In most situations, you should wear your best business suit. Even if your participants are dressed very casually, you should still wear a jacket when you present. Make sure your clothes are clean and pressed, and your shoes are polished

Pay extra attention to your hair and grooming, and especially to your hands. Make sure your fingernails are in good shape because they will be in full view.

Be rested and nourished

Try to relax the evening before and get a good night's sleep. Eat nourishing food for energy, but don't overeat if you want to be at your peak energy level.

Meet and greet

At the presentation, try to meet and greet people as they enter the room. Shake hands and introduce yourself. This goes a long way toward creating a rapport with the audience. Once they've met you, you will begin to establish a relationship. As a result, they will listen more carefully, and you'll feel like you are talking to friends rather than strangers.

Provide handouts at the end

Hand out any necessary materials at the end of the presentation, not at the beginning. If you give them out before your talk, people will start reading them instead of listening to you. Before you begin speaking, let people know that you'll be giving them a handout, so they won't be frantically taking notes.

Canadian Business Concept: Speaking well to a group is an important skill to everyone in business. You may have to present to a client, to your department, or to the entire staff at a company meeting. An excellent way to learn to speak more powerfully is to join Toastmasters, an organization that helps people feel confident speaking in public. You can find chapters in almost every city.

How to speak effectively
Using your voice to connect with your audience

Sanjay was preparing to update the sales and marketing personnel on the results of his market research. He was normally a fast speaker, and his rate of speech tended to increase even more when he was nervous. Combined with his accent, he could be difficult for his co-workers to understand.

His manager coached him before the presentation, and signalled him during the presentation whenever he began to speed up. Once he became aware of his speech patterns, he worked on modifying them. His professional presentation at the meeting raised his profile within the organization.

The human voice can communicate powerful messages. People learn to use their voices in many different ways. They also use words, phrases, and gestures in specific ways that may be common to people from one culture, but alien to those from another.

When we hear other people speak, we unconsciously register the quality of their voices, as well as the words they use. We react negatively to a variety of intonations and speech patterns, including voices that are monotonous or too high-pitched, and speakers who mumble, speak very quickly, or speak very slowly.

"When you come from a different language background, it's important to slow down for the first few minutes when you speak in public," says Montreal voice coach Sheelagh Freeman. "Every language has its major and minor tones, and people have to become attuned to the nuances of your speech before they can understand you.

"Language is formed in different parts of the mouth, and when you don't open your mouth much, you tend to speak more rapidly. However, you will have less vocal variety (high and low tones), and you can easily end up speaking in a monotone. This tends to distance you from your audience, and people disconnect and become bored."

When you speak to a group, try to be aware of the following vocal elements:

Vocal variety

Having too much vocal variety will make you sound as if you are singing, but not having enough variation will make you sound monotonous. Canadian professionals value a voice that has energy. They regard a person who speaks in a monotone as lacking enthusiasm, or being tired or bored. This directly impacts your professional credibility.

People from some countries minimize vocal variety and think that Canadian speaking styles are overdone. A recent immigrant from India observed that "Indians tend to speak in a monotone, while Canadians have more highs and lows in their voice. It took me some time to understand this. Listen to people's voices carefully and try to adjust your voice so they understand you better. Remember that people like and feel comfortable with people who are like themselves."

Canadian Business Concept: People from some cultures speak with a great deal of vocal variety, while those from other cultures limit their voices' ups and downs. Listen carefully to the speech patterns of people you work with. Do they use more or fewer ups and downs than you do? Try to adjust your speech to match the people around you. It will help them understand you better.

Tone

Your tone of voice mirrors your emotional and physical state. When you are feeling positive, strong, and healthy, the tone of your voice will be upbeat and energetic. When you are feeling unhappy, negative emotions can come through in your voice as well.

Sheelagh Freeman says, "If you want to persuade and motivate people, your tone needs to be warm, inviting, and collaborative. To do this, it's necessary to open your mouth, lips, and jaw. If you don't open your mouth (enough) when you speak, your voice may sound cold, directive, and less enthusiastic and collaborative.

Volume

Try to keep your tone warm and inviting.

In Canada, people who speak too softly can be perceived as being nervous or lacking in self-confidence. In a one-on-one exchange, however, softer voices can make the speaker seem more friendly and approachable. People who speak more loudly are perceived to have confidence and leadership abilities, but a voice that is too loud can be intimidating.

To connect with people, mirror their speech patterns. When they speak softly, try to speak more softly as well. When you speak to a crowd of 200, you need volume to project your voice to the back of the room. Make sure to hold the same volume right to the end of your sentence, so your voice doesn't fade away.

Pitch

Pitch refers to how high or low your voice sounds, and it is the easiest way to add variety. Low-pitched voices are pleasing to the ear and are equated with trustworthiness, credibility, and control. High-pitched voices are associated with youth and with strong emotions such as nervousness or agitation. High-pitched voices tend to lack professional credibility in western cultures.

"Culturally, Asian women are expected to speak in a higher pitch, but this can make it difficult for them to establish their credibility in Canada," Freeman says. "As well, when people are excited or nervous, their pitch naturally goes up.

"I teach people to lower their pitch, which you can do to a certain extent. This makes your voice easier to listen to, increases your credibility, and helps you get your message across with more impact."

Be careful to avoid using a rising inflection at the end of your sentence when you are not asking a question. This will make you sound hesitant and unsure of yourself. Instead, your pitch should fall on the final word of a statement.

Be careful, however, not to fade out vocally in the middle or the end of a sentence. This can make it sound like someone is pulling the plug on you. To avoid this, keep your sentences relatively short and keep your energy up, right to the end of the sentence. Finish one idea before you begin another, to help people retain what you are saying.

Speed

Some people try to fill every gap with conversation, and talk too much and too quickly. Talking quickly adds energy to your voice, and shows enthusiasm, up to a point. If listeners can't follow you or get a word in edgewise, they will lose interest. If you normally talk quickly, slow down a bit. You'll appear more friendly and approachable.

"One way to slow down is to pause. This allows time for your thoughts to reach the audience, and makes you intelligible. Deal with one idea at a time. Remember that you know what you're going to say, but your audience doesn't. They need time to process the information as you speak," advises Freeman.

People who take forever to get their thoughts out can be equally frustrating. Slow talkers may appear tired or bored, or even self-absorbed. If you speak slowly, you may want to increase your speed, particularly when you're conversing with a person who speaks quickly.

Accent

"Look at everyone as if they were an immigrant. In Canada, most people were immigrants one or two generations back," says Michele Caba, Senior Technology Career Manager, BMO Financial Group. "Try not to be self conscious if you speak with an accent. Chances are you aren't the only person who is not speaking your mother tongue.

"If you don't feel confident speaking in public, an excellent resource is Toastmasters. We had a foreign student working with us who had an introverted personality. It was hard to get her out of her shell. She joined Toastmasters, and eventually worked her way to the top of her Toastmasters group. As she became more confident speaking in public, her true personality emerged, and she was very successful in her job."

If English is your second language, speaking without an accent will be nearly impossible unless you began speaking the language at a very early age. If your vocabulary and grammar are fine, your accent will not greatly affect how well you are understood.

Try not to be self-conscious about your accent. People will respect you for what you do in the workplace, and you'll find people with many different accents working together in Canada.

If you are concerned that your co-workers have difficulty understanding you when you speak, you may want to do some vocal preparations prior to important meetings or presentations, paying attention to your vocal clarity.

You can identify your vocal characteristics by recording yourself reading your presentation, and playing it back, or by asking a trusted friend for feedback.

Before a meeting or presentation, make sure to practise what you will say out loud, not just in your head. This will help you pace your speech well, and you'll learn when to project more enthusiasm, and when to pause for emphasis.

If you find that you have a lot of difficulty being understood, look for a teacher or voice coach who can help you.

From powerless to powerful phrases

 Lin, Vice-President of Sales and Marketing, was giving an update on the new product launch. The power of her voice was captivating. She stood tall and spoke positively. She talked about new opportunities, and her confidence that the company would be successful.

Several years ago, Lin spoke with hesitancy. She hedged her phrases with, "I guess maybe we could ..." Vocal coaching helped her eliminate distracters in her speech and learn how to use powerful language that projects authority and confidence.

A phrase such as, "I was wondering if we could ...?" shows a lack of confidence. To succeed in the Canadian workplace, learn to say what you think, politely and firmly. This can be especially difficult for women who come from cultures in which they were taught not to express their opinions.

Here are some weak phrases to avoid, and some suggestions for ways to rephrase them more powerfully:

Weak phrase	More powerful phrase
I'm wondering if we could ...?	Could we ...?
I'm not sure about this, but we could ...	We could ... / Let's ...
I suppose / I guess, perhaps ...	Let's ... / I suggest that we ...
This may be only how I feel, but ...	Please consider ...
I guess my question is ...	My question is ...
I'm not sure, but maybe we could ...	My research shows that we should ...
This is only my opinion / suggestion ...	In my opinion / I suggest ...

Speech habits such as saying *uh* or *um* every few seconds or using the words *like* or *okay* in every sentence make you sound unprofessional in the workplace.

Don't begin your questions with, "This might be a stupid question ..." It's probably a question that many other people have, but are afraid to ask. Besides, whether or not it's a stupid question, you've just suggested to everyone that it is.

To change speech habits, you first have to become aware of them. Ask a friend to signal you every time you use your problem word or phrase. You may be frustrated at first, but once you become aware of your habits, you'll be able to break them.

Please consider this

Now please consider the effect of a few more powerful words: *please, thank you*, and *consider*.

Inviting others to consider your idea gives them a choice, and *consider* is one of the words least likely to provoke resistance.

Please and *thank you* convey appreciation and gratitude. They are words we have been conditioned to use since childhood, and are associated with rewards and favours.

Think about the simplicity and power of the following sentences: "Please consider my proposal to work on this project. Thank you."

Business Buzzwords

- big idea
- bring something to the table
- engage the audience
- hijack a meeting

Chapter 17 Action Plan

1. In Canada, employees are expected to participate actively in meetings. Write three ways you can participate at a meeting more effectively.

   a) _____

   b) _____

   c) _____

2. Write three ways you can improve your presentation skills, to create more impact in your next presentation.

   a) _____

   b) _____

   c) _____

3. Write three ways you can change your speech patterns or the words you use to speak more clearly and powerfully.

   a) _____

   b) _____

   c) _____

Words of Wisdom on Achieving Success

Take responsibility for your career

"You are the hero of your own story. When meeting with a prospective employer, it becomes apparent within 30 seconds whether or not you believe in yourself.

"Most people in business have to fire on all four cylinders. Immigrants need all their cylinders, plus a turbo charger. This means you have to do everything you can to succeed. Immerse yourself in this new culture. Network to build connections, and strive to ensure that both you and those in your network are successful.

"Turbo-charge your career by delivering above and beyond expectations."

—**Tej Singh Hazra**, Senior Manager, Corporate Diversity & Inclusion, IBM Canada Ltd.

"Be brave and put your hand up.

"In Africa and Asia, often the village or community is your family. Canada is more individualistic, so you may feel isolated at first. The best way I know to make friends and improve your work experience is to volunteer. Employers will recognize the value of your experience, whether it's maintaining a website for an organization, being on the board of directors, or managing a project.

"As an immigrant, you have to take the first step. Volunteer for committees at your workplace. Join community associations. You'll build a sense of family by working with people, and be recognized for your leadership—which will help you succeed in Canada."

—**Yasmin Meralli**, Vice-President of Diversity and Workplace Equity, BMO Bank of Montreal

"Invest in yourself. A large part of this is managing your time. Immigrants from some cultures tend to make their job their whole life. You have to pace yourself, or you'll get burned out and be disappointed with the results you get.

"Spend 80 percent of your time and energy in your job, and 20 percent in learning. Don't accept where you are as being fate. If you say, 'I'm going to stay here, it's too difficult to change,' you will. Spend time reading, networking, and speaking to other people. Your first job may not be what you like. You may have to retake exams, or learn how Canadians speak. Find your own path and invest in yourself. Your career will progress more quickly."

—**Paresh Vyas**, Consulting Architect, IBM

"Leverage your assets. If you speak a second or third language such as Cantonese or Mandarin, let your employer know that you can deal with clients and understand their cultures. This is a big asset in Canada."

—**Srini Iyengar**, Director Multicultural Markets, GTA Division, BMO Bank of Montreal.

"Always look for ways to improve. For example, request formal or informal training from the company. Formal, scheduled coaching sessions from your boss will help you break into the Canadian working environment in the shortest time possible. Take courses that relate to your tasks, to demonstrate your commitment to your employer and your passion to do a better job. Come to your boss with your study plan and its benefit to the company and its customers.

"Express your thoughts on own career development. Look for opportunities in your organization and let your boss know, respectfully and politely, about your desire to advance. Your boss may be preoccupied with his daily routine and won't read your mind, so you have to say what you want. Canadian bosses are very open and do not mind when you openly discuss career advance opportunities at the right time."

—**Adrian Cheung**, Director, Multicultural Marketing BMO Bank of Montreal

Understand the Canadian workplace culture

"In Canada, it is okay to say *no* to your boss—politely.

"In many cultures, people never say *no* to the boss. But in Canada, your boss will appreciate your input. I tell people in my department, 'Don't say yes to everything I say. Tell me if you have a better idea. I can be wrong.' Canadians recognize the value of different opinions. Saying *yes* all the time here can be perceived as a sign of weakness."

—**Haakon Saake**, Information Technology Manager, Toromont Industries

"To succeed in Canada you have to understand your company's culture and environment. Take a proactive approach to integrating into your organization by getting involved in company activities. Remember that succeeding in the Canadian workplace works two ways: both the employer and the employee have to play their parts."

—**Lynn Palmer**, former CEO Canadian Council of Human Resources Associations

Improve your English communication skills

"Concentrate on your English. If you know you aren't speaking perfectly, it will affect your self-esteem and you won't push as hard to achieve your goals.

"Find out your weaknesses, and get help. For example, do you need to learn how to write better? Is accent your biggest problem? Get a language coach, or take ESL courses.

"Immerse yourself in the English language. Put down your Chinese newspaper and read the *Toronto Star*. Talk to co-workers in English, because if you speak Mandarin at home, and talk to your Chinese co-workers in Mandarin at work, you'll never improve your English.

"You can also join one of the many language clubs where you meet someone who wants to learn your language. You discuss a topic for one hour in your native language, and another hour in English.

"Another tip is to offer to do presentations in English. This may be very hard for you, but it's an excellent way to learn to express yourself and gain confidence in speaking English."

—**Haakon Saake**

"Using appropriate Canadian language is the first challenge. Newcomers entering the Canadian workforce have to learn the way Canadians say things. In general, Chinese people tend to be quieter at meetings, especially when they are the only Chinese person in an English environment. When I first started working in Canada, I would attend meetings and not say anything. I had many good ideas, but I felt I could not express them properly, so I kept my ideas to myself.

"The keys to overcoming the obstacles are listening to radio and TV, and mingling with Canadians at various social settings, plus constant practice. According to feedback from Canadian friends and business associates, most Chinese newcomers do not articulate clearly. The last syllable of the word is often dropped or pronounced too weakly. To improve, practice by reading articles aloud, recording yourself, and playing it back."

—**Adrian Cheung**

Network and build relationships

"Always be sensitive to other people's cultures. We often assume certain things about a culture. Try not to make assumptions. Educate yourself. Ask questions. Most people are willing to share.

"I work in a team that includes people from India, Pakistan, China, Tibet, Greece, and Canada. We try to define our commonalities: how many things do we share? This helps us connect."

—**Rania Llewellyn**, Vice-President of Multicultural Banking, Scotiabank

"Attending office, business, and social events is a good method of finding out about your company's culture. This is a good way to quietly observe how your company operates."

—**Sharon Wingfelder**, Vice-President of Human
Resources, Diversity and Resourcing, CIBC

"We rarely make small-talk in my culture. I realized that making small-talk is important in Canada. People talk about the weather, sports, and other topics. When I came here, I learned about the (Toronto) Blue Jays and the Raptors. That made it easy to start conversations. Take time to learn about Canadian sports and topics that people discuss. Mention their achievements and give praise when it's appropriate. Attend all the events that your company sponsors, and get involved. You'll find it much easier to make connections, and you'll see the Canadian community in a different way."

—**Rakesh Kirtikar**, Senior Manager of Multicultural
and Local Marketing, Scotiabank

Have a positive attitude and good work ethic

"As a new immigrant, often the biggest barrier is yourself. Ask yourself what you are afraid of. Do you need to improve your English? Take more language courses. Be patient. Remember that it takes time to settle down and integrate into a new culture."

—**Catalina Duque**, Graduate Leadership Program Associate, RBC

"Be positive at the workplace. Everyone has problems outside of work, but bringing them into the office is one of the biggest mistakes. You are there to work, not to be solving personal problems at your desk. This also includes not using the phone for personal calls, surfing the Internet or using instant messaging during working hours. If you have a cellphone, turn it off at work and check your messages on your breaks or at your lunch hour."

—**Karen Wallis-Musselman**, HR Independent Consultant

"Take courage a step father. It took courage to come here and leave behind your language, culture, families and all things comfortable. When you are beginning a new job, keep up that courageous spirit. If you gravitate to people only from your cultural background you'll miss opportunities and exposure to leadership, different team dynamics, and a chance to grow in ways that you may not have known to be possible. Meet new people, work hard, and learn the skills you need for your new life in Canada."

—**Gita Clarkson**, People Exchange

"Attitude is very important. If you have a question, don't ask people from your cultural background, because everyone will say something different given that they migrated at different times. What may have been true in their experience may no longer be the reality now. Ask Canadians. You'll learn the Canadian perspective, and this will help you transition better to Canada.

"There is nothing wrong with being with people with whom you share your cultural background, but when you unconsciously seek your comfort zone by being with them, it prevents you from exploring new opportunities with Canadians, and finding out what the new culture can offer, which is important for your growth in the new environment."

—**Ringo Morella**, Senior Manager of Human Resources,
Mead Johnson Nutrition

access badge: a card or other piece of identification that lets people into buildings or through locked doors

accountability: responsibility for quality of work, meeting deadlines, etc

ace a presentation: give the best presentation you can

active listening: focus attentively on what someone is saying

admin: abbreviation for administration

American style: the style of eating common in the US and Canada

armed with (a plan): to bring your plan or suggestions with you to a meeting

ASAP: acronym for "as soon as possible"

awry: if something goes wrong, we say it went awry

baby boomer: a person born shortly after World War II

backfire: go wrong, often with the opposite result than you intended

beat around the bush: speak indirectly to avoid saying what you mean

bellhop: a hotel employee who takes luggage from the car or taxi and delivers it to your room

beneficiary: the person who will be able to use your benefits, such as medical and dental coverage, and who will receive money from your life insurance if you die

bereavement: the state of mourning the death of a loved one

best practices: the most effective way of doing something

big idea: an important idea or message

big picture: the project or company as a whole

bigwig: an important person in the company

birthright: to own something or have certain rights since birth instead of earning them

board of trade: a local network of businesses that work together to promote business interests

body language: non-verbal communication through posture, gestures, and facial expressions

boost someone up the ladder: help someone get promoted

bottom line: the company's net profit or loss; the essential details

bounced around (on the phone): to be transferred from one person to another on the phone

breathing space: extra time; personal space

bring something to the table: come to a meeting with ideas and suggestions

broaden your horizons: create new opportunities for yourself

brownie points: imaginary social points awarded for something you've done to please someone

business casual dress: a style of dressing that is both professional and relaxed

business speak: language that is overly technical

BYO: acronym for "bring your own"

call to action: request for an audience, a reader, or a person to do something

camaraderie: mutual trust and familiarity among friends

canapé: a cracker or piece of bread topped with cheese or a spread, served as an appetizer

caps: capital letters

carry-on bag: a small bag that you can take with you onto an airplane

cat will be out of the bag: the secret will be exposed

cell yell: speaking too loudly on a cellphone

chamber of commerce: a local network of businesses that work together to promote business interests

charisma: the ability to attract and influence people

chatterbox: someone who talks all the time

cheat sheet: a small piece of paper with essential information to help you remember something

chew up time: take up too much time

chief executive officer (CEO): the company's leader

chip in: contribute money towards a gift for someone from all or most employees

chit-chat: light conversation

civic holiday: holiday on which employees get the day off or are paid extra to work

closed body language: withdrawing and placing physical barriers between yourself and someone else

comfort zone: physical space around us that we only let certain people into

concierge: hotel employee whose job is to respond to guests' needs, such as booking theatre tickets or finding a restaurant

connect the dots: say something in an obvious way to help someone understand

Continental style: a style of eating common in Europe, often considered to be more sophisticated than American style

controversial: causing disagreements or arguments

corner someone: put someone in a position where he or she cannot leave

corporate survival: continued employment in a company or industry

cover for someone: lie to protect someone

cubicle: a small space in an office that is separated from other spaces by low, temporary walls

culture: the values, social practices, rituals, and ways of communicating of a country or organization

demoralized: lacking confidence and enthusiasm

dermatologist: a doctor who specializes in diseases and problems related to skin

direct communication: saying things as clearly as possible, using few words

direct deposit: method of depositing money directly into employees' bank accounts instead of giving them cheques

directives: instructions

discreet: careful not to cause embarrassment by attracting attention

dishing the dirt: gossiping

do your own thing: do whatever is important to you

do's and don'ts: the things you should and should not do

doorman: hotel employee who handles the arrivals and departures of guests and gets you a taxi when you need one

downcast: unhappy; looking downwards

drone on: talk about something for so long that it becomes boring

dynamics: the way people interact in a group

eat and run: leave as soon as you are done eating; generally considered rude in Canada

eh: an expression used at the end of a sentence when asking for agreement

elbow room: space to move around

emoticon: symbol used in an email to represent a facial expression

enabler: someone who can help you

engage (in conversation): begin a conversation with someone

engage the audience: keep the audience interested and involved

enunciating: the way someone pronounces words

estate: all the money and property that a person owns, especially everything that is left when he or she dies.

euphemism: polite way of saying something unpleasant

ex: person you used to have a romantic relationship with but don't anymore

eye contact: looking directly into someone's eyes

fire off: send quickly, especially an email

flats: dress shoes with a flat sole instead of a raised heel

flextime: schedule in which employees work a set number of hours but have some flexibility in when they begin and end their work day

flip-flops: casual, open-style shoes that are held to the foot by straps between the toes

gender-neutral: treating women and men equally

get a word in edgewise: make comments while speaking with someone

get to the point: say what you mean directly

give-and-take: willingness to compromise

go the extra mile: do something extra for someone

go to bat for someone: help or support someone

go with the flow: stop worrying and do what needs to be done

go-to person: the person to talk to if you have questions about the company

grapevine: the way people pass gossip along

grind to a halt: stop abruptly

ground rules: guidelines participants must follow

hard feelings: resentment or anger

hat hair: hair that is messy from being under a hat

have the executives' ears: have the attention of the executives, the executives are willing to listen to your ideas

header: title at the top of a memo or other document

heads-up: a warning that something might happen

hidden agenda: secret motive

hierarchal: organization that has ranks from lowest to highest and tends to be very authoritarian

high-maintenance employee: employee who requires a lot of attention

high-touch society: society where people touch each other frequently

hijack a meeting: take over a meeting that you are not leading

hog the floor: talk for so long so that others don't get a chance to speak

hold a grudge: be angry towards someone for something that happened in the past

home away from home: place where you feel as comfortable as you do at home

home team: local sports team

hot button: sensitive topic that may make someone upset or angry

human resources (HR): the department in a company that is in charge of employing new workers and taking care of all the workers in the company

image consultant: someone whose job is to give fashion advice

impersonal: not having or showing emotions or personality

imply: suggest something without actually saying it

in a bind: in a difficult situation

in good hands: being taken care of by someone responsible

in jeopardy: in danger

in someone else's shoes: in the same situation as someone else

in the loop: aware of important things that are happening

in the same boat: in the same situation

indirect communication: using facial expressions and body language to get your meaning across, while avoiding saying what you mean directly

information overload: too much information

information technology (IT): the study of computer systems for collecting, storing, and sharing information

instrumental: very important in helping someone or in getting something done

insurance claim: a request for payment from an insurance company if you've been sick, hurt, etc.

interpersonal space: space between two people that determines how closely people stand to each other

intimidate: make someone feel afraid

intranet: computer network within a company or organization

inundated: to be given more than you can deal with

jargon: special or technical language that only people from certain groups or professions understand

keep a low profile: try not to attract attention

keep a straight face: avoid showing any emotions on your face

keep your eye on the ball: focus your attention on what is important

key phrases: useful phrases that you can use in many situations

kill someone with kindness: be very kind to someone

land the job: get the job

learn the ropes: learn how to do your job correctly, learn how your company works

learn to live with something: accept something unpleasant

lend a hand: offer to help

like pulling teeth: very difficult

look (or feel) like a million bucks: look (or feel) extremely good

lose track: forget about the time; become unfocused

low talker: someone who speaks quietly

lunch break: time off from work in the middle of the day to eat lunch

mannerism: way of speaking or body movement that is typical of a specific person

maternity leave: paid time away from work for a mother after having a baby

medicare: medical care that is paid for by the government

mission impossible: task that can't be accomplished successfully

mix and mingle: network, meet lots of different people

movers and shakers: people who make things happen

netiquette: etiquette on the Internet

network: (noun) a group of people or organizations who work closely together; (verb) to create relationships with people who may be able to help you in your career

new-hire folder: information given to new employees about the company

new thread: new email conversation with a separate subject line

nickel-and-dimed: asked for money often

non-verbal: communication through body language is called non-verbal

norm: customary way of doing things

object of your affection: someone you have romantic feelings toward

objective: goal or purpose

off the ground: started

off-colour: offensive (comments or slogans)

on the right foot: to start something well

on the wrong foot: to start something badly

open body language: facing someone and making eye contact to invite interaction

opening line: way to begin a conversation

optometrist: healthcare professional who tests your eyes and tells you what kind of glasses you need

orientation: the process of learning about something, like a company

out of the running: not being considered for the job

out the window: disappeared

over-accessorize: wear too much jewellery

overtime: time at work after regular working hours end

pad your account: put extra expenses on your account, beyond what your employer would normally reimburse you for

paternity leave: paid time away from work for a father after his partner has a baby

payroll: list of paid employees; the department responsible for paying employees

pea jacket: coat that is made of wool, with two columns of buttons down the front

pension: money you will receive when you retire

pepped up: full of energy

per diem: daily allocation of money for meals and other expenses while on a business trip

performance appraisal: evaluation of your performance at work

perks of the job: something extra you get from your employer in addition to your salary

philanthropist: rich person who gives money to people in need

physiotherapy: the treatment of injury or disease by massage, exercises, etc

pick up the slack: do work that someone else should be doing

pick your battles: decide which things are worth fighting for

pig-out: eat too much

play the devil's advocate: get into an argument for the sake of arguing

play to one's strengths: focus on things one does well

poised: sure of oneself

porter: someone who carries your luggage at the airport or on a train

post-mortem: review of your work after it's done

president: the person in the highest position at the company

pre-existing condition: condition that existed before you were covered by insurance

priority: something that is more important than other things

prolonged: going on for a long time

pros and cons: the good and bad aspects of something

protocol: specific way of doing things

provoke: cause a certain type of reaction

public relations: the work of creating a good relationship between a company and the public

pumps: women's shoes without laces or straps

punch a clock: use a special clock to record when you arrive and leave work

put someone through (on the phone): connect someone to the person he or she is trying to call

put two and two together: figure something out

put out fires: calm people down

ramble off topic: talk a lot about something unconnected to the topic

red-eye: night-time flight

reinvent the wheel: create something that has already been created

religious holiday: day that is important to members of a religion

reply to all: function that allows you to send an email to everyone on the original email list

road warrior: someone who spends a lot of time travelling

room service: items delivered to your room at a hotel

round-the-clock service: service that is available 24 hours per day

RSVP: reply to an invitation

save face: avoid embarrassment

scrap a project: decide not to complete a project that has already been started

secret Santa: gift exchange in which employees randomly choose another employee's name and buy a gift for that person

self-directed: work that is done without much guidance

sentiment: attitude or opinion that is determined by an emotion

server: a program that manages information shared by a group of computers

sexual harassment: inappropriate or offensive comments about sex in the workplace

sexual innuendo: something said about sex in an indirect way

shorthand: expressions used to describe common business issues

shrill: a sound that is high-pitched and piercing

shrug one's shoulders: raise shoulders up to signal that you don't know or care, or that you are bored or uninterested

sigh of relief (breathe a): become free of worry caused by a certain situation

silent signals: communication shown through body language

sincere: honest, genuine

sink one's teeth into: start something that is challenging enough to keep you interested

slacker: someone who doesn't work as hard as he or she should

smart business dress: professional way of dressing that is a bit more casual than a formal business dress

SMART goal: goal that is specific, measurable, achievable, realistic, and timely

space bubble: personal space around people that they don't let many others into

spaghetti straps: thin straps on a woman's shirt or dress, inappropriate for a business environment

spell out: clearly communicate something

stand one's ground: refuse to run away or back down

status: professional position within the company

statutory holiday: public holiday set by law

stay on track: focus on what you need to do and get it done on time

step on others: do things that hurt others so that you can succeed

stew about something: feel upset about something for a long time without saying anything

sticky situation: difficult or unpleasant situation

stroke someone's ego: praise someone so he or she feels more confident

subordinate: someone who is less important

suck up: praise and try to please someone who is in a position of authority

take someone under your wing: show someone how to do things

take the brunt of the fall: take most of the blame

take the high road: do the honourable thing, act maturely

talk shop: talk about business

territorial space: arrangement we make with furniture such as chairs in an offices or other environments

terse: said using very few words, often unfriendly

three-dimensional: complex and real

tickle the funny bone: make someone laugh

time flies: time passes quickly

time is money: time is valuable and wasting time costs money

to the letter: exactly as you were asked or instructed to do

Toastmasters: an organization that helps people improve their public speaking skills

to-do list: a list of important things to be done

tolerate: allow someone to do something

tongue-tied: unable to find something to say

turnoffs: things that cause disgust

twiddle your thumbs: do nothing; waste time

two's company, three's a crowd: a saying that teaches us not to interrupt two people who are talking, but to find a group of three or more people to sit with

under wraps: secret

underhanded: deceptive or sneaky

underlying: fundamental or basic

undermine: hurt someone's reputation or make them weaker

underway: in progress

unwritten rules: rules or ways of doing things that are implied, not said

up front: at the beginning

utmost: the greatest amount

valid: legitimate

vent: talk about things that are frustrating or annoying

vice-president: the person in a company directly below the president

void: empty space; invalid (cheque, for example)

wake-up call: phone call to wake you up, usually at a hotel

way with words: express yourself well

wet blanket: boring person

will: legal document that outlines what will happen to someone's money and property after he or she dies

win-win strategy: strategy that everyone benefits from

work ethic: the principle that hard work is good for you and should be rewarded

workaholic: person who works a lot and finds it difficult to stop working and do other things

wrap up: complete

wring one's hands: hold one's hands together tightly to show that one is upset

zip-out lining: layer inside a coat that is attached by a zipper and can be removed for warmer weather

You're Hired...Now What?
Information for immigrants who
are new to the Canadian workplace
www.YoureHiredNowWhat.com

Bromgold Workplace Diversity
Information for employers of
immigrants
www.BromgoldWorkplaceDiversity.com

ACCESS Employment
Resources to help immigrants integrate
into the Canadian job market
www.accesemployment.ca

BNI Canada
Professional marketing organization
specializing in word-of-mouth referrals
www.bnicanada.ca/

Canada's Privacy Legislation
www.priv.gc.ca/fs-fi/02_05_d_15_e.cfm

Canadian Chamber of Commerce
www.chamber.ca/index.php/en/

Canadian Human Rights Commission
Information on employee rights and
safety
www.chrc-ccdp.ca/

Canadian Rotary Clubs
www.rotaryclubmembers.com/pages/
club_country.php?club_country
=Canada

Dress for Success
Not-for-profit organization that offers
services designed to help clients find
jobs and remain employed
www.dressforsuccess.org

Gandy Associates
English communication training
www.Gandy.ca

Kiwanis Foundation of Canada
Nonprofit charitable foundation
supporting a variety of causes
kiwanisfoundationcanada.org/

LinkedIn
Professional networking website
www.LinkedIn.com

The Office Life
Business jargon dictionary
theofficelife.com/
business-jargon-dictionary-A.html

Toastmasters
Organization that helps people become
more skilled and comfortable speaking
to an audience
www.toastmasters.org/

TRIEC (Toronto Region Immigrant
Employment Council)
Programs for immigrant employment
www.triec.ca

Index

Quotations

Tina Bakin 290, 365
Sandra Bizier 45, 290
Karen Bowen 123, 156
Shelley Brown 30, 42, 229, 263, 264, 265, 269, 283
Loreli Buenaventura 24
Nazia Bundhoo 304
Michele Caba 365, 382–383
Baljit Chadha 5, 189
Adrian Cheung 214, 217, 387, 389
Gita Clarkson 391
Marco Della Rocca 298
Catalina Duque 17, 289, 390
Nicolas Fagnard 35, 52
Sheelagh Freeman 380, 381
Cory Garlough 287
Judith C. Hart 190, 288
Srini Iyengar 139, 187, 309, 387
Alan Kearns 28, 291
Rakesh Kirtikar 123, 390
Lynn Lapierre 6, 15
Jane Lewis 290

Rania Llewellyn 25, 389
Thomas Manuel 236, 318
Teresa McGill 11
Yasmin Meralli 188, 272, 386
Ringo Morella 391
Gautam Nath 289
Anais Nin 22
Nick Noorani 3–4
Lynn Palmer 388
Jean-Rene Paquette 264, 281, 284
Jeannine Pereira 6, 15
Felix Quartey 48, 60, 305
Haakon Saake 230, 388–389
Rhonda Scharf 278
Tej Singh Hazra 273, 386
Judith Thompson 14, 129, 185
Paresh Vyas 108, 387
Karen Wallis-Musselman 6, 37, 41, 42, 51, 318, 391
Sharon Wingfelder 8, 25, 390
Dessalen Wood 11, 191, 226
Marvi Yap 5, 123, 303

A

accents, 382–383
acronyms
    in emails, 157
    workplace language, 29–30
adaptation, to workplace rules, 28
agendas (schedules) for meetings, 369–371, 373
agendas (planners). See time management: tools
alcohol
    expensing policies, 35
    holidays, 205, 352
    not drinking, 188
appearance, professional, 43–45
appointments
    phone calls, 140

punctuality, 319–320
arguments
    avoiding, 192
    cultural differences, 109–110
    meetings, 374
assignments
    asking questions, 13
    organization, 323–325
    project meetings, 363
    time management, 334–335

B

balance, work and personal, 336–337, 344
benefits. See rights and benefits
bereavement, time off, 36
body language, 87–104

bosses. See managers
breaks
    policies, 36–37
    timing, 50
buffets, 248
business cards, 300–301
business casual clothes, description, 67–69
buzzwords, 115–118

C

casual days, clothing, 61, 68–69
casualness
    clothes, 44, 60
    friendships, 18
    greetings, 110–111
    workplace, 26–27
cellphones, 145–148
clichés, avoiding, 159

clients
  gifts, 206
  how to dress for
    meetings, 70–71
  introductions, 299
  making a good
    impression, 238–240
  relationships with,
    235–239
clothes
  as small-talk, 306
  conferences, 350
  cultural and religious, 60
  dress code, 43–44
  dressing appropriately,
    59–77
  meeting clients, 70–71
  mistakes, 76
  presentations, 374
  shopping, 73–75
  special occasions, 83
  travelling, 342–343
collectivism, 14,15, 194–195,
  201
communication
  active listening, 127–128,
    306–308
  conversation patterns,
    307–308
  directness, 9–11
  faxes, 169–170
  letters, 171–176
  memos, 166–169
  miscommunication,
    275–276
  non-verbal, 87–104
  on the phone, 132–148
  small-talk, 303–311
  styles, 214
  thank-you notes,
    176–177
  verbal, 107–129
  verbal conflicting with
    non-verbal, 95
  voicemail, 142–145
  while travelling, 343
  with teammates, 196
  written, 151–181
conferences, 348–351
confidence
  meeting clients, 238–239
  posture, 102–103
  speaking, 378

conflicts
  avoiding, 108–109
  resolving, 276–279
conversations
  networking, 306–311
  patterns, 307–308
  styles, 112–114
  summarizing, 237–238
  topics to avoid, 308–310
co-workers
  building relationships,
    185–206
  dining out, 359
  dinner parties, 355–356
  first meetings, 45–48
  gifts, 205–206
  problems with, 272–285
  small-talk, 123–125
criticism, receiving, 193, 273
culture, your workplace,
  3–4, 24–38, 54–56
customers. See clients

D
dating co-workers, 263–269
deadlines
  and holidays, 204
  time management,
    321–325
  working overtime, 324
dining
  American and
    Continental styles,
    246
  co-worker's or manager's
    home, 355–356
  etiquette, 241–249
  expenses, 34–35
  hosting a meal, 250–251
  with co-workers, 359
direct deposit, paycheque,
  30–31
directness
  communication, 7, 9,
    108–109, 113
  euphemisms, 118
discrimination. See
  harassment
documents for human
  resources, 30–31
dress codes
  events outside the
    workplace, 351, 352

first days on the job,
  43–44
  selecting your wardrobe,
    69–70
  your industry and
    company, 61–67
driving
  cellphones, 148
  getting to work in winter,
    53–54
  See also travelling

E
electronic organizers.
  See time management:
  tools
email
  personal, 36
  signatures, 160
  use of, 154–166
emergencies, time off, 36
emotions
  heated discussions,
    109–110
  managing yours, 189, 192
equality, men and women,
  13, 16–18
etiquette
  guidelines, 241–249
  office, 56
  on the road, 345–346
  See also specific topics
euphemisms, 118
exercise
  company teams, 189
  health,336–337
  travelling, 344
expenses
  policies, 34–35
  travelling, 342, 344
eye contact, 94, 100, 377–378

F
facial expressions, 92–94
faxes, 169–170
feedback
  asking for, 56
  from your manager,
    226–230
fingernails, professional, 82
first impressions
  greetings, 46
  positive, 43, 54–56

food
    at networking events,
        302–303
    at parties, 353
    at photocopier, 199
    at your desk, 49, 202
    dietary restrictions, 242
    for meetings, 369
    in refrigerator, 200
    to avoid, 244
    unfamiliar, 355–356
    See also nutrition; dining
formal clothes, description,
    62–64
friendliness
    body language, 94
    in emails, 161–163
    on the phone, 134
    small-talk, 123–125
    smiling, 99–100
    toward co-workers,
        190–191
    versus romantic interest,
        265

G
gestures, 92–96
gifts
    co-workers and clients,
        205–206
    dinner parties, 357
    office parties, 203–204
glasses (eye), 78–79
goals
    business trips, 345
    setting, 321–323
gossip, avoiding, 191, 260–
    263, 353
greetings
    daily, 35–36, 110–111
    first day, 46
    phone, 135
    voicemail, 144–145
grooming, 79–82

H
hair, 44, 78, 82
hands, body language,
    101–102
handshaking
    etiquette, 97–99
    meeting co-workers, 46
    personal space, 88

harassment
    offensive behaviour,
        280–285
    psychological, 281–282
    sexual, 282–283
    touching, 90
    unwanted attention, 265
health, 336–337
hierarchy
    introductions, 299
    perception of initiative,
        15
    roles, 235–236
    workplace culture, 7, 12
holidays, 32–33, 204–206
    parties, 352–354
honesty, 187
hugging, 90–91
human resources
    documents, 30–31
    filing a complaint,
        283–284
humour, 310

I
idioms, 115–118, 318
inappropriateness
    clothes, 76
    harassment, 280–285
    habits, 96
    offensive comments, 274
    topics, 309
    touching, 90–91
indirect communication. *See*
    directness: communication
individualism, 14–15,
    194–195, 201
informality. *See* casualness
information, researching
    your company, 27
initiative
    hierarchal style, 15–16
    making decisions, 212
    making use of free time,
        51
insults, harmless, 112
introductions
    clients, 299
    hierarchy, 299
    on the phone, 135

J
jewellery, 44, 76

job description
    from your manager,
        42–43
    going beyond, 237
    performance reviews,
        228
job performance, 20

K
kissing, 90–91
kitchen, etiquette, 200

L
language
    acronyms, 29–30
    difficulty understanding,
        107–108
    improving speaking
        skills, 128–129, 383
    powerful, 118–122,
        383–385
letters, 171–176
listening, 127–128, 306–308
loyalty
    to your manager, 216
    work relationships, 187

M
managers
    communication styles,
        212
    conflicts, 278–279
    dating, 266
    dinner parties, 357–358
    egalitarian, 210–211, 212
    gifts, 206
    harassment, 283–284
    hierarchical, 13, 210–211
    offices, 89–90
    supervising styles,
        218–224
    supporting yours,
        215–218, 258
    travelling with yours,
        347–348
    women, 17
    working with, 209–232
maternity leave, 33
medical exam,
    pre-employment, 34
meetings
    efficiency, 328
    etiquette, 364–365

lunch or dinner, 249
networking, 290
participation, 365–367
phone, 367–368
problems, 372, 374
punctuality, 320
salary review, 231
types, 362–364
your manager as
    presenter, 215
memos, 166–169
men
    communication style, 114
    with female managers, 17

N
names
    accuracy, 175–176,
        301–302
    learning, 55
    remembering, 46
negativity
    dealing with, 273–276
    using the wrong words,
        125–126
networking
    conferences, 350
    etiquette, 295–303
    following up, 312
    groups, 292–295
    overview, 287–290
    small-talk, 303–311
    versus gossip, 261
    within your company,
        290–291, 353
    with people outside your
        company, 291–295
nutrition
    health, 336–337
    prior to presentation, 374
    travelling, 343

O
odours
    body, 80–81, 91–92
    breath, 79–80
    colognes and perfumes,
        82, 91
    feet, 81–82
    food, 49, 92, 200
office politics, 254–260
offices
    clients, 238–239

territorial space, 89–90
onboarding, 25
organization
    assignments, 323–325
    daily planning, 326–328
    emails, 165, 201–202
    making a good
        impression, 218
    meeting clients, 240
    meetings, 368–375
    time, 317, 319, 321–325
    travelling, 341
orientation sessions, 30
overtime
    meeting deadlines, 324
    pay, 32–33

P
paperwork for human
    resources, 30–31
parties
    clothes, 83
    in the workplace,
        203–204
    outside the workplace,
        351–355, 359
    promptness, 18–19
paternity leave, 33
payroll, necessary
    documents, 30–31
PDAs. See time management:
    tools
performance reviews,
    227–230
personal information
    in emails, 157
    on voicemail, 139
    small-talk, 124
    to avoid discussing, 114,
        191–192
    to remember, 55, 217, 331
phone calls
    answering, 138–139
    appointments, 139
    calling in sick, 37–38
    etiquette, 132–148
    meetings, 367–368
    personal, 36
photocopiers, etiquette, 199
physical contact. See
    touching
picnics, 355
piercings, 76

policies
    breaks, 36–37
    dating, 264
    expense accounts, 34–35
    time off, 32–33, 37–38
politeness
    Canadian value, 26
    cellphones, 145–148
    clients, 238–239
    controversial topics,
        109–110
    conversations, 112–114
    dining, 241–249
    dinner parties, 357–358
    emails, 156–157, 159
    meetings, 366–367
    office etiquette, 198–204
    on the phone, 135–137
    outside the office, 345
    presentations, 384–385
    promptness, 318–320
    thank-you notes, 176–177,
        354, 358
    using names and titles,
        175–176
    with co-workers, 45–48,
        188
positivity
    about problems, 224–227
    assuming the best, 276
    phone calls, 134, 137
posture, 102–103, 378
preparation
    daily, 326–328
    conferences, 349–350
    first days on the job,
        41–45
    not getting a raise,
        231–232
    performance reviews, 229
    phone calls, 135–136,
        142–143
    spare clothes, 70
    topics of conversation,
        304–305
    travelling, 332
    unexpected delays, 331
presentations, 375–385
privacy, 50, 201
priorities
    important calls, 147
    your manager, 213
    scheduling, 326–328

pro-activeness, 12–13. *See also* initiative
problems
    clothes, 76
    co-workers, 272–285
    criticism, 273
    gossip, 260–263
    impossible tasks, 325
    managers, 218–227
    meetings, 372, 374
    misunderstandings, 114–115
    office politics, 256–257
    solutions, 217, 275–279
    uncomfortable topics, 111
    words to avoid, 125–126
procedures
    breaks, 36–37
    end-of-day, 37
procrastination, 335–336
professional clothes, description, 64–66
professionalism
    bad habits, 96
    clients, 238–241
    dating co-workers, 263–264, 269
    dressing well, 59–77
    emails, 155–157
    general, 4–5
    grooming, 79–82
    networking, 295–303
    parties, 352–354
    powerful language, 118–122
    reliability, 21–22
    resolving conflicts, 276–279
    ring tones, 147
    speaking, 379–385
    travelling, 341
    workspace, 48–50, 202
    what not to do, 191–193
    writing, 178–181
promotion, not received, 225
public recognition, 14, 15
public speaking, 375–385
punctuality
    Canadian value, 18–19, 317–318
    meeting clients, 239–240

parties, 352, 357
work hours, 50–54

Q
questions
    about assignments, 13
    about your company, 27–28, 41–43
    avoiding misunderstandings, 114–115
    conversation starters, 305
    inappropriate, 282
    open-ended, 16, 212
    performance review, 229
    sign of interest, 128

R
raises
    asking for, 230–232
    disappointing, 225
reading suggestions, 128–129, 304–305
receptionists, interaction with, 137–138, 290
relationships
    clients, 235–239
    co-workers, 186–206
    establishing, 56, 190–191, 303–311
    friendly, 18
    managers, 211–218
    networking, 312
    office politics, 254–260
    romantic, 263–269
    solving problems, 275–279
    teams, 194–197
reliability, 186
religion
    food, 242
    holidays, 32
    respecting, 205, 274
researching your company, 27
respect
    being reliable, 21–22
    for co-workers, 45, 197
    from co-workers, 189
responsibility
    employees, 14–15
    for mistakes, 188
    from your manager, 216
    within teams, 195

rights and benefits
    medical coverage, 33–34
    time off, 32–33
    travelling, 340
romance at work, 263–269
routines, daily, 53
rudeness, dealing with, 275–276
rules
    company-specific, 28
    meetings, 369
    unwritten, 24–26

S
salaries, 230, 231
schedules, 50–53
self-direction, 12–13
sexual harassment. *See* harassment
shyness
    asking for a raise, 230
    conversations, 113
    dealing with shy people, 374
    networking, 297–298
    overcoming, 47
    participating in meetings, 365
    small-talk, 123–125
sick days, 37–38
silence and talking, 111–112
slouching, 103
small-talk
    building relationships, 123–125, 303–311
    parties, 353
    ritual conversations, 110–111
smart business. *See* professional clothes
smells. *See* odours
smiling, 99–100
    presentations, 377–378
    talking on the phone, 134
softening phrases in emails, 160–161
space
    between people, 87–89
    territorial space, 89–90
    speaking, 107–129
sports, watching and playing, 189. *See also* exercise

style, looking up-to-date, 78–79
summer clothes, 73
supervisors. *See* managers

T
tact, 125–126
tattoos, 76
teams, 47, 194–197
thank-you notes, 176–177, 354, 358
time
    spent working, 19
    time-consciousness, 37, 317–320
time management
    assignments, 323–325
    efficiency, 332–333
    meeting clients, 239–240
    organization, 321–325
    personal time, 337
    priorities, 326–328
    procrastination, 335–336
    punctuality, 18–19, 50
    setting boundaries, 333–335
    tools, 329–331
    travelling, 341

tipping, 346
titles, personal, 175–176, 301–302
touching, 90–91
trade shows, 348–351
training period, 27
travelling
    expenses, 34–35
    getting to work in winter, 53–54
    preparation, 332
    professionalism, 341
    safety, 346–347
    tips, 340–345
    with your manager, 347–348
trust
    establishing, 109, 186
    teams, 196

U
uniforms, 43–44
unwritten rules, 24–26

V
values, 27–29. *See also* work ethic
vegetarians, 242

voice, speaking effectively, 379–385
voicemail
    etiquette, 142–145
    leaving messages, 136
    outgoing, 144–145, 332

W
weather
    as small-talk 124, 305
    getting to work 53–54
    summer clothes 73
    winter clothes 71–73
women
    communication style, 114
    equality, 16–18
    managers, 17
work ethic, 7–8, 19, 209–210, 318
workspace organization 48–50
writing, 151–181
    emails, 154–156
    faxes, 169–170
    letters, 171–176
    memos, 166–169
    thank-you notes, 176–177

Photo Credits

BigStockPhoto.com; 88 Stephen Coburn / BigStockPhoto.com; 92 iStockphoto.com / Izabela Habur; 93 Vladimir Mucibabic / BigStockPhoto.com, Nikola Bilic / BigStockPhoto.com; 94 Boris Djuranovic / BigStockPhoto.com, Yuri Arcurs / BigStockPhoto.com; 95 Mark Aplet / BigStockPhoto.com, Jarek Miarka / BigStockPhoto.com; 96 Marcin Balcerzak / BigStockPhoto.com; 97 Tatjana Krstic / BigStockPhoto.com, Simone van den Berg / BigStockPhoto.com, Ron Chapple / BigStockPhoto.com; 98 Ljupco Smokovski / BigStockPhoto.com, Jeffrey van Daele / BigStockPhoto.com; 101 L David / BigStockPhoto.com; 102 Geo Martinez / BigStockPhoto.com, Edyta Pawlowska / BigStockPhoto.com, Keith Brooks / BigStockPhoto.com, iStockphoto.com / Rick BL; 103 iStockphoto.com / Justin Horrocks, iStockphoto.com / Justin Horrocks; 104 Erwin Purnomo Sidi / Dreamstime.com; 106 PhotoAlto; 110 Phillip Jarrell / Image Source; 111 Digital Vision; 115 Stockbyte; 119 iStockphoto.com / Sheryl Griffin; 120 iStockphoto.com / Fred Goldstein; 121 iStockphoto.com / Izabela Habur; 122 iStockphoto.com / Anna Bryukhanova; 124 Pando Hall / Digital Vision; 125 Sigrid Olsson / PhotoAlto; 128 iStockphoto.com / Oleg Prikhodko; 131 Comstock; 134 Digital Vision; 136 Leah Warkentin / Design Pics; 139 BR Ramana Reddi / BigStockPhoto.com; 143 Stockbyte; 145 Andrew Twort; 150 Gareth Boden; 152 iStockphoto.com / Mehmetali Ertek; 154 Photodisc; 165 Tom England; 169 Odilon Dimier / PhotoAlto; 173 iStockphoto.com / Stefan Klein; 176 Carlos Arranz / BigStockPhoto.com; 183 Yuri Arcurs / Dreamstime.com; 184 Sigrid Olsson / PhotoAlto; 186 iStockphoto.com / Paul Kline; 187 Digital Vision; 189 Will van der Zyl; 194 iStockphoto.com / Neustock; 199 iStockphoto.com / Xin Zhu; 201 Jonathan Ross / Dreamstime.com; 203 Dmitriy Shironosov / Dreamstime.com; 208 iStockphoto.com / Jacob Wackerhausen, iStockphoto.com / Bravobravo; 212 iStockphoto.com / Eliandric; 213 iStockphoto.com / Gradts; 215 Sean Justice; 219 iStockphoto.com / Patrick Breig; 222 iStockphoto.com / Jaimie Duplass; 225 Milos Jokic / BigStockPhoto.com; 229 iStockphoto.com / James Tutor; 234 Nick White / Image Source; 238 iStockphoto.com / Marcus Clackson; 243 Yuri Arcurs / Dreamstime.com; 244 Julie Homenuik, Julie Homenuik, Julie Homenuik, Julie Homenuik; 247 Julie Homenuik, Julie Homenuik; 248 Yuri Arcurs / BigStockPhoto.com; 250 iStockphoto.com / Phil Date; 253 Sigrid Olsson / PhotoAlto; 255 Lisa F. Young / BigStockPhoto.com; 260 Stuart Miles / BigStockPhoto.com; 263 Sigrid Olsson / PhotoAlto; 268 iStockphoto.com / Pidjoe; 271 iStockphoto.com / Brad Killer; 277 Dean Mitchell / Dreamstime.com; 279 Stuart Freeman / Dreamstime.com; 280 Konradbak / Dreamstime.com; 284 iStockphoto.com / Jacom Stephens; 286 Michale Flippo / BigStockPhoto.com; 288 Radius Images; 290 Schultheiss Selection GmbH & CoKG / Digital Vision; 294 iStockphoto.com / Vinko Murko; 296 iStockphoto.com / Webphotographeer; 299 iStockphoto.com / Kathye Killer; 303 Julie Homenuik; 308 iStockphoto.com / Steve Luker; 310 iStockphoto.com / Jacob Wackerhausen; 315 Arne9001 / Dreamstime.com; 316 iStockphoto.com / Pali Rao; 320 iStockphoto.com / Zhu Difeng; 323 iStockphoto.com / Alex Slobodkin; 326 iStockphoto.com / Ericsphotography; 329 iStockphoto.com / Jacob Wackerhausen; 330 iStockphoto.com / Pali Rao; 333 iStockphoto.com / Wojciech Krusinski; 339 iStockphoto.com / Outsourcing Design & Multimedia; 340 iStockphoto.com / Dmitriy Shironosov; 342 iStockphoto.com / Gene Chutka; 344 iStockphoto.com / Webphotographeer; 346 Photodisc; 348 iStockphoto.com / Sheldon Kralstein; 356 iStockphoto.com / Royce DeGrie; 357 iStockphoto.com / Chris Schmidt; 361 RubberBall; 364 iStockphoto.com / Zsolt Nyulaszi; 366 iStockphoto.com / Daniel Laflor; 367 iStockphoto.com / Phillip Jones; 374 iStockphoto.com / Marcin Balcerzak; 376 iStockphoto.com / Ben Blankenburg; 378 iStockphoto.com / Jon Helgason; 381 iStockphoto.com / Steve Debenport